THE GREAT MUCKROCK AND ROSIE

Ross C. Detwiler

www.thegreatmuckrockandrosie.com

abbott press®

A DIVISION OF WRITER'S DIGEST

The Great Muckrock and Rosie

ISBN: 978-1-4582-0308-3 (sc)
ISBN: 978-1-4582-0309-0 (e)
ISBN: 978-1-4582-0310-6 (hc)

Library of Congress Control Number: 2012906275

Abbott Press books may be ordered through booksellers or by contacting:

Abbott Press
1663 Liberty Drive
Bloomington, IN 47403
www.abbottpress.com
Phone: 1-866-697-5310

Printed in the United States of America

Abbott Press rev. date: 01/18/13

Cover by Anders Lejczak (www.colacola.se)
see last page in book

CONTENTS

Thanks to Dr. Dean Echenberg, (more on Dean inside the book) and to Mr. Bill Garvey, Editor in Chief of "Business and Commercial Aviation" Magazine. Their early editing and content advice was instrumental in the telling of this story.

To John Wittman for help with the web- site, thanks for your enthusiastic support.

And especially thanks to Sharon for listening to ALL the old war stories, again. Your support is "the rock."

—Ross Detwiler

INTRODUCTION

"**B**ROADWAY" FRED OLMSTED (CLASS OF 64, AF Academy) was an F-4 Phantom pilot with two air-to-air victories over North Vietnam. Fred's description of flying combat was simple, "*This ain't no puss game!*"

In war, a combatant's senses feast on stimulation available nowhere else. Each day brings struggles that are for "all the marbles," that "really count," that are "where it all pays off." These surfeits of stimulation, these experiences, these events are so far beyond day-to-day life that they are virtually impossible to describe to those who have never been there.

Oliver Wendell Holmes, after nearly dying in the Civil War, expressed Broadway's sentiment with a bit more literary skill. "*We have shared the incommunicable experience of war. We have felt, we still feel, the passion of life to its top.*" "*In our youths, our hearts were touched by fire.*"

While not wanting to argue with the medical community, I think the cessation of that feast of stimulation, in the case of combat veterans, leads to a post-stress reaction—not, as it's been called, a disorder. I think the severity of that reaction is related to how people processed the amount of horror they witnessed firsthand, how often they felt the surety of their own demise, and how much they shared their thoughts with their comrades. At its most debilitating, this "normal" reaction leads to flashbacks and periods of severe depression that can last for years or even a lifetime. At a far less severe level, the reaction—through the spontaneous sharing of fears, thoughts, hopes, and love for each other during the struggle—makes these men special friends for the rest of their lives.

"*The pageant has passed. The day is over. But we linger, loath to think we shall see them no more together—these men, these horses, these colors afield.—Joshua Lawrence Chamberlain*"

My "reaction" has led me to feel like Chamberlain. So I wrote this story. It is about my friends and me preparing for and flying fighters during The Vietnam Conflict. It concentrates on our first tour, as that's when the most of us were involved, but does include vignettes from the second as well. . I want to simply state how proud I am to have been with them during the times in this story, and to let you know how much we cared for and helped each other while preparing for and engaging in war. I want you to note that these are not famous men, just good men. They are not "war lovers," that curious breed that finds joy in death and destruction, but they are warriors.

The men in this story, who were my friends, were called to battle and went, aggressively answering the challenge of those who stood in the way of their country's objectives. When trained, motivated, and engaged, they were unbeatable—absolutely unbeatable. Unfortunately, they were betrayed by the very top of the chain of command, and from behind by those with other agendas.

If they survived, my friends went on with their lives and continued being valuable members of society. They do not consider themselves extraordinary, but when the character of such men is woven deep into the fabric of a nation, that nation is extraordinary, strong, and free. This story is for them—just to say, "Hey guys, remember this?"

You'll notice that all my war stories begin by discussing the goings-on around the air base from which the pilots departed, the routine procedures to get to and start the planes, the procedures pilots went through each time they flew a combat mission, their thoughts before reaching a target area, and their feelings in the target area and at a point of potential disaster.

I wanted to build in the reader's mind a feeling for the daily life of a fighter pilot in a combat theater. Things go on in a routine manner, missions are flown in a routine manner, results come back in a routine manner, and then, suddenly, instantaneously, the pilot is in a life-or-death situation that he does or does not survive.

You'll also note that whatever the story is about, my friends are always involved in it with me. I was going to see one of them or flying with one of them or talking about one of them or sharing thoughts with one of them. They were always there.

That was the way our lives went.

"Muckrock" was the nickname of my friend, Tom Mravak. This story is not "about" Tom, but attempts to recognize what a strong remembrance he created for himself in my life and the lives of some of the "gang" I tell about in this story. I think of Tom virtually every day. That, too, is part of my "reaction." The last words he ever spoke to me were, "I love you." It was a simple phrase at the end of a phone call that he and Sandy made to me while he was home from Vietnam on leave. He was dead a month later. Those words have stayed with me for the forty years since he spoke them. Tom realized long ago what Thomas Merton wrote:

> *Every moment and every event of every man's life*
> *on earth plants something in his soul. For just as*
> *the wind carries thousands of winged seeds, so each*
> *moment brings with it germs of spiritual vitality*
> *that come to rest imperceptibly in the minds and*
> *wills of men. Most of these unnumbered seeds*
> *perish and are lost, because men are not prepared to*
> *receive them: for such seeds as these cannot spring*
> *up anywhere except in the good soil of freedom,*
> *spontaneity, and love.*

We were planting seeds in our lives that would grow into cherished memories. Tom seemed to know how precious those moments would become, while the rest of us just lived them and enjoyed them. He knew that, above all else, caring for each other was most important.

I know nothing of what any of these men did in private with their "serious" girlfriends or wives, so I made those parts of the story fit the character of the good people I knew them to be. Anything I wrote about conversations that they had with the women in their lives, when I was not present, is fiction.

But when the story deals with their times with me at the Academy, in pilot training, and in Vietnam, the stories are true even if a few of the names have been changed because I don't know their families. I was there with them or back home waiting for their return.

In the mid-sixties, nothing was settled, nothing was quite complete. The war was on, and it was where we were or were just back from or were going again soon. For those who didn't make it, their story ends here. For those who did, this entire book is a chapter in their lives that closed after the war, just as you will close this book when you're done reading it and go on with your life.

CHAPTER 1
Early June 1968

There were some missions that could be termed "milk runs." These were flown to areas that presented no threat to the fighters and involved placing ordnance for reasons other than killing people or destroying war goods. Such missions gave us fighter pilots the chance to do what we loved most in life—just fly the plane. The mission described here was flown in support of a small garrison of soldiers posted to the east of Pleiku in the Central Highlands, Republic of South Vietnam, 1968.

*H*EAT.
The one word to describe Vietnam for the uninitiated is, was, and always will be *heat*. If you were a "new guy" who happened to come in-country in the warmer months of the year, it felt like you had walked, in full gear, into the steam room of an athletic club. A new guy would think this was impossible, that there must be some secret to it, something the "old heads" did to help them function in the overpowering heat.

The truth of the matter is that wars are fought by young men. And a young body is incredibly capable of adapting itself to varying climates. By the time a young man had been in-country for a month or so, he was able to at least function on a routine basis in the heat. Function, yes; be comfortable, never.

In the torrid June heat of 1968, around 150 army guys—"grunts" in the fighter-pilot lingo—sat through the day at a Special Forces camp in the "Punchbowl" area just east of Pleiku, South Vietnam. They did what army guys do when there's no water to make mud: they ate dust. The day-to-day chores in a place like that were probably mundane, but enough to keep the mind occupied, and thus keep it from going adrift while the body waited for the next dose of combat.

Picture this place from above, a tiny outpost of red-brown dust in a verdant sea of green jungle, like a tiny fly surrounded by a labyrinth of spider trails, waiting for the spider to wake and try to eat it, but with one major difference: The fly had balls. The fly bit back. The fly only died when you overwhelmed it with webs, poison, and numbers.

On that day in June, the men waited for an air show timed for the arrival of our two F-100 Super Sabres. We were out of Phu Cat Air Base, east of their position. At that time, Phu Cat had about three thousand horny guys, a squadron of C-7 Caribou (small transports), and four squadrons of the "Hun" (F-100) to offer the war effort.

The creation of a landing zone for helicopters between two roads just south of the camp was our assignment. Landing-zone preparations were milk runs for fighter jocks because they were done in a place where helicopters could fly, and that meant that there would be nothing hairy about the ground fire that we would encounter.

That is to say, there was nothing about the ground fire that would be hairy for us, in the fighters. The story was different for the FAC we would be working with that afternoon.

FACs—forward air controllers—were the eyes of the fighter pilot in the days before targets were found by GPS and bombs were guided by various sources of energy. At the speeds and the distances that we attacked, it was nearly impossible to see people or small firing emplacements. Though the firepower of a fighter is awesome, when applied to land combat, it is like leading a blind man with a hammer toward the place where you want him to swing it. The FAC got in low and slow, in a light airplane, nose to nose with all the automatic small-arms fire, talked to the folks on the ground, and saw and dove upon the target, firing at it with rockets tipped with white phosphorous ("Willie Pete") warheads. The phosphorous exploded and sent up a plume of smoke that we fighter pilots could see and attack. If there were friendly troops near the action, the FAC usually circled over them or had them deploy a colored smoke, which we had to identify before attacking.

Try telling a guy in a chopper or a slow-moving FAC that there's no danger in small arms when those small arms are within a thousand feet of him, he's only moving through the air at about 150 knots, there's sometimes hundreds of them, and they're automatic. I know how tough it was for these slow speed FACS. My brother, Gene, and Tom Maguire, who was my best friend in later life, were both FACs, as was another close friend, Howard Silkman. I've heard their stories. I can picture these men, so close to me, working their trade, whenever I tell this story. They managed three radios: one to talk to air-traffic control, one to talk to the soldiers on the ground, and a third to talk to the fighters, all while dodging ground fire from enemy soldiers below.

The FACs were guys who wanted nothing more than to fly a fighter, but often there were not enough fighter slots available at the time a class completed pilot training. Most all of the FACs had done well enough in pilot training to have had a fighter assignment had it been available. Virtually all of them volunteered to be FACs because it was where the action was if you weren't in a fighter.

Landing zones were often cut out of the jungle with bombs. If you took a 750-pound bomb and dropped it into the jungle with an instantaneous fuse, you could move some lumber. The trouble was that even with an instantaneous fuse, the bomb would be several feet into the ground before it went off. This mixed a lot of mud in with the trees. If it was raining, which it often was, the mud and the water left you with adobe and lumber. Tough stuff for a grunt to move out of the way after the bombers were done. Enter fuse extenders.

Fuse extenders were thirty-six-inch-long pipes added to the front of a bomb with the instantaneous fuse screwed into the end of it. This meant that when the bomb exploded, its casing was very near the surface, and so only trees were moved. A 750-pound fuse-extended bomb could pound out a hundred-foot circle of trees that looked like a stockade fence around a lawn. I'm sure it was rougher than that for the poor bastards who had to get in there with chain saws and clean it up, or land helicopters in it, but it looked pretty clean from a fighter. Usually, in preparing a landing zone (LZ), the F-100 dropped four 750s at once, leaving a small-sized baseball field in the jungle. The first guy flying in had it easy. He only had to drop his bombs near the spot desired. It was up to the second man to get his four bombs near the first four. The grunts got downright upset if they had to spend the day hacking out vegetation because some yahoo fighter pilot missed.

When the military first tried an LZ prep like this, it was a raging success, creating a nice clean LZ in no time at all. This led to the thought that if a 750 made a good LZ, then what would a thousand-pounder do, or a two-thousand-pounder? And so it went until one day a huge sky-crane helicopter took off with a ten-thousand-pound bomb, fuse extender in place, swinging in the breeze below it. I guess when the crew got over the desired location, surely at a very high altitude to avoid knocking themselves down with the bomb blast, some poor sergeant had to reach out and saw the rope. The resulting LZ probably looked like LaGuardia Airport, but the trees were supposedly so smashed around the sides of it that the troops couldn't get out of their fort. It made for a good story, anyway.

Above the Special Forces camp that day, the FAC droned in a lone Cessna O-2 Skymaster. This is the little airplane with a propeller in front and a propeller in back and two long booms coming out from the wing and holding the tail in place. It's a very strange-looking machine and even stranger sounding, but it was a good plane for FACs.

The landing zone was to be about half a mile from the clearly visible fire camp. The forward air controller circled lazily overhead, with his home base of Pleiku in sight off to the west, a warm can of Coke in his hand, and the voice of the ground commander coming over his FM radio.

The commander told the FAC, "When these guys are done, how about asking for a flyby? My guys have been out here for about a month without sight of any of the rest of the force, and it would be good for morale."

"They're checking in now," said the FAC. "I'll ask."

My flight leader that day was a well-respected and highly experienced major in our squadron. He keyed the microphone to check in with the FAC.

"Hello-o Covey 22 [the FAC call sign], this is Elect 41 and 2 coming to your control from Peacock (The radar agency that followed us to the target area) with two Fox-100s."

"Go ahead with your lineup, 41!"

4

"Rog, two Fox-100s with eight 750s, fuse extended, mission number 4401. The drop tanks are just going empty, so we can give you at least a half hour of playtime."

"Two, go extended."

All that was jargon for two assigned fighters, F-100s (Fox stood for "F"), an assigned mission number, their ordnance, and how long they could hang around for "playtime" while the FAC and the ground troops sorted out what they wanted done. By putting his wingman in extended trail—in other words, following along behind him about a mile back—both fighter pilots could look at the target while the FAC was describing it instead of having to fly in formation. Also, it made for two targets instead of just one if there was any ground fire heavier than small arms in the area.

"Won't need to hold you up at all, Elect. We've got an LZ prep down here. I would like your runs along an east-west axis staying at least a half-mile south of the Special Forces camp. Let's make it one pass and haul ass. There's been very little activity down here in the last two days, but my buddy took about forty rounds of automatic weapons off the hill south of the target last week. If you follow the little path out of the camp south about a half a mile you can see where it forks off to the southeast and the southwest. They want the LZ right between the forks of the road."

"Two's got the target area in sight."

"Hold on, Two, let me get around to that side and have a look."

The major wasn't going to let me go first if he could help it. First guy in doesn't have to be as accurate as the second. He was smart. That's why he was leading.

"Okay. Lead's got the fork in the road, and I'll be in from the west."

"You're cleared, Lead. Got you in sight."

"And all the friendlies are in the camp, right?"

"Affirm."

"Leader, I've got four away.

"Lead's off to the south."

"Rog, Two in from the east, got you pulling off leader."

The bombs hit, fairly close to where the FAC wanted them.

"Nice hit, Lead; now, Two, I want you to make another circle on the west side of Lead's and just connect them in the middle, got that?"

"Rog, I've got four away, and I'm off to the south for the rejoin."

"I'm coming around to the right at your eleven o'clock high, Two."

"Got you in sight, Lead."

"Join on the left side."

"Nice bombs, Two. Just left about ten trees in the middle for the boys with the chain saws. Real nice. Let me know when you're ready for your BDA, leader." (BDA stands for bomb damage assessment.)

"Go ahead."

The FAC came back, "On target at 43 past the hour and off at 48 past the hour. You were 100 percent on target with smoke and foliage."

Smoke and foliage meant that the only visible damage was burning trees. It was a common phrase.

"Got it, and we'll be heading out."

The ground commander called the FAC, "How about my flyby?"

"Elect, the guys down below want to know if you could give the camp a low flyby. The commander says they've been sort of out of touch for a month or so and feels it would be good for morale."

"Happy to. Go trail again, Two, and wait until I'm off before you fly by."

Lead rolled down and flew about a half a mile to the west of the camp at a thousand feet above the ground, lit the afterburner, and as he pulled the nose up, did a roll.

The disappointment in the voice of the FAC was obvious. He said, "Okay, Lead, thanks a lot for the air show," but what he meant was, *These guys want a moral booster, not a fucking wing wag from a mile away.*

I had seen Lead pull off and heard the disappointment in the FAC's voice. Determined to make Uncle Sam's Air Force proud again, I was planning to sneak up from behind the mountain northwest of the camp. To the boys on the ground, I guess my plane looked like a giant swept wing wasp just falling out of the sky before it disappeared behind the mountain.

Here I was, at the controls of the second F-100, Lieutenant R. C. "Rosie" Detwiler, fresh out of the Air Force Academy, twenty-four years old, four hundred hours of logged flight time, twenty-three combat missions, and ready to rewrite the book on flying fighters, if I didn't bust my ass first. I had the low-frequency radio tuned to the Armed Forces Vietnam Network in Qhi Nhon and had been listing to the unbelievably sexy voice of a woman named Chris Noel as she introduced a Beatles song. I had a second's worth of reverie as Chris's voice reminded me of the woman I'd spent my last weekend with in the States.

God, she was beautiful—tall, slender, beautiful long legs, tiny little waist, short, short, dark hair. I'd always liked short hair on good-looking women. She had blue eyes that I just melted into when I looked at her. I'd met her at one of the Friday-night Luke officers' club parties, which were famous in those days throughout the entire air force. The front gate at Luke was open for single women and they came in generous numbers. When I left Phoenix, I figured we'd never see each other again, but she called me at home and set the hook by saying, "It's a shame you didn't get to see my new nightie before you left. I bought it with you in mind."

I came to Phoenix like a puppy to a bowl of warm milk.

We'd gone up to Flagstaff, Arizona, for a weekend in that beautiful little town. Being the end of March, it snowed lightly the whole time we were there.

After a romantic dinner out, we came back to the hotel and got into bed "to watch some TV." She excused herself to put on the new nightie but came out in a pair of flannel pajamas.

"Hey, what happened to the 'skimpy' little gown I was going to see?"

"Too cold," she giggled.

"Oh. Well, hop in. I'll get over it."

She came into the bed, and we snuggled for about three minutes. There was plenty of heat to ward off the cold.

She got out and stood up. "Is this what you came for?" She pulled off the flannels and the new lingerie was underneath. She was right. She would've have been pretty cold walking around in that outfit.

"That'll do just fine ..."

"Two, where are you?"

The FAC had lost sight of me while he was watching the lead aircraft go by.

"I'm coming around the hill to the northwest, in the trees and smokin'."

"Let me turn around. Holy shit, kid. Allow me to get out of your way."

What the FAC had seen was the oval nose of the F-100 coming at him from about two miles away. And I was, in fact, "in the trees" and "smokin'," Just like the F-100 on the cover of this book. As I pulled back on the stick to level over the trees, the wings of my fighter condensed the moisture-laden air, and two willowy contrails of vapor silently marked my path. I glimpsed them briefly in the canopy mirror. It was beautiful and spellbinding.

On the ground, I was too low to be seen, still behind the hill.

I burst on the scene, coming from behind the hill, into the clearing, right at the camp. Catching sight of the thirty-foot-high watchtower in the middle of the camp, I aimed right at it, indicating just over 480 knots and smiling. *God, don't let me fuck this up.*

There was an unwritten law in our young fighter-pilot world that you took care of the grunts. If they had a "troops in contact" situation, you let it all hang out. If they wanted an air show, you gave them an air show. The kids on the ground were nineteen and twenty years old, and we kids in the jets were twenty-three and twenty-four years old. The army worshipped the fighter pilots, and the fighter pilots knew, in our hearts, that we deserved it.

But there was more to it than that. We knew how hard these guys on the ground had it compared to us. While we might be the protector coming out of the sky to save their butts, we went "home" afterward, cleaned up, took a shower, got into fresh clothes, and went to a club. We lived on a base kept almost as safe as the US through the efforts of young soldiers in the field, and we knew that the guys out there had their faces in it day after day and week after week. There was no break from the war for these guys. In fact, the junior officers' council at Phu Cat came up with the great idea of taking some of the combat soldiers on a mission with us in return for spending a night at their location. Though we took many of them, few of us found the time to get back out to their fire-control bases or their outposts or their hilltop clearings. These guys have my admiration. From the Revolutionary War to today, it's been the grunt who never gets his face out of the combat, that bears the heaviest burden in war.

I was about five hundred yards to the northwest of the camp. Close, the noise of the jet, from the front, more of a growl than a roar. It was at once terrifying and exhilarating. All the fear and frustration and loneliness that the men had been feeling for the last few weeks leapt onto the plane and rode it. They grabbed each other with pride and joy. Then they were overcome by the noise and presence of the fighter. They instinctively ducked for self-preservation. Two guys in the tower started to shinny down and just jumped off from about ten feet in the air. My fighter engulfed them, overpowered their senses and lifted them from the morass in which they had found themselves. I took their spirits with me as I pulled up, hard, disappearing in the moisture cloud generated as the air was squeezed for lift. Right above the camp the afterburner went off and they all hit the ground, screaming with joy. God, it was a beautiful sight.

I tried to time the lighting of the afterburner just right. I was going so fast, and I wanted it to sound like I lit it right over the top of them. That's what I wanted, but I had to nudge the throttle outboard and then pull it to the lowest range of afterburner operation until it lit. The J-57 engine had a bad habit of compressor stalling if the burner was lit at high power settings. There was more to this than it appeared.

As the burner lit, I pushed the throttle back up to full and started to pull hard—six g's hard.

"Take that, grunts, compliments of the 416th Fighter Squadron," I screamed into my mask, laughing as I pulled up, looking to the left, grunting hard, and waiting for the horizon to go from horizontal on the canopy to vertical. Then, straight up, I eased off the back pressure and started rolling. The noise, the vapor trails corkscrewing, the sheer joy of life was all on beautiful display.

Finally, far below, all the noise was gone.

On the ground, the sheer exultation had turned to quiet pride. "Take that, fuckin' Charlie." It was such a beautiful sight. "God bless A-fuckin'-merica."

The FAC came on the air. "That was beautiful. These guys are out of their minds. Can you do it again?"

"Hold on, I'm a little busy right now."

By this time I was at thirteen thousand feet, with no airspeed left, the engine compressor stalling as I rolled slowly, ever so slowly, over onto my back, looking down at the ground and the camp through the top of the canopy. I moved the throttle inboard, out of burner, and back toward idle. As I eased the stick forward, the entire canopy filled with ground, and I let the nose fall through the horizon inverted, zero g. Then I slowly aileron-rolled upright, eased the power forward, and started to accelerate.

Not bad, I said to myself and turned up the volume on beautiful Chris.

The leader was heading home. Time for the join-up.

"Maybe another time."

The camp was left with only two specks in the sky as the second airplane, me, diving to gain speed and catch up, wagged its wings at them. We headed east for Phu Cat.

"What a show ... what a beautiful show. Did you see that guy? Holy shit. Holy shit, man. Oh God, I wish I was in that son of a bitch. Oh man."

Everybody wanted to be a fighter pilot.

CHAPTER 2
Reflections

I think the memories of my friends stay so close because of the relationships developed during the quiet times, the lulls in the action or training. During those times, because what you're doing has such a high probability of being fatal, you lay your frustrations, fears, dreams, and hopes out to your friends and they to you. You intertwine your lives in ways that most folks never do, because they never need that type of support so vitally. That intertwining of your lives can never be unwound. It is why we stay "special."

NEAT STORY ABOUT THE FLYBY, isn't it? We flew a lot like that during pilot training and during our time overseas. The Great Muckrock always seemed to be present in those tales, either as a participant or as one being talked about. When we talked about such flying or when we laid out our dreams and hopes about what we were doing or what we were going to be doing, Tom was there. He was the leader of the gang. I met Greg Parker at a reunion after his "resurrection" (more on that later). He asked me how often I thought of "ole Muckrock." The answer for both of us was the same: just about every day.

A devout Catholic, Tom was raised by a single mom who adored him. He would wonder aloud if organized religions were missing the point. That point, according to Tom, was that you should take care of your friends and family and always give life your best shot. That's what Tom did. That's what all the friends I talk about here did.

But Tom could turn back to the roots of his religion also. On one occasion, in 1967, he said to me, "Wouldn't it be the biggest surprise on all of today's pontificating intellectuals if they were to die and there was old St. Pete with a huge book of their life? It's Judgment Day, just like the Bible says, and the saint goes through their life day by day, event by event, screwup by screwup, good deed by good deed. When he's all done, Pete looks up at the guy standing there with his smug little grin, sure that all his religion would get him into paradise. He starts to tell the saint about his achievements. The old man says, "That's nice," pulls a lever, and drops him into a huge pit. He's just plain fucked. He's not able to argue, intellectualize, or discuss his point of view like they love doing. He's out of there."

Looking back, Tom did more than just go through life. He thought about the big picture, about how he and the band of us fit into a plan. If I could meet up with Tom or any one of the pilots or weapons-systems operators I flew with, in less than a minute we would be back to old times, enjoying each others' company, telling war stories, laughing, and catching up.

When you are engaged in a life-or-death proposition, those standing shoulder-to-shoulder with you become very special, because that venture is measured with such finality, the highest stakes. ."

My nickname was Rosie, and Tom Mravak was nicknamed Muckrock. That's because people that he met usually butchered his name so badly, we just took to calling him Muckrock, one of the more common mispronunciations. He got the nick-name at the academy, I think, and kept it through pilot training and on to Vietnam because of men who loved him. I got my nickname in pilot training when a letter arrived addressed to "Miss Rose Ann Deviler." Mike "Hurtin'" Heenan saw that letter and said, "Well, Rosie it is from now on." I wear it proudly now because of its association with my friends. We all had nicknames, shortened names, a "y" added to the back of our name, or "big" put in front of it. We were a band.

We arrived in Vietnam in late spring of 1968. At that time, most of us fighter pilots and the GIs on the line believed in the correctness of the mission. We believed that we, like our parents in Europe and the South Pacific, were in Vietnam to help. We volunteered to do it, and we looked aggressively at the challenge the mission presented.

By the time I had been in Southeast Asia for eight months, I was an old hand. Combat is a place where the only qualification that matters is the ability to go into harm's way and have a relatively good chance of leading others into there and out with the least amount of problems for the conditions. Combat is not a one-time adrenalin rush, done in front of news cameras to be played in the next election. It is about the constant, close, and very real possibility of dying on the next mission. It is a "grind you down" experience. Facing that threat day after day and still coming to the briefing table is where the difference lies between warriors and fools.

Regardless of the reason that men found themselves there, there was, after the war, a common image that few, who could have, did anything to decry. That image was that all these men came home broken and beaten. They fell into drug-induced comas or showed up at public gatherings in old fatigues looking for handouts.

I always thought that image was particularly unfair to the young combat soldiers, both volunteers and draftees, the vast majority of whom performed so well during their tour. There is no denying that there were problems as the Me Generation fed into the services and as the country's commitment to its soldiers and the Vietnamese mission waned, but on the front lines, where guys were squeezing triggers, there were far less pronounced problems.

Yet after all that they'd been through, all they'd suffered and all they'd overcome, there was thought to be something wrong with them. They'd been affected in some terrible way and were not normal. Post-traumatic stress is called a "disorder." I think, in this instance, it would more accurately be termed a reaction to what "normal" people, put into combat, have seen. Some, most, can compartmentalize it and go on with life. Some need some help. Most are reacting normally.

. We are not a nation of professional soldiers, as admirable a career as that may be in this country. We are a nation of reluctant soldiers, men who want to finish what they've been challenged with during any given war, have the guts to go, have the mindset and ingenuity to take charge in the field and make decisions when they must, are virtually impossible to beat in any armed engagement, and mostly just want to get back home. The American soldier fights for something he freely believes in and wants to protect. That's why he has never been beaten.

None of us mentioned in this book care whether anyone approves of our actions in Vietnam. We were there, we did it, and most of all, we know who we are. When we see each other, we are able to smile, shake each others' hands, look into each others' eyes, and know and respect. We went. We were not the country's "greatest generation," but we held up our end of the bargain just as our parents in the greatest generation did. We honored the greatest generation, not by talking about them, but by emulating them.

CHAPTER 3
Fighter Pilots Are Different

In the eighties, I was a liaison to various high schools in the area for the Air Force Academy. As such, I would travel to those schools with members of other services. I remember on one such occasion, a young girl asked the Marine who was with us, "Why do Marines consider themselves different from all the rest of us?" The young Marine, much closer to her age than I, looked at her and asked, "Do you consider us different?" When she answered with a sheepish, "Well, yes," he just smiled and said, "There you have it."

Fighter pilots are different for the same reason. Not everyone can do what we do.

WE WILL BE THE FIRST to tell you we're different. When you step, alone, over the canopy rail of the highest performance machine that your nation can produce; when you sit down in that machine and strap it onto yourself; when you watch as the crew chief pulls the ladder away and leaves you alone; when you look around at all the mighty machinery that you, and you alone, are about to put into motion; when you feel the vibration, hear the turbine whine, and smell the smoke of jet fuel—you know. You are different because the mere contemplation of performing the action that you love is about as close to doing so that most men will ever get.

The crew chief hand signals checks that must be accomplished before flight. Activity around your airplane increases as taxi out of the revetment gets nearer. The noise, without a headset, is almost deafening. Then your flight checks in on the radio, you call the tower, you are cleared, the power comes up, more noise, dirt flying, and the machine inches forward. Turning the corner onto the taxi line, the crew chief salutes, suntanned men watch as you pull out and salute, mouthing, "Go get 'em."

You run up the engine at the end of the runway, check the gauges, and look to your wingmen. They nod back at you, a silent signal that means they're ready. You release the brakes, ease the throttle into afterburner, and announce, "Lead's rolling."

You're on the way.

People put amazingly complex instrument panels in automobiles and drive around like fools just because they are reaching for the type of performance—and, more importantly, the reason for performance—that they can only imagine. The type of performance that is only available in a fighter.

We fighter pilots will be the first to tell you just how great we are. But when we are alone together, when we can let down our guard, talk, and express ourselves to each other, we do so in a way that the façade does not allow.

"Oh man, this is a real bucket of shit we're getting into tomorrow."

"Jim was so nervous last night, he threw up." (But Jim showed for the mission.)

"I don't know why we have to fly the last day we'll be in Southeast Asia. It seems like you're just sticking your finger in the eye of fate. Fuckin' army brings guys back to base when they get this close to going home." (That may or may not have been true.)

"I rolled in so scared I could hardly make the call, but I was determined to get the shit in there for those grunts. Man, that was close."

"You know, I really don't hate those little guys. They're just doing what they've been told and trying to stay alive. That's all I'm doing. But when someone shoots at you, all that shit goes out the window. My one thought is, I've got to kill this guy. If people back home don't like that, they shouldn't start a war. As far as I'm concerned, they started it, and I'm going to fucking finish it."

"What the captain means ..."

So there we are: arrogant, cocky, fearless on the outside but leaning heavily—with the aid of jest, good humor, some alcohol, and camaraderie—on our friends. Afraid often, determined always to not give up, and more importantly, not to fuck up.

And always, we are checking with our friends.

Fighter pilots, or any pilots in a combat theater for that matter, have a great advantage over field soldiers. As I've said before, pilots face whatever they have to face during the day or night and then come back to the base. Other than the ejection into enemy territory and capture, if their life ends, it ends instantly in a puff of smoke or a fire spread across a quarter mile of jungle or rice paddy. But when they make it through a mission, when the day's work is done, they come "home."

The Grunts were stuck in their area, they remained "dirty" for days with nothing but a towel to wipe sweat on—not because they wanted to, but their lives were organized into the most basic of priorities. Anything that wouldn't make you more certain to be alive tomorrow morning wasn't important. Stay alert, watch for the gooks. Wait.

I remember Thanksgiving 1968. Army choppers were bringing young troops out of the hills and jungles around Phu Cat AB for a big traditional feast. I stood in line and saw a bunch of these guys come out of the chow hall and go right back again to the end of the line for another meal. It dawned on me and the two pilots I was with that we were standing between them and their second good meal. The second, and only the second, good meal they'd had in months. We gave them our spot and went over to the club (such as it was). I remember a friend, Bob Fitzsimmons, who did the same and joined us later. As he came to the table with a grilled bologna and cheese, he uttered, "Happy fucking Thanksgiving." We laughed, and we felt good about it. It was a miniscule effort to realize the sacrifice those soldiers had given all of us.

We called them grunts, but that was not a derogatory term to us. It was a term that showed we knew they were in such a dire condition that all they could do was grunt to the task and try to stay alive.

Let nothing I ever say, talk about, brag about, joke about, write about, or mention be interpreted as me thinking I look down on those guys who were in the field, regularly struggling for days to stay alive, to protect us—both the "us" at home and the "us" on the giant air bases of Vietnam that were kept safe by the infantry and the air police who manned the perimeter. The foot soldiers, Marines, air police, special forces, and so forth are the workhorses of any military engagement. They are the reason everyone else is there. They, their ancestors, and their progeny are the reason this country is here.

Fighter pilots are the tip of the air-force spear. But we exist to help soldiers occupy space. We clear the air of enemy fighters so that, heavily laden, we can freely bomb supplies to help the grunts face an enemy less well-equipped. We take off and come in close to where they are engaged with the enemy to help them push that enemy back. Had our soldiers been allowed, they could've been in Hanoi, with some help from us, in less than a month.

We slept in air-conditioned comfort, clean at day's end, because of the sacrifice of the grunts. We live clean, as a nation, in total freedom, because of the blood sacrifices they make to this day. We are different from them but no better. God bless them.

CHAPTER 4
Noncombatants and Their Roles

If the fighter pilots are the tip of the air-force spear, there is a lot of support behind that tip. There are others who were "noncombatants" who form a big part of my memories.

For most noncombatants, life on a huge base like Phu Cat was as safe as working in a small stateside town. When an attack on the base was underway, we seldom even went to the bunkers. We knew the grunts would keep us safe.

For noncombatants, life had a 365-day chunk clipped off it that they would spend in agonizing slow motion doing routine chores and waiting for the DEROS, "date of expected return from overseas service." Life was lonely and boring, but safe.

There are certain noncombatants who stand out in my memory. For example, the maintenance troops who spent day and night, if necessary, keeping the jets ready. After a few weeks on station, they worked in a tropical environment that they would have been hardly able to stand up in previously. They'd work all night, turn their plane, fall asleep in a revetment waiting for it to get back, and then start in on it again when it got home.

I talked to an old master sergeant with the Sioux City Air Guard from Iowa. They'd been activated to go to Korea for the Pueblo Crisis but wound up in Vietnam. I asked him how long he had been working on F-100s.

He answered with a question. "Do you mean F-100s in general, lieutenant, or *that* F-100? I've been on *that* F-100 for eight years." That's the air guard. Their youngsters learned from old NCOs like that one, they melted right in with the regular maintenance hogans, and they all, active and guard, did a terrific job. I remember getting back from the rescue pickup after I had been shot down, and the old line chief saying to me, "Every swinging dick on that flight line was worrying about you and waiting to hear you were okay." We felt that close to them also.

Little aside here, speaking of the maintenance guys. They used to take the three-inch-round little Styrofoam containers in which bomb fuses were shipped and put cold beers in them after a day "on the line" or at a squadron get-together. Those containers kept the beer cold for hours. This was several years before I ever saw Styrofoam coolers on the home front. These guys were ingenious.

There were other support people worth remembering. We had a flight surgeon, Dean Echenberg, who regularly flew missions with the squadron. As if that wasn't enough, he was our flight surgeon in the Misty Forward Air Controllers, performing as was required of the second pilot in one of the planes in that operation. He didn't just ride along, choking down his breakfast; he "flew combat." I don't think there was anything in the regs that said he had to fly combat at all. He was a doctor, for crying out loud, but he flew. And he flew some of the toughest combat missions there were at Phu Cat.

Dean was also "out and about" and wound up with some of the most beautiful women we'd see for the year we were there. And there were no women at Phu Cat. If you ask him about it, he'll just smile with a sort of "you can't imagine" look.

I was out with him eating lunch recently when another customer, at another table, started choking. As is usual in such a circumstance, everyone just sat and watched the poor man choke. I started to get up and give a shot at helping him when I heard a loud smack on the table behind me. I knew exactly what that noise meant. It meant that Dean had thrown himself into the problem and would fix it. He did just that, performing a Heimlich maneuver to perfection. Dean gave that guy medical attention without hesitation and saved his life. Remember, a doctor is not covered by the Good Samaritan law, but Dean just helped, no questions. He's a wonderful person.

We had a chaplain, Ted Graves. I think he flew in my backseat in an F-model two-seater on a mission in South Vietnam. He could pop in around the squadron and people just said, "Hi Ted" and went on about their business or stopped to spend a few minutes with him. He never proselytized or lectured. He was just there. He was welcome. He was one of us, a "Father Mulcahy" in Vietnam. I asked him about the idea of a man of God going on a combat mission, and his answer was simple: "I'm here to take care of you. I go where you go." Forty years later, his words and his ideas of service still remain.

I believe God is the power, the force, the reason and the logic behind this universe. All the equations, theories, formulas and medical research man derives are merely an effort to understand that power. We picture God as a father to relate to the power. We talk to God, in prayer, for our sake, not God's. God is Love. The type of love you have for your family, for your comrades. Read the epilogue. That kind of love. When you feel that type of Love, you're in the presence of God.

Somehow Ted Graves seemed to me to be a man that "had the Power" and "reflected the Love."

.

THERE WERE THE PE GUYS and the intel troops, especially in Misty, where the intel guys would stay up all night working on target analysis and coordinating with Saigon about where and when the next strikes would occur. These guys carry their commitment to this country and us with them as strongly today as in the sixties. They show up at reunions as equals; some visit the places we once attacked and represent this country in those endeavors as "former soldiers." And they represent it well. More on this later.

AT PHU CAT, WHERE I was stationed, there were virtually no "round-eye" women until late 1968, only the little "mama-sans" who took care of our quarters. The two or three of them I knew were mothers and wives and somehow remarkably able to keep laughing despite the misery they had seen in their lives. Their teeth often stained black from the constant chewing of local nuts, they lived and functioned as mothers and wives in a maelstrom that makes getting the kids to soccer on time look irrelevant.

Chatting away constantly, cleaning the laundry, wiping the trailers out with little reed brooms, trying to get you to use your dollars to buy the Military Payment Certificates they constantly picked up as tips so they wouldn't lose out when the MPC were reissued—they were all over the base in droves.

The little woman who cleaned our trailer and did our laundry had a family that had been decimated by the Vietcong. I remember a day she came in and was crying about a friend or family member killed. Two days later, she was back to her chatty "normal" self, somehow having compartmentalized another round of horror and gone on with her life.

When I was in Vietnam, many of the American women were at the monster bases like Cam Ranh, Tan Son Nhut, Bien Hoa, and Da Nang, or smaller but well-protected places like Qui Nhon. That's where either the medical services or the major headquarters were. They were there because women were noncombatants then, and the big bases were safe.

But nurses in some of those places went out into the field and came back, risking their lives for soldiers who were wounded. They served very bravely, facing not only their own demise but the heartbreak of young lives ending. Doing that on a daily basis would wear most people down. Somehow they kept it together over there. Some took the grief out on themselves for years when they got back home.. How does a nation reward that kind of service?

Also, there were the American Red Cross volunteers—young ladies who had volunteered to provide some company, or a quiet place to sit with other human beings. They also went out to the very front of the line, to the fire-support bases and camps in the jungle. There are many places where they went that I'm sure the enemy could hear them talking to the troops. They were the "Donut Dollies." Their proud history and their name go back to the First World War.

When you bring a young woman to an area where men act as savages to survive, it is possible for a deranged person to want to be able to control someone soft and tender. In one or two cases, that control went way to far, even causing the death of one of the women.. That cloud hangs over all of us, forever, but for the most part, they just spent time with the guys and reminded them that the world still had warmth and friendliness and sweetness left in it. Many of the fighter pilots had them over to the squadron areas for parties. Some of the guys married them. There were none stationed at Phu Cat, and I only saw them there once or twice. I ignored them, not because I had anything at all against them, but what was the use? They were going to leave in an hour or two and go back to Qui Nhon. I found it easier to be in Vietnam with no "close" attachments. As nice and as sweet as they were, I always considered them working, and they were, when they were around. They didn't have time to socialize with the likes of me.

I don't think there's a man or woman that served overseas in the last sixty years, that doesn't hold Bob Hope up as a special person, a gift, a man who just gave to us so we could forget for a few hours. The women he brought with him were "mind candy" as one of the guys said. You looked at them, you had pleasant thoughts about them or other women as beautiful, then you put all those thoughts back into storage, and you went on alone.

And there were the flight attendants on the Airlift Command Charter flights. One of them told me they used the term "stood-up" to mean the remaking of an old acquaintance in the lav of a 707 rather than a guy missing a date. They were all young. They were virtually all good-looking, and we met them when we took planes to maintenance facilities in Taiwan or the Philippines.

These were "the fighter pilots of the female world"—always ready to party, always ready to drink, often ready to love, and always gone after a day or two. Some guys, myself included, tried to make them "my girl," but many a guy's "girl" was making a new acquaintance while he was waiting for a letter. They were the female reflection of our own attitudes about life at the time, which was to enjoy it while you can because it can end in a heartbeat.

CHAPTER 5
Scotty Robertson

There was a fairly regular process that new guys went through when they first got in country. It was a tough time, because you were trying so hard to impress the guys that had been there a while, trying to get your feet under you, and trying to fit in to a new organization. Scotty was a new guy when this story takes place. He'd just arrived.

SCOTTY WOKE UP. THE ALARM went off in the porta-camp trailer he had been sharing with his old buddy, Marshall Clinkscales.

Scott had finished a class behind the rest of us at Luke AFB in Phoenix. He arrived about six weeks later, and we all took a great deal of pleasure in welcoming the "new guy." Scott was a tall, thin man with angular cuts to his chin and brow line, blue eyes, and sandy blond hair that finished the look of a college track star. There wasn't an ounce of fat on the man, and he constantly worked to keep himself in that shape. He looked like the kind of guy who would go on to be a business executive in a large multinational company and the president of the local school board.

Scott was a health nut—that being anyone who didn't smoke and only drank three or four beers a night. That morning, he put his shorts on over his skivvies and jock, reached under the bunk, grabbed his sneakers and athletic socks, and headed out of the trailer into the heat. He got outside and had to catch his breath. It was six a.m., and the heat would knock over a small child or an old woman. It was overbearing. Scott started loosening up for his run.

Being new in-country, Scott knew to limit his exertions until he had better acclimated to the heat. He started walking for about the first hundred yards and then went into an easy jog and finally a run. He ran out of the porta-camp fighter-pilot cantonment area to the right and down the hill toward the flight line and the oxygen plant. Like most of the fighter pilots on the base, he felt absolutely safe while on the big installation. There were security police out in the brush, patrolling and guarding. There was mortar radar, Korean patrols, and trip wires all through the scrub bushes between the road he was running on at the time and the perimeter of the base. Off in the distance, he could see the tiny little mobile-control unit that was at the north end of the runway at Phu Cat.

Earlier in the year, during Tet, several enemy sappers had broken through the perimeter by that mobile unit to get to the planes on the flight line and maybe to the fighter-pilot housing. None of them made it within a half mile of the sleeping pilots before they were chopped up by the security forces.

Scotty headed south, paralleling the installations along the main taxiway. To his left, Phu Cat spread out like a brave new world with construction going on everywhere, clusters of aluminum buildings like the new BX and the dispensary cluster. All of this sat on a reddish compact soil with scrub bushes everywhere.

Scotty looked up over the approach end of the runway to see four F-100Cs from the Sioux City Air Guard, call sign Bat, coming down initial. They were clipping along at about 325 knots, and the whine of their four individual engines blended to one purr as the lead snapped into a left break, with two, three, and four following at ten second intervals. They rolled out just past Scotty and lowered the gear and flaps and started into the final turn. As Lead crossed the threshold, Two was halfway through the final turn, Three was just beginning it, and Four was just rolling out on downwind. Perfect.

He was here. He was in combat and had finished his first "dual" mission in the two-seater, and here were four guys returning who had just finished a mission.

SCOTT HAD GROWN UP IN a small farming community in northwest New Jersey in the fifties. As things went in rural America in those days, he lived in a town called Fairmount, had a mailing address of Califon, and went to the Consolidated School in Tewksbury Township. To further muddy the waters, the consolidated school at Tewksbury was not built until 1952, so he actually attended first and part of second grade in the old schoolhouse in Oldwick, New Jersey. This was a stately building in the middle of town that housed all nine grades in four rooms, with the kindergarten wedged into what had at one time been a closet for cleaning supplies. Towns were small. The big war had just ended. The Baby Boomers had not yet started school.

On any typical day in his family, all would come to breakfast and sit together. The radio was on and tuned to WOR in New York—which for them was a different world, a place where important things happened. Nothing important happened out in Califon. Scott's dad used to listen to the news for fifteen minutes each morning and fifteen minutes each night. Later in his life as all the "talk news" began, he stayed to the same habit.

"There's only fifteen minutes of news a day worth reporting," he'd say. "The rest is talk about news by people who know no more about it than the rest of us. They're jerks." *Jerks* was a one-word dismissal he'd use for anybody he thought was wasting his time.

On a school day, Scott and his brothers left home at about eight in the morning and headed up over the hill from the old farmhouse, past the big house on top of the hill owned by rich Dr. Mage from Mt. Sinai hospital in New York. (This was a lovely older couple named Sig and Becky, but they seemed weird to the kids in the neighborhood, as they only came out to the place on the weekends and for stretches in the summer. Imagine having such a beautiful place and only spending two days a week there.)

The brothers walked through the back field, over the fields of the Smith Farm, down past their beautiful new sheep barn—one of the largest structures in the township—and onto the Fairmount Farmersville Road near the Smith driveway.

The hill in back of the Smiths' big barn was a source of winter fun for years. Borrowing the Smith's toboggan, they'd load up on it, shove off from the top of the hill, and then come racing down that hill and fly over a mound that had been built at the bottom to protect the barn. Into the air they'd go, at breakneck speed, four kids hanging onto the ropes on the side of the toboggan. When the sled landed, they had about two seconds to decide whether to ride it out or bail out just like a fighter pilot would before the sled hit the barn. In the front of the sled was Buck Hall, who would later spend two years with the Marines in constant combat in Santo Domingo, Guantanamo Bay, and Vietnam. He was with the first Marine unit that landed at Da Nang. Buck's brother was also in the military, as were Scott's brothers (combat tour of duty in Vietnam and navy carrier pilot). There was never a thought given to the fact that the Smiths were nice enough to lend not only their hill but their toboggan every time the kids wanted them. People gave what they had for each other. Lending a sled to a kid wasn't even considered a favor. It was just done. The sled was returned to the barn every time, and the Smiths were thanked every time, and they never once worried about anyone suing if one of the kids got hurt.

Anyway, back to the walk to school. From the end of the Smiths' driveway, it was about a quarter mile to the Halls' house. There the brothers stopped and walked with those kids the remaining half mile to the bus stop at the end of their road and Route 517. The wait for the bus was usually no more than ten minutes. The bus came through and picked them up for the ten-minute ride to the consolidated school. On the very few days that a kid missed the bus, he was expected to keep on walking and take his knocks for being late when he got to school.

Total time from leaving home to arriving at school—including walking to the bus stop, waiting there for ten minutes, and riding from there to school—was about forty minutes. School began at nine o'clock. Not once in all of the elementary years that the kids made that walk did an adult stand on the corner to protect them from evil people. They had been made aware that such people could exist, but the extent of their instruction was "Don't get in a strange person's car, ever." And they wouldn't do so, but they lived a life unafraid.

Fights between kids were commonplace, - were quickly settled, and usually resulted in the two parties playing again by the next day. Never did a fight lead to more than a warning from a teacher, or on bad occasions, the threat of "I'll tell your old man. What do you think he'd do?" That solved the problem. Bullies were put up with, often with the admonition that kids had to learn to take care of themselves.

In the winters, kids donned secondhand ice skates and skated on the ponds owned by the Smiths and the Popovics, good neighbors. One time, Scott's brother fell through the ice at the Popovics'. All the kids helped him get out. Then, he was on his own for being dumb enough to fall through the ice. He walked nearly a mile home with his ice skates still on, crying. Tough.

In the summers, they would swim in those same ponds.

Thoughts like these of home went through Scotty's mind, I'm sure. They were there with all of us. We talked about them in times of stress and in quiet times together. They were our common backgrounds.

SCOTTY CONTINUED DOWN THE FLIGHT line past the control tower and base operations. Next to base ops was the passenger terminal with its "no hab" café, so named for the response that awaited anyone who ordered anything but a cheeseburger, a hamburger, or fries in a pre-filled bag—red for hamburger, yellow for cheeseburger, and orange for fries.

The fighter pilots rarely ate there. It was a place that was used by transient personnel and aircrews, but once in a while, when there was nothing else to do, the pilots would drive over to the passenger terminal and have a "bag burger." They thought it was great fun to order a rare steak, fresh salad, and an ice-cream dessert. The little Vietnamese, after months of this, knew he was being had and joined in the game.

"No hab steak."

"Okay, fresh lamb, mint jelly, and baked potatoes, please."

"No hab lamb."

"Okay, how about a hamburger with fries?"

"No hab hamburger. Cheeburger hab."

"Right. Gimme one cheeburger, hold the chee."

"Yes, sir." (Nitwit.)

Scott ran on down the line past the maintenance hangars, the protective cover for "Pedro" the crash-and-rescue helicopter, and down past the squadron buildings where he would brief in about an hour and fifteen minutes. He continued around the buildings past the dispensary and up the small hill around the mess hall and onto the porta-trailer area again.

By this time, Scott had worked up a good sweat and walked off the exertion of the thirty-minute exercise. When he walked in the trailer, the cool air hit him hard.

"Morning, Sunshine. You're up early."

"Yep, got my first solo today. Going out with Mac for a local area with snake and rockets."

Major Mac MacCathun was a senior officer in the 416th squadron at the time, , well respected by everyone. He was a short guy, bald on top, with years of fighter experience as I remember. I went out on my first combat mission in the backseat of an F model that Mac was flying after I'd been in-country about four days. I remember how I felt as we pulled out of the chocks and the crew chief stood up straight, saluted, and mouthed the words, "Go get 'em." That chief made me feel that I had finally made it. I was operational.

The first time he rolled in on a target with me in the rear seat, Mac pulled the nose straight up in the air, rolled over to the left, pulled the aiming sight down on the target while in the inverted position, and continued the roll until he was in a steep forty-five-degree dive with the target dead in his sights. He released the two outboard bombs and began an immediate pull-up.

"You have to keep changing the direction in which the plane is moving," he said to me. "That's the secret to not getting hit."

I agreed with a meek sort of, "Yes, sir."

Prior to that point in my career, I had delivered all my ordnance on a range in southern Arizona under perfectly controlled situations, with squared-off turns at each corner of the pattern and easy roll-ins when the target came up on the left side of the cockpit. Major Mac's roll-in was sort of a barrel roll that ended with the plane pointed at the target, and then right back up into the sky. It was a new survival skill I'd be emulating within the next month.

Anyway, Scott and Mac briefed the mission thoroughly. The F-100 squadrons at the time were made up basically of two kinds of pilots. There were the ex-Europe and Far East guys who had years of experience in the "Hun" and the brand-new guys right out of pilot training, like Scott, myself, my friend Chris Kellum, and about half the others. Many of the "old heads" were nevertheless relatively young men who had only had several years of experience in the airplane and had just made flight leader when their orders for Southeast Asia came through. In combat, a young pilot could become a flight leader in several months.

Some of these younger old heads referred to my friends and I as "baby rabbits." That was a derogatory term that in the peacetime air force referred to a new guy who an experienced older pilot like themselves had to watch over. The new head, obviously, was supposed to listen reverently. That worked for about three weeks. After three weeks in combat, if you were still alive, with the exception of not being as highly qualified as the old heads on instruments, you were as good as anyone else with fewer than three years in the airplane. There were no baby rabbits, only fighter pilots. The term quickly melted away.

We had four of those younger old heads in the squadron—Noel Duncan, Dave Arndt, George Franzen, and Leo Mansuetti. I think they used the term baby rabbit because they knew it lit up guys like me, but they were great pilots and good guys who had a lot to teach us newer fighter pilots. George, as I remember, used to say that everything that happened to him after the night he aborted at Cannon Air Force Base in Clovis, New Mexico, where he had missed the barrier and went out into the desert at over one hundred miles an hour, was "gift time." I think he went on to be a two-star general, the Adjutant General, for the state of Iowa. He and I flew a mission into Cambodia a year before "President Nixon today extended the war, for the first time, into Cambodia."

Leo Mansuetti was a short Italian guy who was a tremendous flight leader, highly experienced and capable. The F-100 was taxied on the ground by engaging a button on the stick and using the rudder pedals to steer. The guys used to tease Leo about having to taxi the airplanes by engaging the nosewheel steering and using the rudder trim switch on his side panel because he couldn't reach the pedals. Leo was an avid photographer, taking and developing his own pictures all over the base.

But Mac was a leader for all of us. One of those guys who flew an unbelievably good airplane, was a quiet man, and was teased about wanting nothing more than to get back to Phoenix and grow tomatoes. He'd seen it all, digested it all, and was capable of giving that wisdom back to you if you were smart enough to listen. I remember one day seeing him actually get mad at someone else in the squadron. Everyone within earshot just tried to get out of the way. He was generally such a quiet man that when he blew, it scared the shit out of all of us.

Scott came through the front door of the 416th and met Mac at the counter that was right inside the door. Mac was talking to Lt. Col. Rupert Scott, the 416th squadron commander, and Elmer Follis, the ops officer. These were two old jocks who went way back. They were good leaders, and Scott felt he'd drawn a couple of winners in these two. He, and the rest of us, had drawn good leaders. The wing commander was Leroy Manor, the man that would become a two star general and command the raid on the Son Tay Prison later in the war. Manor was assisted by Evan "Rosie" Rosencrans, another old, old fighter pilot.

Scott saw Mac. Mac smiled at the lieutenant and said, "Ready to do this by yourself?"

"I sure am. Let's give it a shot."

They briefed and went over all the switch settings and the area to which they would initially be sent to meet with an FAC and to where, from that area, they should head if they were hit and had to bail out of their airplane. The FAC, or Forward Air Controller, was needed because of the speed and altitude from which the jets attacked. It was nearly impossible to see targets as small as individual people in tree lines or machine-gun or mortar emplacements. The FACs went in close to the ground troops to direct the jets into the target area.

There were a myriad of details to be covered, and Mac went over them one by one for Scott. They went out to their airplanes, started, and took off.

I can imagine what was going through Scott's mind, as the same thing had gone through mine about six weeks earlier. I was there; I was alone in a frontline fighter doing the work of the United States of America. I was proud, and I'll bet Scott felt that way on that day also. He was a proud guy with a young wife and kids at home.

I never had any attachments the whole time I flew both tours of duty in Vietnam. I hand it to the guys who did, as they had an extra thought traveling along with them all the time. They had to try to compartmentalize the thoughts of an adoring wife waiting and worrying back home and one, two, or three tiny kids at her feet growing up without Daddy. What would they do without him if he died? That thought would've eaten at me constantly. I cannot give credit enough to the young men and their families who went through it then, and the young men and women who go through it over and over again today as volunteers. It was as tough for some of the older guys who had preteens or even teenagers at home when they left for the war. So much was being missed. I was glad to be alone. I'm sure my parents worried much more about me than I ever did about them. Not having a significant other was, for me, one less rock in the sack.

The target for Scotty and Mac that day was a suspected VC location from which the local town had taken mortar fire several times that week. The term "suspected," which was applied to about a quarter of the targets that we struck, meant that the FAC had seen something there, or else an electronics airplane had triangulated radio talk to be coming from that location in the recent past, or perhaps that some other airplane had taken ground fire from that location. The FAC that morning had gone out and flown around and not been able to see any action. Nevertheless, he would put the fighter power in anyway, as "something" had been there. Sometimes this netted results, sometimes it didn't.

The ordnance that the two fighters were carrying that day consisted of rocket pods, each carrying fourteen 2.75 inch diameter rockets, on the outboard two wing stations, and "snake," or five-hundred-pound high-drag bombs, on the inboard pylons. The outboard pylons, because of their distance from the center of the airplane, were almost always dropped simultaneously. If you had heavy ordnance outboard, you didn't want to have an 840-pound can of napalm hanging out on the end of one wing without a counterbalancing weight on the other, so you dropped the outboards together.

But rockets were different in two ways. They were light enough that one wing pod could be fired at a time, and the rockets didn't have to be "armed." They fired at the target and the impact at such a high speed set off the explosive in the end of the missile. You would usually fire a pod of rockets at one time. To the front of the pod was attached a cardboard nose-cone fairing, which made the front round and provided streamlining.

The rockets merely fired through this fairing, destroying it in so doing. After the rockets were fired, the pod was jettisoned.

This cardboard rocket fairing had an interesting trait if you happened to fly through rain on the way to the target, which happened often in Vietnam. The fairing would just sort of turn to glop. As the rockets came out of the tubes, the little stabilizing tails on the back were supposed to pop out. When they went through the goo of the soaked fairing, some popped out and some didn't, and rockets could go all over the place. Mac probably had his eye out for showers that day, as he would have wanted to minimize this problem for his new wingman.

In addition to rockets, we also dropped napalm and bombs. Dropping a bomb "armed" from the F-100 meant that the pilot had thrown a little switch down and along the left side of the cockpit. This switch had three positions: "safe," "nose and tail," and "tail only." These positions were chosen depending on whether it was desired that the bomb explode the instant it hit the ground or that it penetrate the ground for about twenty-five feet before exploding.

In addition to all this, some of our bombs were high-drag bombs. Mac and Scott were carrying high-drag bombs that day. On these, there was a four-bladed paddle that was banded around the outside of the bomb when it was loaded. Arming the bomb allowed those paddles to open like an umbrella and create a tremendous amount of drag on the bomb as it fell. This drag slowed the bomb and allowed the fighter to get in much closer to the target, drop the bomb, and have enough separation speed to get away from it before it went off.

If you dropped a bomb unarmed, it would travel along and impact the ground with no explosion. It was beat into all of our brains that dropping an unarmed bomb was about the worst mistake you could make. To do so gave the little brown people hundreds of pounds of high explosive that they could fashion into weapons that would kill guys on our side at a later time. *Do not* drop an unarmed bomb.

I think these two facts—that the rockets didn't have to be "armed" inside the airplane and that we were never to drop an unarmed bomb— came together that day with catastrophic results for Scotty. The bomb he dropped on his third pass was found to have come off the airplane unarmed. I think he remembered about not having armed the bomb the instant after he released it. This same thing nearly happened to me.

In my circumstance a month or so later, with the same load, I fired the two pods of rockets. We had been briefed to "arm" the rockets even though we didn't have to, but I did not do so. I thought about it rolling in with the first rocket pass, but blew it off, as I was busy. I forgot the switch until the third pass. On the third pass, I felt the left side high-drag come off and instantaneously remembered that I had not thrown the arming switch. The bomb came off without being armed. I looked down at the switch on the left side of the cockpit for an instant and then remembered to pull out. In that half a second or so, I had traveled dangerously close to that target and nearly hit the ground myself. The FAC that we were working with at the time warned me, "Two, that was as close as I ever hope to come to seeing a plane crash."

On the first two passes for Scotty, everything went fine. On each pass, he fired a pod of rockets, and all the ordnance appeared to hit where the FAC wanted it to. But on the third pass, his airplane started to pull out and then just flew forward, hitting the ground, spreading fire for two hundred yards..

Maybe Scotty took a bullet in the cockpit that distracted him. No one will ever know. I know what I think must have happened to Scott. He made the exact same mistake that I had made, the bomb he dropped on his last pass was not armed. Yet I got away with it. A young man with a wife and family dies, and a young man doing nothing in his spare time but drinking and chasing skirts lives because he pulls out of a dive a fraction of a second sooner.

EVERY PERSON THAT WENT TO Vietnam went with the prayers for survivial of his entire family behind him. For most those prayers were answered with a "yes". For Scotty, and fifty thousand others, the answer was "no." Why? I know of no other explanation except that whatever God is, is perfection. Knowing God is not controlling the all-encompassing power, but rather, it is submitting to the perfection of God's judgements.

In these instances, God is the absolute perfection of the laws of physics. If you wrap a man in a metal tube and hurl him at the ground at over five hundred miles an hour and he pulls out, those laws are not violated. If he does not pull out in time, the laws are violated and forces are encountered well above the ability of the flesh and blood of that man to survive. God is not absent in such an undertaking, rather present in the perfection of the laws of physics.

DOES THAT MEAN THAT ONE pilot was more deserving than the other to live? I know from my case that this is not true. I would like to think I am as good a man as Scott, but I know I'm no better. Yet I have had forty-four wonderful years since those days in 1968. I have lived to raise a wonderful family and enjoy a wonderful life and have a wonderful career, and Scott got spread along a thousand feet of rice paddy and died in an instant.

PERFECTION IS INVOLVED, AND PERFECTION affects all of us the same. If I knew why God took Scott back and gave me such a wonderful life, I would be God. I'm not. If death were the final answer, death would be God. That is not true.

If that could happen to someone as good as Scott, what might be in store, at some point, for a real prick in the eyes of God? I assume Scott is in the type of place I talk of in the last few pages of this book. I only hope to be as lucky some day. Other than that, you press on and hope to please the "Big Guy" and try, if not to please "Him", not to piss "Him" off.

It was awfully lonely around the squadron for us new guys for the next few days. I remember asking Mac if we were going to cancel the party we had planned in the squadron hootches (homes) that night. A party occurred once every month or so and was a chance for all the pilots to eat and have a beer together.

Mac was sitting alone, smoking a cigarette, and looking pretty dejected himself.

I said, "Scott was a friend of mind, and I don't think having a party is the right thing to do."

"It is the right thing to do, because if Scott were here, it's the thing we would do. If you're going to be in this, you can't change plans because a good man dies."

I went to the party.

CHAPTER 6
Leading into the War

"If a man puts a donation in a church plate that is later stolen, what does God think of him after? What does God think of the thief?"—Muckrock, 1966, talking about religion, not about the war.

IN 1957, THE SOVIETS ORBITED a little grapefruit-sized device called a satellite. Its beeping sounds were transmitted into the souls of Americans as the ticking of destruction. That satellite could fly over any part of the US, and there was nothing we could do to stop it. The Soviets could use the same missiles that launched that satellite to carry a thermonuclear device to any place in the world. These guys were getting ahead of us and could launch missiles to eradicate our cities. They wouldn't have to have airplanes. They could annihilate us without even losing a single soldier. News programs pointed out the obvious: "They have a missile that works and we don't. They have a satellite in orbit and we don't."

My family had taken in a boarder. As a member of the school board, Dad knew that a bright young man who would teach seventh grade needed a place to stay. George Kobrick spent the year arriving each week on Sunday night and leaving Friday afternoon. He had been a college football quarterback, and we three boys worshipped him. It was with him that we got up in the middle of one cold fall night in 1957 to watch Sputnik pass through the heavens overhead. It was ominous. This silent light sliding through the night sky over us, and there was absolutely nothing we could do to stop it.

The fifties came to a close with our President Eisenhower being embarrassed by the shooting down of a US spy plane over Russia. This allowed the Russian leader, Nikita Khrushchev, to have the upper edge briefly in public opinion as the one trying to reach for peace despite the provocations of the former general and his country.

Khrushchev had taken the shoe off his foot and pounded on a desk at the UN like a madman shouting, "We will bury you," but the relative success of the two systems was seen in the look in his eye when he visited a supermarket brimming with food. Still, hungry people with an A-bomb and satellites posed a menacing threat to the whole world.

These were necessary evils that had to be borne. That country could not be trusted. They were testing nuclear weapons and had a satellite orbiting the earth.

With the dawn of the sixties came a new president. A new generation took over. Kennedy became president, and few around where I lived could believe it. "I can't find a single friend who wanted this guy." That could be read as a statement of what the young people, by this time, knew about how their folks voted. When it was announced the day or two after elections that even though Nixon took California, Kennedy had won, the entire high school was quiet except for a cheer from many of the young teachers.

So the Kennedy years began. Although JFK was considered radical by my parents, his stand on most foreign-policy issues would be considered very conservative today. He'd been in the military. He'd been in combat, something that hardly a politician alive today has given a thought to doing.

"The torch has been passed to a new generation" and "let every nation know, whether it wishes us well or ill, that we shall pay any price, bear any burden, meet any hardship, support any friend, oppose any foe, in order to assure the survival and the success of liberty."

People can talk all they want about how they knew that Vietnam was wrong; that they knew the Vietnam War was a waste; that it was a civil war, not an extension of a global strategy. And you can say all you want about what a dirt bag Kennedy appears now to have been in terms of his treatment of women and I would agree. But in 1960, the ruler of "Camelot" spoke the above lines. He said any price, any burden, any hardship—not ones we picked and chose, but *any*.

Whether you liked Kennedy or not, he spoke for the country. The sacrifices of the men and women who went may have been robbed for political considerations, but whose fault is that? Certainly not those who went; not those who answered the president's call to protect freedom; not those who shouldered the mantle as their parents had.

In the early sixties, there were several hundred US servicemen helping the Southern Republic of the now divided Vietnam build a defense against Communism. All the pieces were coming together. They all fit.

CHAPTER 7
Learning to Fly

In high school, I had the normal amount of success or lack of success with girls and sports. In my sophomore year, I started taking flying lessons. I had always wanted to be an airline pilot like my father. Dad always said that if you wanted to be a pilot, do it the right way. Let the military train you. The orbiting of Sputnik and the "missile gap" that the news ginned up over it motivated me even more to want to learn to fly in the military. While that was my goal, I was determined not to wait until after college to learn to fly.

I'D GROWN EVER MORE ENAMORED with flying. My mother had soloed during the war, and Dad had spent many nights over Latin America in Pan American Airways "Clipper Ship" so and so. I would mow grass and do chores during the week and spend what I made on flying lessons. It took about ten hours of mowing grass to buy a half hour of flying lessons. Half of what I made had to be saved for college, so the ratio of work to fly was about 20 to 1.

Nevertheless, after my first ride, I had the checklist for the little Champion 7EC airplane memorized and could go through the routine in my head. After the first ride with "familiarization" penned in my new logbook along with the instructor's signature, I sat up for an hour, as my two brothers listened attentively in the bedroom we shared, repeating the steps involved in getting the plane off the ground.

I soloed after less than five hours of instruction, and that started what would be a primary occupational interest for the rest of my life. I loved flying and saw a poetry in the endeavor.

The day of my first instructional ride was July 8, 1960. I came home that night, overjoyed by what had happened, and wrote:

It seemed even the sun had turned out to watch my first ride.

I'd come to this airport before, pedaling a bike for fifteen miles to go for a ride, but today I drove with my family and would be flying an airplane. Today I would be the pilot.

There's Al, he'll be the instructor. Everyone knows he's the instructor in this operation. He has his own airplane, can do acrobatics, has a glider operation, and has been an instructor for as long as you can remember.

He doesn't know me.

Here we go. This plane sure doesn't look this fast from the outside. Faster and faster we go. Up past the family who were looking. I wanted to look, but then my two brothers would know I wasn't doing the flying.

Al says something about aileron drag, something about looking around, we do a glide, a climb, there's a short story about the boy who used to live in that farm, a nice short ride up over home, and then the airport was just under the nose again. God this guy could fly. When he said turn here or do this or that he could do it so smoothly it looked like it was second nature. It was. A little bump and the landing is over and we're rolling down the grass strip. Don't look at the family, too busy, don't look. Shutting it down and looking at the gang. Try not to smile too much. Oh heck, go ahead and smile, they all are. Sure is a wet shirt. Hope nobody notices. That's it. That's the beginning. Ride one.

About a month later, I soloed. My instructor had changed the second time I came to the field for a lesson. It was a young twenty-one-year-old named Tom. I wrote this after Tom soloed me:

"Not bad. Not the greatest landing in the world, but certainly improving," said my instructor, Tom. We taxied back to the end of the runway for another takeoff and traffic pattern.

As the power came in for the takeoff and the tail came up, I could see Pop out of the corner of my eye, watching. He seemed proud of this whole operation, although he never did anything to encourage or to discourage it. I guess if it hadn't been for him, I'd have spent every dime I earned on this little airplane.

Tom said something about getting that wing up. He yelled something about getting that wing up. I'll never forget it. He had never raised his voice before. Now he had suddenly changed the subject, was asking if we had gotten the student certificate all straightened out and the medical exam. He knew I had. I had had them complete after the first day of flying. What the heck kind of a time is this to ask a question like that? Another landing. This time to a full stop, and we taxied back.

At the end of the runway, it happened.

"You don't need me anymore."

I answered instinctively, "Yes I do. Get back in here."

Tom said, "Take 'er around three times then taxi back down here and pick me up." And then the door slammed shut. Jeez. I wanted to ask Tom if this was legal, but he was already walking away.

"Just get this thing going in a fast taxi," I said to myself. "When it's too late to stop, we'll take off. Once we're off, we'll have to land." Okay. Power. Noise. Speed. Tail up. Faster. Airborne. As I turned to the crosswind leg of the pattern, I looked at the empty seat behind me. Oh boy. I'm doing it.

Downwind. In the whole world, only that green strip of grass mattered. Around the corner, slowing down. Power off. One landing complete. I taxied back. Tom made a mock gesture with his arms covering his head. Up again and back. Two patterns.

One more time and I'll have done it. I'm on final now. Go easy. This is the one that proves it all. I come across the gulley at the end of the runway. Power's off, and I start coming back on the stick. I could hear Tom, "Hold it off, hold it off, hold it off." And then the gentle rumble of the wheels in the grass ... I DID IT.

I had flown an airplane by myself.

From now on, it was all downhill.

I had arrived. I was a pilot. I had stalled it, turned it, learned about it, worked for it, dreamed of it, and done it. I had soloed an airplane.

There was Pop, smiling and walking toward the plane. I almost got out without turning it off. Down the runway came Tom. I had, of course, forgotten to taxi back and pick him up, but he said he'd overlook it."

I STILL HAVE THE RECEIPT for the flying time that day. What a purchase. What an accomplishment.

CHAPTER 8
Halton Ramsey "Vince" Vincent

Vince grew up with the same values as me—he told me so many times during the years we were squadron mates and roommates at the Academy. Vince was a good, good person; I remember a high-school classmate's entry in a memorial log about Vince, "For those of us still around, you will forever be 18 and the nicest guy in the Class of '62." To the A-1 drivers, this is a story about Vince, not A-1s. I regret that I may not have the A-1 details all correct; the closest I came to you during the war was when you flew low overhead and helped save my life on the day I ejected. You know you have my respect.

VINCE WENT TO VIETNAM WHILE I was home. I have pieced this together from the parts of his life I did know, from knowing his wife, Linda, and from what I've learned on the Web since. Any conversation in this narrative between Vince and anyone but me is fictional. I did this because I think I know how Vince would act in those situations.

VINCE HAD BEEN IN SOUTHEAST Asia about three days and had not yet become used to the heat. It bothered him less than the day he arrived, but it was still difficult. He was used to heat, having been raised in Louisiana, but the heat and the stress of his first combat mission were a tough combination. By the time he finished his preflight, his entire flight suit was as wet as if he'd jumped in the Mekong River, which ran by his home base of Nakhon Phanom, Thailand.

Vince had been assigned to the A-1s at "Naked Fanny." The base was the home of special-operations air forces—older propeller-driven airplanes and helicopters. These craft were vital to the types of operations

43

that were going on in Laos at the time. The base was right across the Mekong River from Laos so that the slower aircraft based there could get to the action faster. The flying was tough, and the heat was unrelenting. Vince hoped to one day be able to finish a mission like old heads did, with only a little bit of wetness under their arms and in the small of their back. Right now, heat and Vince were having a tough time, and heat was winning. He paused and sat on the left front tire of the huge war bird. The A-1 was powered by a huge radial piston engine that swung a monstrous four-bladed propeller. It had originally been built for the navy around the time of or just before the Korean War. The airplane had been used by the air force ever since we got into the special-operations type of warfare. It was slow but carried huge amounts of ordnance and, unlike a jet, could remain in a target area for hours. There were basically two types of A-1: the A-1E had a huge cockpit with three or four seats in it, and the A-1H was a single-seat version with a bubble canopy. Firepower was delivered from seven pylons under each wing or through 20-mm cannons in the wings.

It's funny the things that go through your mind when you're going into combat. Vince was normally a pretty calm character, but today he was thinking back for some reason to home and his family and just wishing he was there instead of where he was. It was a lonely thought, and Vince put it off to nerves.

The crew chief came over and started a conversation.

"How many is this for you, sir?"

"This is number one. It's the thirtieth of the month, and the old man just wants me to get the September combat pay. I actually just got here a few days ago." He looked at the crew chief. "How long did it take you to get used to the heat, Sarge? You walk around out here without a shirt and in long pants and hardly seem to break a sweat."

"Shit, sir, I'm from Texas. This isn't anything compared to what I'm used to."

Vince smiled. Yeah, heat and him seemed to go back a ways also. He had come out of the Academy in 1966 with me, Tip, Wheels, Beck, Hugh, Kenny, Jerry, Tom, and the rest of the gang, and went to pilot training for a year in Columbus, Mississippi. His initial assignment out of pilot training had been to T-38s at Randolph Air Force Base in San Antonio. That lasted four years. He'd made his way back to Craig a couple of times to visit me when I was an instructor there in the T-37, having finished my combat tour in the F-100.

Vince flew the F-100 as part of his checkout in the A-1. First the gun school at Luke in the F-100 and then on to Hurlburt Field in Fort Walton Beach, Florida, for the big prop.

He and I had been roommates at the zoo and were good friends. I remember the nights he came and visited me in Selma. He usually tried to get there on a Friday night, part of a long cross-country flight with a student or, preferably, another instructor pilot. On one occasion, we'd gone nearly all night, with me dropping him off at the flight line after only about two hours of sleep, not actually drinking that much but "out and about."

"Good thing I'm with an instructor this time. I didn't get much sleep last night."

"Glad we didn't run into him last night."

"No, Jack was here visiting his parents. He was in the sack by ten last night, I'm sure."

"Ya know, Vince, when you married guys come into town, you darn near break me. Bachelors don't stay out all night. Jim and I share a quiet routine." I shared an apartment with Jim Thames, a fellow '66 grad who had completed an F-100 combat tour in Phan Rang about the time I finished mine at Phu Cat.

"Right."

Vince partied hard, but always there was Linda. He never did anything that would hurt her feelings if she found out. Piss her off, maybe, but never hurt her. Wherever he went, he gathered a crowd. He was a "good ole boy", and in Selma, that's about all that was required. But he always came home with me and never left any doubt in anyone's mind that he was a married man.

On the way to Vietnam, he went through Fairchild Air Base near Spokane for the survival school there. That had been in the month of July. Vince had again managed to do something difficult at the hottest temperature possible.

Vince had skied at the academy, but he had not been skiing since then. He was used to warm places.

Now he was back in the heat again and lonely. Oh, how he missed his wife and two little kids. Little ones accept Dad as a natural and always-present part of their world. He's the big voice that comes home every night and talks to them and holds them and plays with them. Vince did that and loved doing it. He never wanted to be a bachelor like so many of us did when we finally got out of the academy. Vince wanted Linda and wanted her to be with him and wanted to have children. And he did that, and he was happy.

He used to tell me that he might once in a while wonder what life would've been like had he not married so soon after graduation, but he could not imagine life without his family. They were on his mind every day, and he planned to take out his little Sony tape player and record his thoughts and send them off to his family as often as he could. I'm sure the plan was for Linda to play them to the kids.

Linda had grown up in Colorado Springs and dated some cadets. Most of the girls she knew who dated cadets would tell you that if you didn't run into some guy who tried to lay you on the first date or at least partially mauled you, you might want to consider marrying him. Vince would certainly be different from most of us. .

If I remember what Vince told me correctly, he had asked Linda to marry him on about their third date. I can only imagine the response.

"Marry you? We've only been on two dates before this."

"I know, but just relax. You like me and I like you. I'm not like the rest of the guys. I've known that if I ever met someone I wanted to marry, I would know it immediately. I almost asked you on the first date. So will you?"

"I don't know."

"Well, that's not a 'no,' so I guess I'll just wait you out, You will weaken. We are going to do this, so why waste time trying to get a given number of dates under our belt? It is just a matter of time. I'll scarf you up like an old dog lickin' a water bucket!"

"What!"

"Hey listen, I'm making this up as I go along here. Work with me."

And Vince was right. He was not an aggressive, in-your-face type of person. Vince was laid-back, easy to get along with, laughed a lot, and gathered a crowd in almost any social event. He was about six-two and thin, a pro-golfer type of build. In fact, he was an excellent golfer and on the academy team. He sort of wove his way into your awareness a little bit at a time because he was so nonaggressive. I visited Linda about two years after he was killed, and she told me she had just started wearing her hair short again, "because he liked it long." That probably meant that he had done nothing more than smile his great big smile and say, " .I like when you wear your hair long."

Anyway, Vince had been right, and they got engaged. About three weeks later, Vince had gone over to pick up Linda. She hopped into the front of his yellow 1966 Chevy Super Sport in a such a good-looking outfit that Vince later told me he thought he would pass out. She was the most beautiful girl he'd ever seen, tall, dark hair, beautiful figure.. As I said, Vince had made it clear he liked her hair long, and it was.

This girl had it all. I would imagine something like this happened. She slid across the front seat, put her arm around him, leaned in close, kissed him, and said, "Yes."

"Yes, what?"

"Whatever you want, the answer is yes."

"Including the marriage thing?"

"Especially the marriage thing".

"Well, you know, the marriage thing was the most important. "

Roger Miller sang "King of the Road" as they left. Later, they'd go over to the Broadmoor Resort for a drink at the ski run. (Keep in mind, I'm making this up from the stars in Vince's eyes when I talked to him and he said he'd become engaged. He told me only that when he first saw her that day, she looked so good he thought he'd pass out. He carried on so much about her for the next few days, I finally had to tell him, "I got it. You're in love. Would you please just shut up."

"You know I want to have children. I want to make the air force a career. I have to go to Vietnam, that has to be done ... I want ..."

"I know. If it hadn't been for all that, I would have probably said yes to you the first time you asked. There's not much room in there for me, is there?"

"It's all room for you. Anything I've mentioned, except the Vietnam, I'd give up to make you happy. I'll do anything for you."

"Why is Vietnam so important?"

"I don't really know. I know I'm not a warrior type, like they keep drilling into us up there. I remember on our basic cadet survival trek, they gave us a live rabbit. I wanted to keep the thing and make it a pet."

"Did you?"

"That little critter was dead, skinned, and barbecued in about four minutes. The first time I said maybe we should keep him, old Nat Sanderson just took him from me gently and said, 'Let me take care of this, Vince.'"

They laughed.

"All my friends are trying to get there. I want to be a part of it. I don't know how I could go through this place, qualify for pilot training, and then say I don't want it. It's part of the deal. It's worth the sacrifice and the potential for the big sacrifice. We should be there. We should be doing that, and they'll train me to do it right."

"I accept."

They were married. I don't remember the details of when and where, but I do know that in the first few years, during the times I saw Vince, they were very happy. They had two children—a boy and a girl, naturally.

Vince was a family man, still trying to get to Vietnam but probably finding himself hoping it would all end before he had to leave his little family. Remember what I said. Although these guys were warriors, they were not war lovers. He was a Southeast Asia volunteer, and the word came through in late 1970 that he'd received an A-1 assignment. On his "dream sheet," he had listed all the fighters in the AF inventory but never thought he'd wind up in an A-1. It wasn't a jet. It was a holdover from the very end of WWII and the Korean conflict. A big monstrous machine that had a propeller on it that was easily fifteen feet across and one of the largest reciprocating engines ever built. The first time he saw it, Vince was intimidated by its sheer size.

"Okay, baby. I'm going to learn to fly you and learn to fly you better than you've ever been flown. This I will do."

The whole course was just over seven months. The first part of the combat checkout was learning to fly the F-100 at Luke Air Force Base in Phoenix and going through the gunnery course there. After that, the entire class was transferred to Hurlburt Field in Fort Walton Beach, Florida. Linda and the kids accompanied him dutifully. All the while, the dread probably built in Linda about the coming day of departure, but she kept it inside. She loved Vince, and the kids had no idea what was coming. All they knew was Dad was still home almost every night. Their life was normal.

The first few rides in the A-1 had been the most intimidating. When you poured the power to that huge radial piston engine, the airplane wanted to just turn around in circles in place. Most jets did not have this torque or propeller effect. In addition to that, most jets had a steerable nosewheel that made them easy to control on the ground. You just pushed a little button on the stick and the nosewheel was attached to the rudder pedals for steering. A kid could taxi a jet on the ground. This monstrous airplane was different. There was no wheel in the front of the plane. In fact, it sat on a little tiny wheel beneath its tail. That wheel was there mostly to keep the tail from dragging on the ground, but it did help control the plane on the ground, along with the brakes. When you took off in the A-1, you had to add power slowly, waiting for the forward speed to create enough wind to make the rudder effective. Then the rudder was used to keep the plane tracking straight.

I wanted to drive down and stay with them over a long weekend in Fort Walton. I really liked Linda, mostly because Vince loved her so much and she made him so happy. I remember several times at the academy, sitting in the back of that Super Sport with my date. For some reason, Roger Miller and "King of the Road" or "Dang Me" come through as the songs we'd all four sing together and laugh over.

We'd talked of doing a formation ride together while he was down at Hurlburt. Vince's instructor knew Vince's capabilities and knew that he could count on Vince. He was a good pilot. Good stick-and-rudder man. But that sort of thing wasn't to be.

Vince headed for Southeast Asia before we could get together again. That was the way of the air force. You stayed friends forever, but you might go years before you saw each other again.

BACK TO THE MISSION AT hand. Vince was through with his preflight. He climbed up into the cockpit. The survival vest was a heavy web material that had pockets for flares—flares that would make him visible to people in the air who might be trying to rescue him if he parachuted. The vest also had a holster in it for a .38 pistol. This pistol was listed, officially, as a signaling device. No one knew why that was. Some of the guys chose to carry a .45 pistol of their own. They wanted to make a bigger signal, was the joke. The vest also contained two survival radios about the size of a brick each. These were for talking to the people who might try to rescue you. Add to this a pouch carrying about fifty feet of line to let yourself down from a tree should you wind up in one, and a pilot ended up with about forty pounds of gear in the olive-green vest.

Vince had an E-model that day. This model had room for up to three people in it, but today it would be flying with just Vince and his instructor. The instructor was three years his junior, but as I've said, that didn't matter. He had the experience. He had survived. He was the teacher.

As Vince had told the line chief, this flight today was just to get combat pay for the month of September. He was merely a passenger on this one. All he had to do was start the engine and then sit in the right seat and watch an old head fly combat.

If you flew on one combat mission in a month, you got that entire month's worth of combat pay, about two hundred bucks as I remember. This fact helped the headquarters guys who came out to the squadrons about once a month to "check in." For Vince, it was just an ops officer doing a good deed for a young man trying to support a family.

Vince would be with an old head, an instructor, in the same type of airplane that Bernie Fisher had earned his Medal of Honor flying.

Bernie Fisher and a wingman named "Jump" Myers had been hitting targets in the heavily defended A Shau Valley in the northern part of South Vietnam. Myers had been hit with so many bullets that the engine of his plane began to fail, and he made an emergency landing on the airstrip that they had been firing around. He was on the ground safely, but being riddled with bullets from the hundreds of soldiers in the grass around the area. When it became obvious that Fisher couldn't provide enough overhead support and that sufficient help would not arrive in time, Fisher landed in that hail of gunfire, signaled his friend over, gunned it, and took off as Myers was strapping into the seat next to him. For this, Fisher got the Medal of Honor. It should be remembered that this medal is given when soldiers perform and act in situations that, if they had turned their back and walked away, no one could have faulted them for doing so. It is given when a fighting man steps into almost certain death to try to help his comrades.

That Bernie Fisher story had happened about five or six years before Vince got into the country. Who ever thought the war would be going on that long?

They were working with an OV-10 FAC today on targets in Laos. These were hot targets that had the most dreaded defenses. Heavier triple-As looked more fearsome, like the three shot bursts of a 37-mm or the long red flames coming out of the end of a 57-mm, but the lighter ZSU and 23-mm quad-mounted guns were four-barreled, carriage-carried defense weapons that could spew out a virtual solid rod of steel, seemingly connecting the bullets nose to tail in four streams of lead. That was the type of target they'd be hitting today, but Vince figured he'd worry about that later.

Vince had sat through a detailed briefing on what was normal, both on and around the home base and on operations in the combat area. He had so much information packed into that hour that he just wanted to be able to remember how to get the damn plane started, just to show his IP he knew something about this machine. After that he could relax and let the IP do the work.

Vince's motto, as it appeared in the Class of 1966 yearbook, had been "Get plenty of sleep and don't clutter your mind with essentials." And he lived that way. Basically, he meant that he didn't sweat the small things.

The giant propeller slowly whirred as Vince held the starter. After it had gone around two times, he turned on the magneto ignition and opened the fuel mixture. The monstrous engine continued turning. Finally, one of the cylinders got enough fuel in it to fire when the plugs sparked. *Bam*. That was it, a puff of smoke. About a turn later, another cylinder fired. *Bam, bam*, and then nothing. Then the explosions came closer and closer together, each one turning the big prop a little faster, increasing in frequency. The big engine roared to life in a cloud of partially burned fuel and smoke from the oil that had dripped into the bottom cylinders and was now burning as the engine started.

"Yeah, baby."

"Hobo 21 flight check."

Vince's "work" done for the day, he watched as the IP hit the little button on the top of the throttle and replied, "Two."

"Channel 2."

"Two."

"Hobo 21, flight check, channel 2."

"Two."

"Nakhon tower, Hobo 21, taxi two."

"Runway 15, 21. Wind 170 at six knots. Altimeter 30.01."

"30.01"

Ten minutes later, they were climbing through a thousand feet, the big engine pulled back to climb power, the gear tucked into the wells, and the flaps slowly retracting into the back of the wings. He had arrived. He was in combat—granted, just watching an old head, but that would change. He would prove his worth. He was at the point that all the years at the academy and all the years in pilot training had led to. He was in the game.

The two fighters banked gently to the left and crossed the Mekong River. Climbing slowly, they got to an altitude of eleven thousand feet.

"Hillsborough, this is Hobo 21 and flight for your control. Mission number 2304, as fragged."

"Roger, sir. Your FAC today is Raven 40 working a truck park up just northwest of you near the south end of the PDJ."

Vince's flight had originally been scheduled for Xepon, but it was changed to the PDJ—Plain of Jars (in French, "of" became "de")—named,

I think, for the way that stone formations looked like giant jars dotting the landscape.

Xepon, their original target, was a word that got everyone's attention. Xepon was the crossroads of the infrastructure that the North Vietnamese used to carry goods into South Vietnam. From the huge mountainous passes to the north, Ban Karei and Ban Phan Nop, and Mu Gia, supplies came to Xepon and went either down along the Ho Chi Minh trail through Laos to southern parts of South Vietnam or to the southeast, toward Khe Sanh and the A Shau Valley and into the northern areas of South Vietnam. These routes were the points of attack during the disastrous Lam Son 719 attack of early 1971. It was heavily defended and considered by some to be a scrap yard of US Air Force fighter airplanes.

Vince was happy when the target was changed to the PDJ. There was no such thing as a safe mission, but the PDJ was a lot easier, generally, than heading for Xepone on your first ride. *Might be nice to get the flow of things before you had to start ducking serious triple A,* thought Vince.

"Raven 40, this is Hobo 21."

"Go ahead 21. Raven 40."

"Two A-1s for your control, mission 2305."

"I have your line up, sir. Let's rendezvous off NKP at 55 miles on the 020 degree. The target is just north of a road intersection. I'll lead you in mark, and you can hit it at your own pace."

"Roger."

FACs had to patrol in the combat area for hours, looking for targets and working flights. To do this successfully, the FACs had to constantly keep turning in high g maneuvers to keep the gunners from being able to hit them. They had to turn every four or five seconds because that was the amount of time considered necessary for an aimed bullet to be fired and reach the four- to five-thousand-foot altitude at which they flew. It was a dangerous mission. It had been done in the Xepone area with slower propeller planes initially, but the defenses got too strong.

Misty FACs had started working the trail in F-100s in 1968, when the US stopped bombing up north. We'd been very successful doing the mission in jets, but even Misty (I'd left by that time), at four hundred knots, took heavy losses during the 1969–70 time period as the defenses in Laos continued to grow.

The OV-10 that Vince and his leader supposed to have worked with today was about the slowest type of airplane regularly used in the Xepon area. It was a little twin turbo propped, twin boomed sort of fighter, much faster than the slower reciprocating airplanes but still about a hundred knots slower than a jet. But in the PDJ, they'd be working with a much slower O-1 single prop airplane. A sign that the target area should be safer than that around Xepone.

Vince and his leader followed the O-1 into the target. Up here, all three should be in good shape.

Only a few minutes ago, he was at a huge US military installation at which he felt as safe as he would've at any air base in the United States. And now, just a few minutes later, here he was in combat, with the base almost in sight at a high enough altitude.

Oh well.

The leader put Vince and his instructor in trail formation. This meant that he followed along behind the leader who was behind the FAC, each with about a mile spacing on the plane in front of them. Too far back and you could lose sight. Too close to the man in front of you could get you hit if a gunner lagged his target by too much.

Vince saw the FAC roll in.

"Smoke's away … the smoke is good. Hit the smoke."

That was the signal that told the strike pilots that the white phosphorous smoke from the rocket that the FAC had just fired was close enough to the desired target that aiming at it would result in a hit that would destroy the target.

The lead came on the radio and stated, "I'm too close, Two. If you want to roll in, go ahead. I'll reverse course and come back from the east."

"Roger, Two is in."

Vince's pilot did the roll-in in much the same manner that Mac had done when I went along with him on my first combat sortie. This was a chance to watch an old head, to learn, to not have to worry about the intricacies of handling the machine, but just watch and enjoy. It was a shallow angle pass for accuracy on what should be a weakly defended target. Piece of cake.

The target came into the sighting piper while they were inverted. They rolled around in about a twenty-five-degree dive and headed for the target. I can imagine that Vince, like I had, was thinking, "I'm here. I'm doing this."

Four thousand feet above the target, then three thousand, just a little closer.

Crack.

Vince wondered what the noise was and almost simultaneously saw the hole in his windshield.

The hole. That must have been a bullet. He looked down and back up. He knew something was wrong, bad wrong. He looked over at the other pilot, but he was just staring ahead.

Take the controls. Try to pull out.

Get out. No, no time. Get out. No time.

Lead saw Vince's plane continue after the explosion hit the front of it.

"Two, are you okay?"

The plane continued down, straight at the target, impacting the ground only a hundred yards long. There was a huge explosion as some of the fuses, bombs, and fuel on the plane all went off at once.

Complete silence for about thirty seconds.

"Hobo 22, if you hear me, come up beeper or voice." There was almost no chance anyone survived, but somehow, someway, parachutes sometimes appeared after all the dust had settled on a crash. In those cases, the pilots hadn't been seen as they were visually so small until the chutes opened. It was at least an exercise that allowed people to function until reality set in. Hobo 21 waited, but nothing happened.

"I'm going home, Raven." Lead pickled his bombs over a "backup" target that the squadron had in the area, as he didn't want to drop anywhere near the primary target in case anyone had survived.

Hope faded quickly. Lead came back and made one long lazy circle around the crash site just in cast he'd missed the chutes.

He hadn't.

Vince had arrived at NKP ahead of the rest of his class. Somehow the airline connections had worked that way, and he finished survival school at Clark early. By the time his classmates from A-1 school got there a day later, Vince was dead.

I read a letter that his mom wrote over two years after his death. The sorrow in her words was all-consuming. It had been that long until she could go over the details of the funeral service Vince had received.

Do we, as a country, realize that the sorrow and the pain never end for those left behind? After the cheers and the hoorahs of the parades, there is just loneliness. Who can thank them? They go on, but oh the sadness.

Dead on his first mission, for about two hundred bucks of combat pay. God ...

I called Vince's son. I wanted to go over everything here with him, just to make sure that nothing I'd said would cause any concerns for the family. He hasn't been able to get back to me. He's deployed someplace where the internet isn't that available. I know there are lots of people and things that influence what a man becomes, but when I heard that, I thought only of Vince.

CHAPTER 9
Class of 1966

Let's go back to the years that led up to those Southeast Asia experiences for those of us who came through the Academy. I'll tell you what drew me to the Air Force Academy and what happened when the Class of 1966, "The Blood that Sticks," arrived and went through our first year.

IN THE FIFTIES, THE US Air Force decided that it should have its own service academy, much the same as the army and the navy had at West Point and Annapolis. Actually, with the air force becoming a separate service in 1947, Barry Goldwater and Generals Arnold, Harmon, Vandenberg, and Doolittle, along with some distinguished citizenry, had started to push for an Air Force Academy. Until 1959, those of us who wanted to go to a service academy and fly had to pick either West Point or Annapolis and hope to make the cut. I had dreamed of attending the US Military Academy at West Point, New York.

When I became aware of the Air Force Academy around 1959, it was the only place I thought of going to college during the entire time I was in high school. It was for me. It would happen.

In early 1959, the entire wing of the Air Force Academy consisted of just a few hundred cadets. They had been through the first couple of years of their existence as an institution at the old Lowry Air Force Base in Denver, Colorado.

During the late fall of '58 or early spring of '59, the entire wing of cadets marched from the grounds in Denver to the new site in Colorado Springs, a distance of some sixty miles. It was an interest piece for most of the newscasts, but it was, to me, simply an inspiring move. That was the type thing cadets did and do. They strove to do the hard act, to laugh at the hard way, to gut it out, to be tough, to be part of something great and a little bit better than everyone else. In the fifties, it was the way to "go to the head of the class," so to speak, for the military service that all must go through.

What they arrived at for home was awe-inspiring. The new aluminum-and-concrete structure rose out of the Rampart Range of the Rocky Mountains like an apparition on a high point. There was a coldness to the setting and a coldness to the architecture that did and does remind a person of high, lonely, and cold skies.

That's just what it was, high and lonely. "Sir, the altitude of the Air Force Academy is 7,250 feet ... far, far above that of West Point and Annapolis."

"And what is Annapolis, smack?"

Fourth-classmen were smacks, dumb smacks, do-jazzes, doolies, dipwads, and just about any other demeaning and lowlife name that could be thought of for them. That was all right. This was all part of the toughening process. "At this place, they take all your human rights away and give them back one at a time as privileges." It was a process that was understood by the parents of that generation. Their "process" had been the Depression.

It was that process that made men out of boys and made fighting men out of normal men by giving them a common core, a thread, a long blue line with which to associate. It would be hard, given this country's history, to argue that only service academies can produce great warriors, but it would be just as hard to argue that the academies haven't helped engender a love of country, unit, and friend—as well as a feeling of commitment to each of those—into their graduates. It was tough. You couldn't make it without a friend or a group of friends. You had to "cooperate to graduate."

But back to the question.

"Sir, Annapolis is a small boat school on the outskirts of the capital of Maryland, with its campus half on land and half in the Severn River."

"And what is West Point, smack?"

"Sir, West Point is an insignificant military school located on the west bank of the Hudson River with 167 years of tradition ... thus unhampered by progress."

Everything about the Air Force Academy was new. And the newness was the reason to push harder, to prove that it deserved to be in existence, to show that the new Air Force could do anything as well as its older sister services and academies.

It's hard to imagine what the place was like in 1962, physically, when looking at it today. Over the last fifty years, the open distance between Denver and Colorado Springs has shrunk to the point where there is almost none. In those last fifty years, there is not a house, a structure, a building, or a sign that has been put up between the two cities that improved the view.

In 1959, the column of cadets could walk the sixty or so miles with far less bother than would today be found on most county roads anywhere. From about the point of the current Tech Center, south to the little burg of Castle Rock, there was absolutely nothing. It was beautiful, God-given country, full of jackrabbits, deer, and elk. At Castle Rock, a little highway veered off the main drag back to the town and then back onto the highway south of town. Castle Rock had about thirty houses. From Castle Rock, there was only openness all the way down to the little six-building town of Monument. All that was there was nothing. All of it was beautiful.

Looking to the east from the academy today, you can see the gradual filling in of the space. Here a group of rubber-stamp houses, there a little corporate park. Here a hodgepodge of junk-food joints. In 1959, there was nothing ... nothing ... it was empty and alone and in the wilderness. It was the same wilderness into which US military forces had first forayed in strength in the late 1800s, less than one hundred years earlier.

If you turned off of Academy Boulevard, just before the south gate, you could wind your way out through the prairie for about a mile to the Academy Air Field or Pine Valley Airport. It had a forty-four-hundred-foot grass airstrip, two T-34s, and a Cessna 182, as I remember. Parts of the old Route 85/87 had been made into a runway at the airstrip, which could be used by "special qualification" people. I would spend a lot of time at this airstrip in the next four years.

Route 85/87 wound around for a few miles from the academy's south gate into the northwest corner of Colorado Springs. An exit led to Nevada Avenue, past a little motel known as the Albert Pick, and then past a dog-racing track, a big power station, and on for about another mile before catching the outskirts of town with Zebulon Pike sitting on his big horse, red balls compliments of the Class of '66 from time to time.

Today, the south gate of the academy feeds under the Interstate, right into Academy Boulevard, Colorado Springs, and on into an expanse of development. Not a house, a building, or an office stands out. While there are still many places of beauty in Colorado Springs, none of this commercial construction can compare to the open prairie and the few houses that stood on that ridge above town in 1962.

Into this pristine beauty of 1962 comes myself. My high-school graduation had been four days earlier, and the ink on the diploma was still wet. I joined about six hundred other young men. Some had gone to the academy's preparatory school for a year, and some had had college or duty in the military prior to being accepted at the academy, but most of us had been attending classes in high school just a week earlier and were away from home for the first time.

I would spend my first long, exhausting day away from home getting to the Albert Pick Motel in Colorado Springs. The alarm had sounded at about five a.m. that day to get the family up and ready for the drive to Newark Airport in New Jersey. My brothers and parents and I had loaded at about eight a.m. and headed out. At the airport, there was the normal checking in and checking of bags. My best friend from high school had come along. An amateur photographer, he snapped pictures of my family and I laughing and clowning around. But the picture that stayed in my mind decades after was one he took of my parents as they walked away, holding hands, quietly symbolizing the loneliness that only a parent can feel when a child leaves home. The parents know the "home" life is over. The kid is so involved in the excitement he tingles.

There were no carry-on bags in those days. Everyone was well-dressed, and everyone checked their bags. Then, in a moment we had all dreaded, there was a last kiss good-bye, a shake of the old man's hand, a pat on the back of the brothers who were already re-dividing the bedroom space, and a quick exit to the gangway and onto the plane.

The plane flew at high altitude to Detroit's Willow Run Airport. Then, after about an hour wait, it went onto Denver's Stapleton Airport. The final leg was a bus ride down the highway to Colorado Springs.

As I recall, the bus driver agreed to let about three or four of us out at the Albert Pick on the way into Colorado Springs.

By the time I unpacked my bags that night, I'd been too busy to even miss my family. It dawned on me that I was a long way from home, that I missed home, and that it would be a long time until I went back. In fact, I would never fully go back. Life had changed, radically, completely, and quickly. Last night, I was just another high-school graduate, still counting on the family not only for love but for sustenance. Tonight, I was on the other side of the country, independent and alone. Although I missed home, I didn't call, because the call would be too expensive. *Save your money. Don't spend foolishly.* A quick letter home and I went to bed.

I lay down and quickly drifted off to sleep, wondering what would be ahead of me but knowing it wasn't going to be pretty.

The next morning, the academy sent a bus around to the three or four hotels in town and picked up all the new cadets going to "Aluminum U."

As I would find to be true in the next thirty-five years in the military, there were three different opinions about what would face us when we got to the academy. None of them was exactly right, and there was just a bit of truth in each. Each was spoken with conviction by so and so, who had heard from a friend who had been there.

As it turned out, there were no upperclassmen to meet us when we got off the bus. Ours was the first class that would be shepherded around for the first three days by NCOs. This was a new idea to let the new cadets get acclimated to the weather and the institution before hitting them with the screaming and yelling that was part of the doolie experience.

Noncommissioned officers took us through the routine of uniform issue, shots, swearing in, rifle issue, and the basics of getting around the academy before the "beast" descended upon us. I will never forget raising my right hand, being sworn in, and right after "so help me God" being told to "stand on that X on the floor." I was hit with a pneumatic shot in the left arm and then the right and then the left again. Welcome to the military.

Actually, it was a pretty good idea to let us get established and get set up and have clothes put away in our rooms before turning us over to the upperclassmen. The first-classmen who were around seethed at us. Seethed like a father watching his beautiful daughter being dated by a bum. These yahoos (us) were walking and sitting and floating around the area without a care. That would change. They would see to that.

CHAPTER 10
Doolie Year, US Air Force Academy

"Bring me men to match my mountains
Bring me men to match my plains
Men with empires in their purpose
And new eras in their brains."
—*"The Coming American" by Sam Walter Foss*

Any of us who attended the academy knew that stanza was behind the "Bring Me Men" lettering on the portal leading down to the parade ground. That lettering had appeared shortly after my class arrived at the Academy, as I recall. It is a stirring poem. It has since been removed in deference to the fact that a large number of women now attend the academy. It's also interesting to note that most of my classmates, in self-deprecating humor, changed the last sentence to "And shit for brains."

SUNDAY EVENING, THE TIME THAT the upperclassmen took over, finally came.

The NCOs walked us up to the Arnold Hall auditorium and shut the doors behind them. We were given a few speeches by the commandant and the director of summer training and told that life was about to change forever. When we saw that first-class cadet standing in front of us, it was like looking at all you dreamed of being but were so far from.

We were about to meet a very big challenge, and it would be a time during which many of us failed for the first time in our lives. The quiet darkness of the auditorium, like a comfortable protective womb, surrounded us, and some wanted to puke. A few even sobbed. Why this?

Why not home with the rest of the gang, chasing bootie and partying? In 1962, most of us hadn't been further from home than the next state. This was a big change.

"You gentlemen will proceed in an orderly fashion through the doors at the front of the auditorium. You will be instructed by the upperclassmen as to where to go."

That was the understatement of the summer.

The director walked off the stage and the side doors at the front opened. You could see floodlights on giant poles illuminating the whole terrazzo area in the late evening sky.

All hell broke loose. There was screaming and mass confusion. The day was old enough that the light of the sun had gone behind the steep mountain directly behind the grounds. The light of the day and the light of the innocence of Mom, home, the gang, sweetness, tenderness, and anything that didn't relate to being an officer in a combat leadership position went out. There were no women allowed, and there was no quarter given or expected. This was to make you tough. This was to make a man out of you. This was to see if you had the balls to be an air-force officer. Smile if you will, but the men who came out of the auditorium that night and their cohorts from other military schools and other officer-training programs were to be among the strongest-willed fighting men ever trained. They were so tough in later years that, when held as captives, they would cause their captors to suffer breakdowns from the torture they had to inflict on men who wouldn't break. It was necessary, it was for the common good, and it worked for academy grads and ROTC grads of that time. We need to think carefully about ever replacing that kind of training.

"Move, move, move, move, move. Get going, mister. What was that gaze for? Do you want to marry me? Stand up. Get your shoulders back and down, roll your hips under your shoulders. Make a dirty movement. Put your hands at your side and put your thumb along the seam of your trousers."

"What squadron are you in? I can't hear you."

"When you speak you will say only one of three things: 'Yes sir,' 'No sir,' and 'No excuse, sir.' You will prefix everything you ever say with 'sir' and you will end everything you say with 'sir.' Do you understand me?"

"Yes sir."

"What?"

"Sir, yes sir."

"You will not speak unless told to speak, and you will not gaze with your puny little eyeballs anywhere but straight ahead or at the ground in front of you. You are the lowest form of life on this planet. You have no life, I own you, you do not do anything without permission from me, do you understand?"

"Yessir."

"What?"

"Sir, yes sir."

"Louder."

"Sir, yes sir."

This had only been going on for about ten minutes, and voices were already beginning to crack. All over the terrazzo, young men were being gathered into separate groups and headed off for their squadron areas for "special instruction."

As I said, I came to the academy four days after high school. It was a pretty mind-numbing experience for me and for guys like me. Guys who had been to the prep school or on active duty as an airman, or even in a college fraternity, had been through all of this before. It wasn't exactly a game for them, but they were able to look at it from one step back from the rest of us. As I look back, I think that level of maturity gave a much better perspective to all the training that was to follow. It didn't necessarily make those guys better doolies, but I think it made them better upperclassmen when it was their turn to administer the discipline. They kept the idea of constant pressure in sight without it ever getting personal. That was a shortcoming many of us straight out of high school, including myself, carried into our upperclassman years.

"Get out of my sight … not fast enough. Drop and give me twenty pushups."

That was bad enough, but then I heard someone get fifty.

Fifty pushups. Was he kidding?

Even for the athletes, fifty pushups was about the most any of us had ever done in one shot. Most of the doolies had had two or three sets of pushups assigned in the first ten minutes they were out of the auditorium. Kids were puking, crying, and running around like skinny little sheep being led to a slaughter. It was awful.

BACK TO THE SQUADRON AREAS.

When you line a group of seventeen- and eighteen-year-olds up in their underpants and shower clogs with their soap dishes in their left hand and towels over their left forearm, you have a pretty skanky looking group. Then parade shouting, hollering upperclassmen in tan khaki "Service Bravo" uniforms that are neat and pressed, with shoes shined to a mirror finish, shirts tailored in, collar stays, ties, everything in perfect place, and you create quite a contrast. Then tell those squats they'll never see the coveted recognition prop-and-wing pins on their collars, they'll never make it through this program, and if they do, the man on each side of them won't, and the first evening's goals have been accomplished. These "recruits" have been taken back to ground zero. They're nothing. They have nothing. They should expect nothing. They hope for nothing except the end of the session, and they can see no further into the future than the end of the hall. You own them, and you make clear that there is but one way for them to survive, and that is to work together as they earn those rights back as privileges.

"Sir, my name is Halton Ramsey Vincent, sir."

"And where are you from, Vincent?"

"Sir, I'm from Sulphur, Louisiana, sir."

"Sir, I'm from Califon, New Jersey, sir."

"Sir, I'm from Brattleboro, Vermont, sir."

"Sir, I'm from Houston, Texas, sir."

"Sir, I'm from Cathlamet, Washington … Reno, Nevada … Russellville, Arkansas … Palmerton, Pennsylvania … Ossining, New York … Anchorage, Alaska. I'm from nowhere and somewhere, USA." The lifeblood of a country, its young, had flowed to Colorado Springs, and we were being hammered. Our past was being destroyed and our life laid in ruins.

"Do you want to go home, little man?"

"Are you going to cry? We've got a crier over here."

Just shoot me.

Even the little voice inside that tells you how you're doing doesn't work under that kind of pressure. You just survive, and you look for lifelines out of the morass. And the upperclassmen tell you where to get them.

"Not from me, do-jazz ... not from Mommy, not from Daddy, your girlfriend, or the minister. The only human beings in the world that can get you through this are your classmates. Never forget that ... never. Only your classmates, your friends, your comrades can get you out of this place successfully. Cooperate and graduate. Or go back to some silly civilian school and rub your noses in the pretty girls' sweaters and tell them your problems ... I could care less. Do you understand?"

"Yessir."

"What did you say, smack?"

"Sir, yes sir."

"Make sure you do."

I was going to be a member of fourth squadron. "Sir, I am in Fightin' Fourth squadron," was the call for the fourth-squadron doolies. It was one little banner to rally around. You weren't anything if you weren't a cadet, and if you were a cadet, you weren't anything unless you were in Fightin' Fourth. Around the corner from where we were learning the insignificant value of a cadet in his first days at the academy, the boys in third squadron, "Thinking Third," were getting their new doolies in line.

"What's your name, do-jazz?"

"Sir, my name is Thomas Anthony Mravak, sir."

"Marvak?"

"No, sir. Sir, it is Mravak, sir."

"Muckrock."

"Sir, my name is Thomas Anthony 'Ma Ra Vack,' sir."

There was something about this guy's voice. It just didn't have the same sound as most of the other voices. It was the doolie, but it sounded in charge.

There was something else ...

"Where are you from, MaaaRaaaVack?"

"Sir, I am from Ossining, New York, sir."

"How old are you, MaaRaaVaak?" The upper classman was mocking the way Tom had pronounced his name slowly and clearly.

"Sir, I am twenty years old, sir."

That was the same age as the man who was screaming in his face.

"What have you been doing with your life, MaaRAAVAAk?'

"Sir, I have been in college for two years."

"You a big fraternity man? You look like a fraternity man."

"Sir, yes sir."

"Well, we got a fraternity at this place, mister, and you just joined, and there's nothing in the frat house for you but trouble. What do you think of that, MaaRaaVaak?"

"Sir, that's fine by me, sir."

"Why are you here, smack. What do you want to do in my air force?"

"Sir, I want to be an astronaut, sir."

"Beautiful, lots of luck. First you gotta learn to be a smack. Think you can hack that?"

"Sir, yessir."

"Louder."

"Sir, yes sir."

"We'll see."

THE NEXT MORNING BEGAN RIGHT where the evening before left off. The doolies had been instructed that when they went to a classmate's door, they were to knock twice. That meant it was a friend. If there was one knock on the door, that was authority, and they were to call the room to attention and be standing looking straight ahead by the time the upperclassman's or officer's foot had crossed the threshold.

About ten minutes before the reveille formation on the first day of basic training, the academy band stepped under the dorm rooms where I was lying in bed across the room from my new classmate, Jim Patterson. The band marked time with a "click, click … click, click, click" on drumsticks. It was like listening to a hammer nailing in the planks on a gallows.

Bang.

Jim and I staggered out of our beds so fast that we almost fell over.

We had finally finished the shower formation the night before at about ten o'clock, gone to our rooms, and had a few minutes peace in the dark before we passed out.

I had begun a pattern that would last the rest of doolie year.

I'd lay quietly in bed and force myself to stay awake for about half an hour. Moments of peace snatched from days of rushing, shouting, and struggling to meet the physical and mental challenge. Moments of peace. As soon as I gave up and rolled over, I slept, and it was, too soon, time to start all over again.

My roommate, Jim Patterson, was a skinny guy from Glen Ellen, Illinois. Turns out Jim had a lot more guts than muscle. He had puked into the wastebasket the night before. I was worried about him. He didn't have that much weight to lose, but he had made me promise not to tell. He wasn't going to wash out of this place ... ever.

"Patterson, quick, get dressed and come with me," the upperclassman said quietly. We couldn't believe that one of the upperclassmen had talked quietly to us, almost in a friendly and warm tone. The spell was burst when he looked at me and said, "What are you staring at with those big teary eyes, smack?"

"Sir, nothing, sir."

"You're calling me nothing?"

"No sir."

"Drop and give me fifty." Unbelievable. The day was ten seconds old, and I was off the tracks.

I got to about twenty-six when the upperclassman shut the door. I immediately got up and put my ear to the door to listen to what was happening to Jim. The door popped back open. The upperclassman, a surly little guy with a back as thick as a linebacker, looked at me like he'd just caught me in bed with his girlfriend. I wanted to melt.

I waited for a trapdoor to open. "Give me an extra fifty, do-jazz, and don't mess with me again, you got it?"

"Yessir."

"Drop."

Jim Patterson was the first of the class to have been given the privilege of shouting the minutes until a formation. Each of the formations of the day was preceded by minutes to first call, minutes to assembly, important events of the day, and days until graduation for each of the classes.

"Sir, there are four minutes until first call for the breakfast meal formation. The uniform is Service Bravo. There are four minutes, sir."

"Sir, there are 365 days until the graduation of the Class of 1963. There are 730 days until the graduation of the Class of 1964. There are 1,095 days until the graduation of the Class of 1965. There are 1,460 days until the graduation of the Class of 1966, sir. Sir, today Marilyn Monroe was found dead at her ..."

"How many days until the graduation of '66, Wad?"

"Sir, there are 1,460 days until the graduation of the Class of 1966, sir."

"How does that make you feel?"

"Sir, I've had better moments, sir."

"Carry on."

All this came from a kid being yelled at each time he opened his mouth for not speaking loud enough, not having enough "balls" in his voice, not remembering what he had just been told ... in short, not having much of a chance to make it through here.

There was a lot of other information that a fourth-classman had to know. What events were coming up this weekend? Who was the president, vice president, and each of the cabinet members? Who were the famous generals of the army and air corps? What did the Eagle and Fledgling Statues mean? What was the mission of the air force? It was all contained in a little red book. Each class had a color: gold, blue, silver, and red. The Class of '66 was red. We were RTBs—Red Tag Bastards. That book was called *Talon* after the claws on a falcon.

In short, there was so much required that a fourth-classman spent his year in a futile attempt to learn everything and was always being asked something about which he knew nothing. He never caught up. That was the purpose. The system was constant unending pressure that could be survived only with a group effort. When you were ahead of the curve, you helped your buddy. When you were falling behind, your buddy helped you.

We went to the athletic fields for physical training during that first week. At the edge of the field was a huge stack of non-creosote telephone poles. The first-classman on the platform in front of us explained that we were to proceed to the piles in an orderly fashion, in groups of four, and pick up one of those telephone poles and bring it back to our current place in formation. It was a heavy job, but doable if all four lifted. If someone gave up for a moment to rest, the load on the other three was unbearable. That's one way to find out who you can count on.

Meals were eaten, or looked at, at a brace. You didn't get to eat unless you were told to by an upperclassman, and that "privilege" could quickly be revoked for not sitting up straight enough, not having required knowledge, not answering loud enough, and a hundred other reasons. Three or four meals could go by without getting more than a mouthful or two in during the entire event. It was estimated at one point that the "activities curriculum" of doolie summer burned more than six thousand calories a day. If you missed a meal or two, weight fell off fast. At the end of the summer, I was down to 159 pounds from about 185. I don't think I'd weighed that little since sixth grade.

You had to serve yourself and pass the plates to the upperclassmen as you announced what they were. There was a "hot pilot" and a "cold pilot" at the head of the table who handled food and drinks for the table.

At the end of the meal, one of the doolies at the head of the table would address the upperclassmen. "Sir, does Cadet Jones, Cadet Smith, or any other gentlemen have any comments for the form O-96?" This was the appraisal of the meal that the waiter would pick up. If there were no special comments on the waiter's service or the food, the form was filled out with the mandatory check marks put into the "fast, neat, average, friendly, good, good blocks. None, none was written into the space for detailed comments."

In one lecture, we doolies had been told to see how long we could hold our arms up. We all stood around for minutes until the last man dropped his arms.

On the second attempt, we were told that the length of time we held our arms up was a direct indicator of our success as cadets and even as officers.

Every man in the auditorium held his arms up for a longer period of time. And that was on the second attempt, with sore muscles from the first. The whole thing had been an experiment in motivation, not a determinant of ability to be an underclassman, upperclassman, or officer for that matter. And it proved only what we all already knew: we wanted this.

During our fourth-class (freshman) year, guys would be assigned special inspections. They would go to their classmates' rooms to help them get ready for a "come-around." This was a formation in front of a specific upperclassman's room where the doolie would have his uniform inspected, recite knowledge, do manual of arms, and discuss current events. All this was done in the fifteen minutes preceding taps, after supposedly having studied for several hours.

Halton Ramsey Vincent, now Vince to everyone, had racked up a ton of these come-arounds with a certain second-classman (junior). One night, Vince had saved an empty shell from the rifle range. That was a move that took a lot of nerve. If the upperclassman took it the wrong way, he was a wiseass, and the shit would really hit the fan.

I had helped, with another classmate, get Vince ready for the inspection. We had come to Vince's room in time to help get his uniform ready. He was so cool about it.

"What are they going to do? Make me a fourth-classman and have to drive around to his room every night? Already done that."

Vince figured he had nothing to lose.

We heard him bang on the upperclassman's door.

"What."

"Sir, Cadet Fourth Class Vincent, HR 4015K, or whatever his serial number was, reporting as ordered, sir."

The upperclassman came out, in full class A uniform, in silence. He ordered Vince to step back a few paces and stand at attention.

"Inspection, arms."

Here it came.

Vince pulled the old M1 rifle to inspection arms. As he slapped the breech back, the shell casing flew out and pinged on the floor a couple of times before rolling off and coming to rest.

According to Vince, the upperclassman looked like he'd just been shot with that bullet, which was the whole subtle message.

He came up beside Vince without a break in his demeanor. Vince later said he felt his future pass in front of him.

"Good show," the upperclassman whispered. He dismissed Vince.

From the first day of training until the day we were recognized, upperclassmen almost always rewarded a shot of determination and guts.

Sundays brought mandatory chapel formations, held in the theater of Arnold Hall because the new chapel with its seventeen spires (one for each of the apostles and one for each of the joint chiefs, so the saying went) was not yet complete. In the cool darkness, the voice of the chaplains was occasionally overridden by a sob or a moan or an outright breakdown. But it was in the dark ... no upperclassmen around. No chance to screw up.

That chapel was dedicated on a hot afternoon in the early fall of 1962, as I remember. We were standing at attention for an awfully long time that afternoon, and I remember hearing guys falling over, passing out from the heat. You'd hear a moan and a sort of *crump* as the body hit the cement. Once you fell over, you were supposed to lay there. It meant one thing and one thing only if you passed out: you weren't going to be a pilot. That chapel dedication stuck in my mind for a long time. I didn't pass out.

Our doolie year ended. The Class of '66 made upperclassmen the following spring after "Hell Week." Actually, Hell Week was a breeze, as most of us had spent the previous year getting in the best physical condition of our lives. We could outrun most of the upperclassmen.

The Class of '66 was fully "recognized." We had the coveted prop-and-wing insignia pinned to our lapels.

Every time you went to a new school in the military in the sixties, the refrain was the same. "Look around you. The man on your left and the man on your right will be gone ... soon."

Yeah, well, we made it, so fuck you.

We weren't gone.

Day after day and week after week, we'd stuck together and met the challenges together, and now we were upperclassmen.

CHAPTER II
Academy Life as Upperclassmen

We spent about 99 per cent of our first year within half a mile of the flagpole on the cadet grounds. In those days you didn't even go home for Christmas as a doolie. As upperclassmen, we were allowed more and more privileges, depending on our rank and performance in academics and military training. We'd journey to Denver, march onto football games, visit US military bases, attend innumerable lectures, travel by rail to Chicago twice—but basically we lived in the high lonely cadet area, studying and waiting for graduation. Waiting, in my case, to fly.

THE YEARS PASSED QUICKLY, LOOKING back. There was a growing feeling of something happening in a place called Vietnam. A group of upperclassmen had made a sign in the squadron area to the effect of, "Here's a war we can get to." We had a former member of the Class of 1959 come back and give us a briefing about the problems and satisfactions of working as an advisor to a Vietnamese Air Force A-1 squadron out of Bien Hoa, South Vietnam. The entire wing of cadets sat riveted to our chairs as he went through his tour of duty. We were ready for war. Naturally. We hadn't been in one yet.

A janitor who had befriended the cadets and been an army infantryman during the Second World War scribbled on the bottom of the above-mentioned sign, "You don't know what you're talking about. You don't want this." He signed his name to it. We laughed it off at the time.

November 22, 1963, was a Friday, and the wing of cadets marched to the noon meal formation. The menu was South African lobster tails. It was to be a big weekend. This was the best meal that had ever been served in my year and a half at the "zoo."

The fourth-classmen were going to be allowed to sit at ease to enjoy the special meal.. It had just been served when the wing was called to attention. All twenty four squadrons of men in the huge dining hall sat in silence, upper class and fourth class, all looking straight ahead.

"Gentlemen, there has been an assassination attempt on the president of the United States. All cadets will return to their rooms and remain there until further instructions.

"Gentlemen, you are dismissed."

AS NEAR AS I CAN remember, no one ate a lobster tail, and South African lobster tails were never served again to the Class of 1966. We spent an hour or so in our rooms, and the word came down that the president had died. My roommate at the time was Cy Young, and he stood in the hall outside of our room as the announcement started. When it was over, he just looked straight ahead, blanched white, and walked into the room without saying a word. What could be said?

My parents and many of the older folks around home hadn't been too hot on John Kennedy as president. But I'd seen him up close when he gave the graduation address to the Class of 1963. He came into the stadium among cheers and drove around the perimeter of the place before ascending the steps to the dais. When he came by me, I was no more than four or five rows back in the seats.

He talked that day about a supersonic transport. He talked with an attitude of, "It has to be done. If the US doesn't do it, who will? We *will* build one. We're the leaders of the world." To us, at that time, he was young. He had been in combat. He had that confidence in himself and his country and his countrymen. He got out in front and waited for you to catch up. That's what we figured leaders should do.

But the day he was killed was tough. It gave us an empty feeling that we'd get used to in the next eight or nine years. The funeral and the mourning seemed to go on forever. Few wanted it to end because it seemed that when it did end, he would be gone for good.

Lyndon Johnson replaced Kennedy on the very day that he was killed.

The transition of authority was complete in hours, as only this country can do. We went on as a nation, but without the same sure hand on the wheel that Kennedy seemed to have given us.

Football games came and went. Wing-boxing championships came and went. Girlfriends at Colorado Women's College, CWC (Cadet Wing), and the University of Colorado came and went. "Down they came from the cattle wagon ... down they came with their knuckles draggin'" as one of the class was to write in later years of one of the mixers.

Cadets and mixers were common. This was the way young women were introduced to the men of the cadet wing. Line up on one side of a wall while the cadets lined up on the other. As you emerged from behind the wall, that was your date for the evening. As people neared the point where they could see down the respective lines, much jockeying took place. The cadets took up a collection called the "ghoul pool." Everyone put in a buck, and the winner was the guy with the ugliest date. Coming in second in the ghoul pool was the worst thing that could happen to you except finding out that your date had won the girls' pool. These mixers took place every time a large group of cadets descended on a place in a single event.

There were field trips to the US military installations in this country and abroad. There was lecture after military lecture and discussion after discussion. During my stay, we had two Army–Air Force football games at Soldiers Field, Chicago, with the accompanying all-night train ride on the Santa Fe. That ride, behind that big diesel, cannonballing across the great plains at speeds approaching one hundred miles per hour, engendered a feeling of what a great and magnificent country this was in which we lived. We'd come out of the academy siding by noon Friday, back in it by midnight Sunday.

The academy had a falcon mascot that thrilled crowds, diving at speeds of a hundred miles an hour at a lure. The army had the dependable caisson pulling mule.

"Let's see the mule fly ... let's see the mule fly."

Later the Annapolis goat, wound up on the academy grounds before one of the intra-academy football games. I remember the commandant telling us that if anything happened to that goat, heads would roll.

At one football game during our first-class (senior) year, Em Roberts and another classmate walked down in front of the opposing fans seats at the University of Wyoming football game. As I remember, the stands had been rowdy during much of the first half, and from time to time a snowball was thrown in the direction of the field. Old Em stood at the goal line on Wyoming's side, threw a snowball at the stands, and started marching down their sideline. He disappeared in a hurricane cloud of snowballs. The cadets, on the other side of the field, watched in silence. When he came out of the storm, at the far goal line, the snowballs stopped and he was not hit even once. He bowed toward the field, and a cheer went up from the cadets and the Wyoming fans.

"We ain't afraid of nothin'."

This spirit was shown by our class in many ways. The way that a flag impossibly wound up on the top of one of the chapel spires, hundreds of feet in the air. The same way that the little X-4 jet that had taken a construction crew a week to put in an enclosed quadrangle was out on the ramp the next morning, the same way that a banner saying "'66 thanks Army" was put on the top of one of the huge parachute-jump towers at the Fort Benning, Georgia, paratrooper school—by daring teamwork.

And as sure as recognition had come after the end of the first year, graduation came at the end of the fourth.

We were done.

We were no longer first-class cadets. Now we were the lowest form of commissioned life, second lieutenants. And the men from the Class of '66 headed off to pilot training. We were split between those who headed off with the young lady who had waited patiently for her man to finish school so they could be married and those who left alone. Many a cadet's bachelor-"officerhood" lasted no more than a few hours. They marched from the graduation parade ground to the arch of sabers at the chapel. Out of the academy, into married life. Tom used to say, "No break, only a new voice yelling the minutes to reveille each day."

So I said so long to friends with whom I'd not only survived but flourished within an environment that could, at times, be extremely challenging. I wouldn't see Nat Sanderson, a great hulking guy who was devoted to his friends, for another thirty years. He'd yell at guys like me out of frustration with whatever difference of opinion we had, but you never doubted he was your friend.

Good-bye also to Frank Andrews, who had been the squadron commander after me in our first-class year. Frank was a close friend, wing-boxing champ, two-term roommate (the only one), and FOB. That was Friend of Benny. Benny was the janitor in our squadron area. As I mentioned above, he also had been an infantryman in the war in Europe, a cook actually. But the cooks also wound up fighting. And they suffered the weather, fears, and accomplishments of the rest of the men. Benny, along with several other of the janitors, had become personal friends of a number of the first-classmen and kept the janitorial closet stoked with coffee and snacks for us "firsties."

So long to Norm Rathje, who I wouldn't see for twenty years. Good-bye to quiet Ron Brooks. So long to Ed Blaess, with whom I went jackrabbit hunting with Frank in Big Spring Texas during pilot training, but haven't seen again to this day. Ed, who married the sister of the girl Frank married, had been a close friend of mine. So long to Pat Maiorca and Dave Hoogerland. Both those guys became doctors, as did Nat Sanderson. Maiorca had all sorts of nicknames that dealt with his "squatty" body, but if you didn't like Pat, you had a problem. He would go to Korat in the back of an F-105 before going off to medical school. So long to Bruce McBride, who would spend hours being shot at working the electronic side of the air war, and to Jim Patterson, with whom I'd faced the toughest first four weeks of the whole four years, and to Ron Morey ("Morals"), always a dependable friend. Steve Eisler was a tough, tough man with inner strengths that would stand him well in challenges to come.

I heard later that Jamie Gough would find himself on the ground in Laos in a shootout with the enemy in an effort to be rescued. I wouldn't see him again for over twenty year when he was a wing commander at Ramstein in Germany and I was flying in Desert Storm.

So long to Carl Womack. Carl was quiet, unbelievably smart, and unassuming. Hailing from Arkansas, with a bit of hesitation in his talking manner, he went on to get a Master's degree and came to the war in F-105s. I met him again at the thirtieth reunion. He probably had more short tours and maybe more long tours in Vietnam than any of us, all heavy-duty combat, all in F-105s. He died shortly after our thirtieth reunion.

So long to Ray Milberg, Dan Heitz, with whom I'd traveled the roads to Denver many times, and big Sam Peshut. Sam and I roomed together for the last semester we were at the academy. I remember the five-day spring break during which Sam drove his new Corvette all the way to Pittsburgh and back, just to show his dad. I remember the argument we got into in our last three days as cadets. Out of that argument, I realized there was no regulation as important as a honest friend, well-served.

And most of all, so long to a little gal I'd been engaged to marry and to her wonderful family. I ran out on her like a mutt with his tail between his legs. Absolutely no class at all in the way I did it, but I did it, and it was better for both of us. I did love her, but not enough to settle down and take on the responsibility of a family the day after I got out of "Aluminum U." Not enough to take her along to pilot training, fighters, combat tours, and all the adventure that was in front of me. That was mine and mine alone to live.

I lost more than she did in that separation.

We were on to the "real" air force. Pilot training.

CHAPTER 12
Pilot Training

After we left the academy, my friends and I joined with a bunch of other brand-new lieutenants and some older first lieutenants and captains from various parts of the military and headed for pilot training. It was probably the greatest party year of my life. I was living with my best friends in the world and flying high-performance jets over the flat prairies around Lubbock, Texas. We, the academy guys and the ROTC guys who joined us, were a remarkably cohesive group of people with very similar backgrounds who were to become very close friends.

One of the advantages of going to pilot training from the academy is that you get to go with so many acquaintances from the school. I had a group consisting of Jan Jaeger, Dan Heitz, Jerry Allen, Mike Heenan, Terry Schmidt, Ken Boone, and P. T. Bingham, also from "Fightin' Fourth." There were other classmates in the other section of the class, but unfortunately we hardly ever saw them after the first few days. When they had academics we were flying, and when they were flying we were in class. When the academic portion ended, they'd be at home when we were flying.

The Great One—Mravak—and I roomed together. Jerry Becker, who was everyone's friend, was there. Jerry was a little shorter than the rest of us and had a mop of dark hair that was always just on the verge of being "too long, Becker."

Hugh Gommel, who had also been a friend but not a close one till that time, was there. Gommel had to have had some Italian or other Mediterranean culture in his recent background. He looked it and was the only guy with a schnoz nearly as big as mine. "Classic," I think he called it, but it didn't hurt his looks a bit in the eyes of the women, apparently. Dark hair, dark eyes, always a sort of grin just about to break out, always ready to stop and talk, not just for a minute but for as long as you wanted to do so. There was a lot of fake tension between him and the Great One over who was the more qualified bachelor, but Hugh had a serious girlfriend, who we all loved, so he had to yield a little in that argument.

Muckrock and Gommel owned the two Corvettes in the group. The rest of us griped continually about the uselessness of having one of these two in a carpool. "Carpooling with Gommel or Mravak means driving alone one day and driving with them in your front seat the next. Their turn is when they fucking drive themselves."

. Muckrock and Becker had organized and played in a rock band called the Flameouts in our junior and senior year at school. Tom was the lead singer with Jerry and Bill Berry, also from Third Squadron. Bill played guitar. Jeff Jarvis was the drummer early on in their stint. I'm not sure he was with the group for very long, but Tom and Jerry picked Jeff not only for his ability but because his Nordic good looks had to attract more women than they would've on their own. When he smiled up on the stage, you expected his tooth to twinkle. There were other cadets in that band, Gary Mueller, did the drums later as I recall, Bill Todd who filled in for Mason Botts, but these were the guys I remember from being at a couple of their shows and singing along with the closer, "We've gotta get out of this place."

Tom, myself, and this group of friends had pulled off pilot-training assignments at the same base—Reese Air Force Base in Lubbock, Texas. Mac Davis, a great country-and-western songwriter, was to later write the lyrics "happiness is Lubbock, Texas, in my rearview mirror." We uttered that phrase many times over the next year. We picked it up from the girls at Texas Tech years before Davis made it into a song. I think he went to school there at about that time or was from there. Any good-looking young woman in Lubbock had heard that phrase at the time, and I'd be surprised if Davis didn't hear it from one of them.

It was a continual party interrupted only by flying high-performance jet airplanes. How much better could life be for a young buck, fresh out of the confines of four years on a hill in Colorado?

Into Lubbock came the Olds 442s, the Pontiac GTOs, the Chevy Super Sports, and the Corvettes. This group was ready to party, ready to fly, ready to fight, and expecting to go to the war in jet fighter aircraft. We figured the fewer people in each of those fighters and the fewer engines pushing each of those fighters, the bigger the set on the man flying it. We had no way of knowing what it took to be a fighter pilot, but we were sure we had it. My lifelong dream of flying large transport aircraft disappeared the minute I started seeing the personal satisfaction that flying high-performance jets alone could bring.

Training began at Lubbock Municipal Airport in the T-41 program. The T-41 was a modified light civilian aircraft that basically allowed the air force to wash out approximately the same percentage of pilots without having to spend the money that it took to wash them out of jet airplanes.

"The man on your left and the man on your right will be gone."

All of that reality was wrapped up in the term "introductory course." If you could fly this plane, you would probably be able to hack the rest of the program. Some didn't, but for the most part, this was a true statement. We flew the mighty T-41 for about six weeks, doing lazy eights and big circles over the western Texas plains. The instructors were an odd mix of ex-military transport pilots, civilians building time for their bid for an airline job, and military officers assigned to monitor the program. The program came to an end, and as we had become accustomed to in our years at the academy, about 40 percent of the class was gone.

"Look at the man on your left and the man on your right. They won't be here."

It was never-ending.

Everything we had done in our air-force careers had a washout rate programmed into it. This was one more. We'd beat it again. Years later, I found out I had washed out on the entrance physical. My sitting height was too tall. Either nobody caught it, or the ever-expanding war in Southeast Asia demanded input that could overlook a lieutenant with a sitting height that was too great.

I did not have problems with the T-41, as I had flown similar airplanes many times since first taking lessons in the summer of 1960 and I had a Private Pilot License. But some of the old gang did have problems. We lost a tight member of the group, Mike Heenan, during the T-41 program. Although he did finally solo, it wasn't in time to make the timeline. I regret to this day that I didn't have the nerve to go with Mike when he offered to rent a plane if I would sit there and let him make touch-and-go's. While I felt I could fly the airplane, I just didn't think I could instruct in it with a fellow student who was having problems learning to land. I was afraid to take on the responsibility of not just flying, but fixing a friend's screwups, with less than a hundred hours total time in my logbook. Dope.

After the T-41 came the Cessna T-37—a six-thousand-pound dog whistle, as the plane was affectionately called. It had all the streamlining of a steam engine, but it served a purpose. It put the pilots in an airplane with a stick in their right hand and the throttle in their left, an airplane with a plexiglass canopy overhead, helmets and oxygen masks in place, and a microphone attached to their face in the mask. You strapped into the T-37 with a wide lap belt and two shoulder harness that came over the back of the seat, through an inertial reel, and down over your chest to the buckle in your lap. This was the first airplane that you put on and grabbed onto the "stick" to fly.

The stick ... there is something incredibly suggestive about maneuvering a machine by hanging on to a pole between a man's legs. "Hold that thing lightly, boy. Don't squeeze it so hard. Treat it like your best friend."

We'd finished a course of physiological training during our time in the T-41. That included another altitude chamber and seemingly endless lectures and movies on the dangers of hypoxia or hyperventilation or the bends and so forth. When we first left the desert ground of Lubbock in the T-37, half of us were convinced we were heading for outer space. The first time I saw an instructor take off his oxygen mask, turn off the flow, and light a cigarette in the cockpit, at altitude, I was stunned. I half expected him to roll over and die of hypoxia, which is the technical term for not getting enough oxygen to continue functioning as a coherent and alive human organism. As a man goes higher and higher into the atmosphere, the available oxygen decreases. We had been trained to believe that at five thousand feet without an oxygen mask, one would begin feeling the effects. No one stopped to think that we had spent the last four years living constantly above seven thousand feet elevation at the academy, all the while moving and exercising vigorously. We were all probably in the best shape of our lives. Terry Schmidt, one of our classmates in the group, summed it up with, "They've got me believing I should put on an oxygen mask to come visit you guys on the second floor."

Nevertheless, as I watched the IP smoke, I figured he'd probably done that before and he seemed to be perfectly relaxed while doing so, conversing and looking around at the flat Texas plains. I had obviously been overtrained on the implications of hypoxia.

On our first altitude-chamber ride at Reese, they asked for a volunteer to take his oxygen mask off while the chamber was at thirty-five thousand feet. Hugh Gommel volunteered. After about thirty seconds, the instructor said, "You're probably beginning to feel lightheaded."

Hugh just looked at him and said, "No. I'm good."

About another thirty seconds, and the instructor said, "How about now?"

"Good, sir. No problems." Hugh gave a thumbs-up. It was the sort of thumbs-up you might get from a guy right after his first six-pack went down.

"Put your mask on, Lieutenant."

Hugh, probably feeling the early effects of hypoxia, started to protest.

"Now!"

Hugh put the mask on and continued looking straight ahead with a sort of *What's his problem?* look.

Years later, I was in an altitude chamber with a bunch of lieutenant colonels, and the hypoxia demonstration was done at eighteen thousand feet. We all had our masks on within twenty seconds.

On my first T-37 ride, I thought I'd never catch up to the plane. I loved the idea of flying it, but I couldn't get over how fast the ground was going by and how fast the proper reactions had to be accomplished. There might be more to this than I had thought. My instructor said, "Detwiler, you were so far behind on the first ride that if we'd hit the ground, you wouldn't have said *ouch* for twenty seconds."

But it sure wasn't all flying. There were the women of Texas Tech University. On the first day of the first weekend that the new lieutenants were in Lubbock, Tom and I drove his shiny red Corvette convertible through the campus, stopping at the student store to meet some of the ladies. Tom spent two years in college before going off to the academy and had a feel for the college scene. I had gone to the academy four days after I graduated from high school. Basically, my social development had been frozen at the eighteen-year-old level. But in the world of sixties dating, I adapted quickly to the fact that women didn't give a shit that I'd eaten meals at attention and marched in parades. They wanted to party and drink. And the dry town of Lubbock and the dry Texas Tech University made it much easier for the lieutenants to get along with the women if we brought them out to the base.

What a party place we brought those women to! The bachelor officers' quarters at Reese in 1966 were old World War II wooden barracks. Mercifully, someone had divided the long buildings into individual units, both upstairs and downstairs, during the mid-fifties. Each unit was entered through a concrete three-step in front of the unit or off a long upstairs porch that was entered via an outside staircase at the end of the building. Each building had a much larger three-bedroom suite at the upstairs end. This was the party room.

Tom, Greg Parker, and I had one of the big rooms, and Hugh Gommel, Kenny Boone, and Jerry Becker had the one across the way from us. We brought the girls out each Saturday night and partied until about midnight as I recall. The parties were held in the three-bedroom units each weekend. There was always plenty of beer, light Scotch for the more "sophisticated" drinkers among us, Lancers in the red crock bottle and Mateus Rose in the green stumpy-looking bottle for some of the girls. The wine industry was laying the groundwork that would pay off thirty years later.

The parties started out with talking and drinking and sometimes cooking something up in the space between the two buildings, and as the night wore on the participants got closer and closer to the floor with what seemed like piles of human flesh writhing and "eating each others' chins," as Beck used to say. Yeah, thumbs-up, brother.

The girls had to be back in their dorms by midnight, but some of them spent many of the evenings getting ten hours of fun into the four or five we were allowed on a Saturday night in the old wooden barracks.

Friendships continued to grow. Places and things done together formed a background of experience and shared times together. Smiles, laughs, parties, women, drinking—and always there was the flying. We'd get together after taking the girls home on a Saturday night. The diner of choice was the local Toddle House. I forget the name of the gal who was on duty each of those nights, but she was a sweetheart. We'd laugh and joke with her for an hour or so. One night, she protested that there were just too many of us at one time for her to handle the orders the way she'd like. Becker hopped behind the counter, eased her into the kitchen, and started taking orders for her. Each Saturday, it was always the same. Same group of guys, same place, same waitress. We loved it.

Tom and I had each dropped the girls off at the dorm one night and met up at a stoplight about a block from the diner. He was in his 'Vette, and I was in the 1966 GTO I had at the time. Someone pulled in between us in some little shitbox. I forget who it was, but he was one of the gang, who was also heading for the Toddle House. When the light changed, Tom and I blew out of the intersection. We were pretty well tied when the next intersection came up and we started to brake. We sat laughing and waiting for the other guy to come up between us, but he didn't.

A cop did.

He pulled us over. As it happened, he pulled us over into the Toddle House parking lot.

"That was a hell of a race, boys. I thought the Pontiac would do a little better. I own one myself. LeMans, though, not a fancy GTO. Yep, thought you could take him. License and registration, please."

There were about nine sets of eyeballs pressed against one of the windows in the Toddle House watching Tom and I get our summonses. We came in to a round of applause.

During the week that followed, we both got the same time off to plead before the judge. The old man smiled when we admitted to everything, admitted to our willingness to pay, and only asked him that the information didn't get out to the base.

"It won't. Promise ya. But if you race in my town again, I'll have your ass. Got that, boys?"

"Yessir, Mr. Judge."

We endured the ever-cooler evenings and days as the late autumn of 1966 led into the winter. The winter was horribly cold. "Nothing between us here and the North Pole but barbwire fences."

After a few more months in the T-37, we went to the next step, the T-38 Talon. The T-38 was a fighter with all the performance of any of the air force's best machines. Below is a piece I wrote for Business and Commercial Aviation, an aviation magazine, concerning our time in the T-38.

Reese Air Force Base, Lubbock Texas, *March 1967.*

This was it. We had arrived. The White Rocket, the T-38. Nobody had their picture taken standing next to a T-37. The 38 was the plane we had waited to fly for a long time.

My first ride was in the front seat and my IP (an ex F-102 interceptor pilot) was in the back. He briefed me thoroughly. He made the first take off. When he lit the burners on that first takeoff, I was like a guy hanging straight out from the rear cargo door of a tractor trailer truck, mouth open with no sound coming out, going by at about 75 miles an hour.

We rotated somewhere around 150, gear and flaps up immediately, nose coming up to about 40 degrees, accelerating through 300. Oh man, life couldn't be better than this.

The next ten rides were in the backseat, doing instrument approaches and then taking an instrument check all the while under a cloth hood that covered all visibility out of the plexiglass canopy. Just shoot me.

Finally, ride 11 was "contact," we were up front, looking outside. Clear plexiglass bubble canopy, hanging on to the "stick" between your legs, left hand on afterburner throttles, g-suit, speed brakes and mike control handled with your left thumb. We had arrived. Now the goal was not to just fly this marvelous machine, but to fly it alone.

The T-38 was just a few years old when we got to it, and it defined "coolness" for a bunch of 22-year-old fighter pilot "wannabes." In fact, it was easy to forget that it wasn't a fighter. I remember an old F-100 pilot that somehow wound up back at Reese as a T-37 instructor. His name was Crockett, nickname, the obvious, Davy. Davy was sitting in the stag bar one night listening to a young T-38 FAIP (first assignment instructor pilot) brag on his T-38's capabilities.

"Davy, this thing will outclimb, out-turn, out-accelerate and outperform that old F-100 you flew in every aspect."

"Tell you what, young fella. Why don't I go up to Cannon (Cannon AFB in Clovis, New Mexico), get recurrent in a hun (F-100), fill it with twenty millimeter bullets, and you and I will meet over Muleshoe and see who shoots who down."

"But Davy, the T-38 doesn't have any guns."

"Best keep that in mind when you're talking fighters, son." Score one for Davy.

Jerry Becker and I made a pact about halfway through the program. Both of us were solo in our airplanes. We would join up in the practice area (non-radar environment in those days), then go to about a half mile spread formation, accelerate to 500 knots at 8000 feet, pull to the vertical and count how many aileron rolls the other did. Winner gets a free Coors. Jerry went first. I followed him up, counting his 11 rolls. We both did low airspeed, vertical recoveries.

Then came my turn.

The plan was obvious to me. I would just keep rolling until I had gone around at least 11 times. Jerry followed along about a half a mile off to my right. I did 13 rolls, found myself at 22,000 feet (Positive Control Airspace, where acrobatics like this would've been illegal, began at FL240 in those days), at 80 knots, quickly decreasing to zero, and out of ideas. I heard Jerry key the mike, breathing hard, nothing else. I eased the stick forward to zero g's and hung on. The T-38 just slowly fell off on a wing and headed back down.

"Recover from the ensuing dive."

Jerry's airplane swapped ends. One minute he was going straight up, the next straight down. All done at 0 airspeed, all with both hands holding

89

the stick neutral, all at full military thrust. We went our separate ways back to the pattern at Reese, shot a few touch and gos, and called it a day. I still remember listening to an instructor tell a guy, "I've had the T-38 down to 80 knots. You just have to keep it unloaded and be real careful." Jerry sucked in on his Winston, looked at me, raised his eyebrows, and we both just smiled.

This was maximum performance flying. While flying formation, you looked out at your friend, in his airplane, looking back at you in yours. As you led him through a formation takeoff or landing, you knew what the word "trust" meant. You could "see" his face even though it was behind a helmet visor and oxygen mask. Four ship in trail formation, fighting wing practice, afterburner climbs, 500 knot loops, "pulling" the plane around the pattern. What a time we had.

Many of my friends went on to fly two tours in Vietnam. Two years of combat. Most made it. Some didn't. I recently watched a program that agonized for a half an hour over whether our generation would ever get over the disagreement about the Vietnam War. What foolishness. Truth is, from the T-38 on, my friends and I saw a job to do, felt we could qualify for it, did it, often scared, sometimes exalted and never really cared how the rest of our generation viewed us. Still don't. The agonizing, it seems, is being done by those that didn't go. We did. We did our best, and we moved on.

As I've said, during this time, I became extremely close friends with a lot of guys. There was Hugh Gommel and his girlfriend, later wife, Kathy. She was everyone's little sister, "Yeah, Rosie, the little sister you want to run away with," as Becker would correct me. She visited often. Later, she followed Hugh to Southeast Asia, where she taught school in Bangkok to be near him. They raised a family together over a period of about thirty years and then went their separate ways. I can only say this about the two of them now: I know I could meet either of them and their current spouse and have as wonderful a time as ever. They are great people.

There was, of course, Jerry Becker. Beck was a Pennsylvania boy with a head of hair that looked, as much as air-force guidelines would allow, like a Beatles haircut. Jer was in on everything, every party that was planned, every flight that was flown, every gag that was pulled. Somehow, Jerry always turned up right in the middle of it. He, Tom, and I drove back to the Northeast together during the Christmas break while at Reese. We had been shown a movie on the perils of driving long distances to get home for the holidays: leave early in the day, don't drink, stop often, get plenty of sleep, and on and on it went. We headed out at about four in the afternoon, after a quick beer, and drove without stopping until we were home. It was a hell of a trip.

After the summer of 1969, the next time I saw Jerry was at Tip Galer's wedding, about 1981. Just like always, Jerry had shown up. He shook my hand and then gave me a hug. "Man hugs" weren't done in those days either, but Jerry was just like Tom. He did and said things because he felt them, not because they were politically correct.

Greg Parker was our class leader. Greg was a captain, a former transport-command navigator, suffering from a recent divorce and struggling to get his legs under him, but he did very well on the flying end of pilot training. He was our class leader and "roomie" in the large three-bedroom we shared. Larry Morris took over for him when Greg got "wrapped around the axle," as they say, late in the program. But none of his problems kept him from being a great pilot.

Also in the class was Ken Rinehart, "Ryno," a good-ole-boy Texan whose dad worked for a brewery, bless him. There was John Mack, who could only be described as a Charleston gentlemen, and his girlfriend and later wife, Helen. Don "Troll" Rapuzzi, , Jerry Allen, and a couple of Iranian guys were all members of the gang. If I was sure it wouldn't get them killed, I'd mention the Iranians' names.

As I said, Kenny Boone shared the three-bedroom on the opposite side of the courtyard with Beck and Hugh. Kenny was editor of the class yearbook at the academy and edited the pilot-training yearbook. Ken's friendship was worth much more than he would ever let one believe.

Clyde Thompson, Bucky Jones, , and quiet Larry Broadhead, later killed in a B-52 midair, were there too.

Beck had a little black-and-white mutt dog that we named Caesar. Caesar spent Saturday night sniffing around and drinking beer out of a saucer that was amply filled for him by the partiers. Sunday mornings found Caesar recovering with the rest of the group.

Caesar was in such bad shape one morning that he walked off the second-story balcony and fell about twenty feet. He just lay there about a minute, got up, and went on as if nothing had happened. Before moving on to Luke, we all went home for leave. I remember flying back to Lubbock to pick up my car and picking Caesar up from the girl who had kept him and traveling in the car with him to Phoenix. That was quite a ride. The little pooch would sit there for hours with his head just up over the edge of the window bottom and watch people as we passed them on the highway. As his head turned from front to rear as the car was passed he'd keep his eyes glued on the driver. People laughed and waved at us all the way to Phoenix. When Jery went to Vietnam, he left Caesar with his parents. By the time he got back, the little pooch had endeared himself so much to the old man that he wouldn't leave. He lived for nearly fifteen years.

THE CLASS AT REESE WAS broken up into two sections, A and B. The B group had most of the bachelors and did most of the partying, but the A group and their wives were all part of the show, and all enjoyed our times there.

When each party, each social gathering, each get-together was over and the married guys and their wives left, there were the ten to fifteen of us bachelors hanging around, talking, dreaming, just not wanting to let go.

Ken Boone—in his typical sarcastic, dead-on-the-mark manner—managed to capture the mood of the group of us in a quote under a photo in our pilot-training yearbook. The picture, which I took long after the civilized folks had gone home, showed Hugh Gommel like a Southern preacher standing in front of his flock with some notes on a piece of paper. Sitting around him was, Bucky Jones, Tom, Jerry, Frank "Wrub" Wrublewski, wonderful Wrub, and Clyde, the whole gang.. The trouble is that the "preacher" and his entire "flock" appeared to be in the bag. The quote that caught the mood perfectly: "The wonderful love of a beautiful maid, and the love of a staunch true man, and the love of a baby unafraid, have existed since time began; but the greatest love, even greater than that of a mother, is the tender, passionate, infinite love of one drunken slob for another ..."

We laughed at that one for hours. Ken had found a "politically correct" way to say we loved each other.

But mostly, there was Mravak—Muckrock. Again, the leader, the man everyone wanted to know and the man who was willing, even anxious, to be your friend.

I think Tom was so popular not because he was Mr. Cocky and confident, but because he was that with enough of an air of human frailty that you just wanted to be around him. He wasn't supernatural. He was just a guy with his doubts, but full of dreams and determined to persevere in making those dreams come true. He'd willingly share those dreams and doubts with you and hear all about yours. Who wanted to be an astronaut in 1966? Tom did.

He had it all. He was several years older than most of the rest of us, yet never stood out as an "older brother."

We all lived through his meeting, dating, courting, and marriage to Sandy. The big guy would never get married—we'd all been sure of that. Marriage was for guys when they got too old to go out and chase women each weekend. Yeah. Marriage was for guys who found someone they snowed and didn't want to let her get away because they weren't sure they could do it again. Yeah. Marriage was for people without enough confidence to just be alone. Yeah. Then came Sandy.

Sandy was a hot little Texas redhead, used to having her way with guys. When Tom first asked her out for a Saturday event, she said she was busy that night but could go out with him on Friday or Sunday night of that weekend. Tom just told her he'd wait until she could fit him in as the "main event," and maybe he'd go out with her then.

The die was cast.

The jousting began.

He was not a gentleman.

She was spoiled.

If he wanted to go out with her, he'd do it whenever conditions allowed.

He didn't play second fiddle to any date.

This would be their first date, who was he?

He was a fighter pilot, live with it.

So was her father, with kills in P-51s in the "big one." That didn't work.

She might call next week, if she was free. She did call the following week, and Tom was busy. Finally, they agreed on a date, and they ran emotionally into each other's arms, beds, and hearts. It was over. The Great Muckrock was truly in love. There were tough times, of course, as Tom fought off the love he felt. He couldn't be getting married. He'd talked so much against the institution.

"Rosie, I've can't believe this girl. She can't do enough to please me. She loves me so much. God, I've got it bad." He sat on our couch looking at his feet, overcome with love.

Coming from Tom, this was such an admission of human emotion that it caught me off guard. I actually felt that he was fooling around with me. This couldn't be the Kahuna speaking.

I remember after our first tour in SEA, meeting up with Tom and Sandy, who were by then married, and Jerry in New York. Sandy was the stay-at-home wife as we boys headed off to New York for a night at Joe Namath's place, the Bachelors Three. We operated out of Sandy's grandparents' place in Long Island, and the next morning I heard, "Rosie, get in here."

There was Beck on top of the bed with Tom and Sandy. He was in his skivvies.

Tom said, "I had a great time with you two last night, but think I'll stick with the Mrs." We laughed. What a group.

Being involved in an endeavor that might lead to sudden and violent death imparted a feeling of wanting to get the very most out of every moment you have with people you love. We were no different. We didn't know it at the time, but we were grabbing for all the love we could.

After that night, Tom and Sandy headed off for George AFB in California for him to upgrade for his second tour, and Jerry and I headed off to become Air Training Command instructors. I often thought how it had to have weighed on Sandy's heart knowing that she would have to live through the love of her life doing another year in Vietnam before he was "safe," if that word could ever apply to a fighter pilot who wanted to be an astronaut.

Tom had grown up the only son. He had a wonderful older sister who I only met once, at his funeral.

But oh, his mom. She doted on him like he was a treasure from the Lord himself. In the hours of conversations that I witnessed between the two, I never saw her look at him with less than total adoration. He was everything that was important to her on this earth, and Tom loved her adoringly also. She would go on and on about him and about what a great boy he was, and Tom never interrupted her, he never stopped her, he just smiled at her. I used to be amazed at such a worldly and mature man holding and caressing and loving his wonderful mother with such deep affection and return of love. It is my shame that I never followed up and visited her, but within a year of Tom's death, I was gone to SEA for another year, and then to the far west, and then she was gone from my life.

But back to 1967 and T-38s at Reese AFB in Lubbock.

At that time, there were ten Air Training Command bases in the US, turning out about four hundred pilots every six weeks. Our class graduated in the late summer of 1967 and got about ten F-100 assignments. At least five of those assignments went to Reese, all to our section. The F-100 was the assignment everyone wanted.

A slew of F-4 assignments came down, which was a bittersweet ending. It was the hottest and biggest and fastest fighter, but the first tour in SEA for most guys was in the backseat, keeping the books, watching the gauges, and trying to help a much older group of men who were being fit into the front seat from various nonflying assignments as the Vietnam War ate into the reserve of first-line fighter pilots.

Class position determined everything. Your class position was made up mostly of how well you flew, but also had an academics portion just to throw another monkey wrench in the works. The top guys picked first. The Class of '68-B was lucky that there were quite a few F-100s in all the different assignments that came down at the time of our graduation.

Hugh Gommel, Jerry Becker, Tom Meishko (Class of '65 at the academy but with us in pilot training), Greg Parker, and I all took F-100s.

All the F-4 guys, Tom included, would have to be willing to go back to SEA for a second tour if they wanted to upgrade to the front seat. That was where he was headed after our night out in New York.

Finally, as pilot training wound to a close in late August of 1967, we were all sitting around the night after graduation and Ken Rinehart just started crying. He excused himself and we all sat around wondering what his problem was.

Only Tom was smart enough to know.

"He's just realized that it's over. The greatest year of our lives and the best friends of our lives, and we're all going in different directions."

We, now with moist eyes of our own, went and dragged Ryno back. Only Tom, without preaching or sermonizing to us, could verbalize the emotion, understand it, and make it okay to display in 1967.

CHAPTER 13
On to the Fighter Schools

The first day I arrived at Luke, a couple of the instructors stopped me in the street and said, "Hey, come on over here a minute. Look, Bert, a second lieutenant with wings. I didn't know they made such people anymore."

We showed up for the first day of academics, and the instructor ran a brief fifteen-second clip of an out-of-control F-100 weaving back and forth about three feet off the runway and finally crashing in a huge fireball. The famous "saber dance."

"Pay attention, gentlemen. We will teach you how to fly this beast so that you do not duplicate that scene."

THE F-100 WAS A CREAM assignment. Up to that time, there was no aircraft changeover in the air-force squadrons to which the fighter was assigned. Sure, people did their tours in Southeast Asia, but when they were over, the guys just went back to the Orient or Europe, flying nuke alerts and gun-range missions in F-100s that hadn't been sent to Vietnam. As time wore on, the F-100s in Vietnam didn't go home, and they kept needing new pilots. With the service policy of only one tour per individual, the only way to man them was by bringing in new pilots. That was us.

Get ready. We'll take over now.

Now more old friends came back into the mix. I shared an apartment with Andrew R. "Wheels" Fornal from the coal-mining area of Pennsylvania. Wheels spent his entire career in fighters and in combat when required. Like me, he had left the academy wanting to fly transports.

Tom Kiser, a '66 academy grad with us, and his great little wife, Bernie, also came. They had a new son, and I remember feeling such wonder for a man who could leave such joy to go to war. The rest of us were bachelors, leaving nothing. Tom was leaving a girl any of us would've loved to have love us, and a new son.

But back to Wheels.

Wheels was a gruff-talking, Winston-smoking ("I'll butt out a Winston on your casket after the service, Rose"), beer-drinking fighter pilot. And he was tough as they came. He had dates, but at that time in his life, he could only be described as having very little use for women. "A broad is a broad, Rose. The sooner you guys realize that, the sooner you'll stop trying to understand them."

If you yelled at Wheels to grab a beer, he'd bring you a Bud, but you had to recite the whole label piece: "This is the famous Budweiser Beer. We know of no other brand produced by any other brewer which cost so much to age and produce. Our exclusive Beechwood Aging Process produces a smoothness, taste and drinkability you will find in no other beer at any other price," or words to that effect. Moreover, there had to be the proper amount of emotion and feeling when you said it or all you got was, "Get your own fucking beer."

Wheels drove an old Jaguar on which the hood release had let loose at some unbelievably high speed, allowing the whole hood to snap up, bending itself over the top of the windshield and smashing a big dent in the roof. In typical fashion, Wheels bent the hood back down, tied it with thick rope, and pressed on, for years. Added to this, the car had a hydraulic clutch, which, because of a leak, usually laid flat on the floor. You had to put your left foot behind it, pull it out, pump it up and down several times by holding pressure against the foot-pedal edge and then, eventually, build up enough pressure to get the clutch plates to separate when you pushed in on it. This was like the old patting your head, rubbing your stomach, and tapping your foot at the same time gig. Somehow it seemed a perfectly normal thing to Wheels. I tried twice and received a "fucking incompetent" from him. But he let me drive it, a badge of honor. Nobody else drove that wreck except Wheels and me.

Stories are told to this day of the pig roast that was held at Wheels's pilot-training base. Tom and Bernie Kiser had been fellow classmates. Fornal had spent the night before tending the roast, as was required, drinking beer and just "hanging out." By the time the guests started to arrive, Wheels was still there, dirty, unwashed, drinking, and feeling no pain. Sort of the pig-roast-troll under the bridge. But Wheels could do no wrong. Everybody loved him because, I think, he was absolutely and completely open and truthful. He never said anything he didn't mean, and he always meant exactly what he said. He would stop what he was doing and spend the rest of a day helping you. He spent the entire night getting that pig cooked. Someone had to do so. Wheels did. If Wheels liked you, you had arrived. The most tact I ever saw Wheels display was when a senior officer asked, "You think I'm an asshole, don't you?"

Wheels just looked at him, smiled, and said, "When a senior officer is talking, who am I to interrupt, sir?"

He was pure of spirit.

There were a bunch of other classmates with me at Luke. Dan Cecil was there. The next time I'd see Dan was sitting in mobile control (remember the little sort of control tower out by the runway?) at Phu Cat when an F-100 nose came sliding out of a monsoon rain. He was rained in with me there for three days. We had a "good review" period together.

Dale Fowler, Wendell Cook, Tom Brandon and his wife, Gail. Tom and Gail had had a bunch of us bachelors out to their place for a wonderful Thanksgiving. Gail was almost in tears at one point because something apparently was wrong with the gravy, or she didn't have any, or some such thing. We just sort of looked at each other. We were a group of guys with nothing in our refrigerators but beer cans and mayonnaise jars, and she had gone to the trouble to cook us a Thanksgiving meal. It was wonderful to the rest of us.

Tom Meishko (Class of '65) was in our class. Jerry and Hugh were a class behind us at Luke There was Art Suro, who I wouldn't see after Luke until the wild party in his trailer at Tuy Hoa the night before I left for home after the year in SEA was over.

Lacy Veach and his sweetheart wife, Alice, were there. Lace would live Tom's dream of becoming an astronaut and actually flew several shuttle missions before cancer got him. I saw him just before he gave a speech at

Stewart Air National Guard Base around 1989. Ten minutes to catch up on over twenty years, and we did it just like I said it could be done.

Tip Galer went through either behind us at Luke or at Cannon Air Force Base in Clovis, New Mexico. Wheels and he were close friends, but Wheels referred to Tip as a hot dog.

Tip was the only one of the three of us who could coordinate a wardrobe. In fact, Galer was probably the only one of us who had what could be considered a wardrobe. He also had a Corvette at that time, as I remember. And his car wasn't half-destroyed. That probably pissed off Wheels more than the wardrobe.

Tip stepped up years later as an element lead in an F-4 flight of four when the leader, Carl Jeffcoat, was shot down. Tip's quiet voice of command and authority over the radio was the perfect example of the right man at the right time.

Now Carl Jeffcoat was an instructor at Luke while we were all going through the F-100 school in the fall of 1967. He'd had a tour in Vietnam in F-100s and went back in F-4s. During the Christmas raids of 1972, he and his back-seater, Jack Trimble, survived the shoot down and Tip took over the flight. I met up with Carl when I came back through Luke, in May of 1973, for F-4 instructor school after my second tour. He was never fat, but like me, he had plenty of meat on his bones. He had lost about forty pounds. "Try eating turnips twice a day for three months." Carl had only been held captive for a couple of months and knew how easy he'd had it compared to guys who had been there for years. But even that had been quite an experience. Trimble, his back-seater, made a reputation for himself sneaking around the Hanoi Hilton late at night getting things out of guards' desks for his fellow prisoners.

These were real life-and-death threats that we faced together. And the humor, intensity, and determination of these guys branded their friendships into my mind forever. With Tip, Tom, Wheels, Jerry, Preston, Hugh, Clayboy, Bill, and the rest, I would expect, whenever we do get together, that there will be just enough time spent introducing all the girls and the curtain will be pulled back on forty years.

The partying continued, and the flying got better. On the day I got promoted to first lieutenant, I managed to get lost on a low-level (fifty feet) high-speed navigation leg. These navigation legs were practice for the mission of flying from European or Asian bases to pre-selected targets in the Soviet Union and striking them with nuclear weapons. The fighters were to go in at fifty feet, below radar coverage, and navigate their way to the target, pop up, and deliver the nuclear bomb.. In reality, it was a one-way trip.

After I got lost on the practice navigation exercise, I climbed up high and made all the proper calls at the correct times, as if I were still flying the proper course. I headed down to the range, which was easy to see at higher altitude, dropped down low, and called the initial point. The instructor, who at that time was orbiting over the range, looked back to see me in a very tight, high-g turn, which meant I had been coming from the wrong direction. Busted. Figured it didn't matter much, as we were not going to be doing nuke low-level deliveries, and they sure as heck weren't not going to send me to Southeast Asia at that stage of the game.

We did daily trips to the gun range south of the Gila Bend to Yuma Highway, or air-to-air sorties over the great open-pit copper mine at Ajo, Arizona. I remember one of the missions with Wheels on my wing as we entered the gun range. We were a four ship formation with lead first, two, three and four each flying, in turn off the next man's wing. I was number two, and Wheels was number three. The instructor pitched out (banked sharply out of the formation) and then I pitched. The right-hand wing tank twisted sideways and flew off the airplane, taking the rocket pod with it. Wheels took a few seconds to compose himself after the tank flew by him. I remember feeling a sudden yaw and wondering what it was, but I was able to maintain control.

"Ah, Lead, a part of Two's wing just flew off and tumbled to the ground. Not sure what it was." We flew back with the instructor on my wing and landed. No problems. Fornal told me that night, of course, what bad form it had been to throw a wing tank at your friend while entering the gun pattern.

As the flying continued, the realization that the party was coming to an end began to sink in. Wheels and I routinely bummed meals at Tom and Bernie's place, and we put Bucky Jones up when he passed through for a few days, but it was time to put up. All the bragging of the last two years had to be backed up. We felt we were ready. Time would tell.

About a week before we left Luke, Greg Parker got married to his second wife. Wheels and I got to the wedding just as the bride and groom were coming out and proceeded directly to the O club for the reception. Greg had purchased two bowls of French 75s, which is a mixture of champagne and brandy, and they hadn't lasted long. About halfway through the third, which cheapskate Parker made us buy, guys forgot the ladle and just started dipping their cups into the bowl. Near the end of the party, there was a cigarette butt floating in the punch bowl. Art Suro or Lacy Veach, I'm not sure who, had regaled the father of the bride with, "Don't worry, sir, fighter pilots trade wives." Then the party was over. It was time to go.

The F-100 "gun school" had lasted about six months. We had reported to Phoenix and Luke Air Force Base in early September of 1967 and were finished in early March 1968.

CHAPTER 14
On to the War

It was an unusual time from the end of the training in fighters to the day that we all got in-country. One would think that the training would end and the lieutenants would receive their diplomas, go home for a week or so, and be on their way to sunny Vietnam. Not so. Just a couple of more hoops to jump through first.

THE FIRST DAY AFTER GRADUATION from F-100s, all of us airlined to Fairchild AFB in Spokane for survival training. This school usually consisted of about a week of academics, PT, unarmed-combat training, a day in the pool, and then a day or two in a fake POW compound. While the operations of that compound are secret, it is safe to say that the training is realistic. It gave the men some idea of what to expect if they were ever captured. This was part of the outgrowth of the dismal lack of training that had been received by the soldiers and airmen who became prisoners during the Korean War. In that war, the term "brainwashing" came into vogue, and the military had been caught off guard. Men broke down, some collaborated, some even refused to come home.

Those of us from the academy had been steeped in Captain Theodore Harris's bravery during the Korean conflict. After being held in solitary confinement in North Korea for months without letup, he was released to go home. Just before he could leave, he was told to sign a statement against the United States. He refused. "If I can't go home with my self-respect, I won't go home at all." But not all had done as well.

This was due to a lack of training, not a lack of guts. The service was determined not to be caught short again.

During the fifties, General, then President Eisenhower had the services adopt the "American Fighting Man's Code of Conduct." It started with the words, "I am an American fighting man. I serve in the forces which guard our country and our way of life. I am prepared to give my life in their defense."

The code went on to say that the American fighting man would never surrender or allow his command to surrender of their own free will. If captured, he would continue to fight through resistance. He would keep faith with his fellow prisoners and give no information that would harm his country or hurt his comrades. He would never forget that he was responsible for his actions and dedicated to the principles that made his country free. He would trust in his God and in the United States of America.

And it worked. The American prisoners of war in the Vietnam conflict wrote one of the finest chapters in American military history. So determined and so brave were they that they psychologically broke down some of their captors. They took terrible beatings for years. Some were beaten to death, but they held to this code, set up a prisoner chain of command that was not broken, established communications that the enemy was never able to decipher, attempted breakouts, refused to give in, and depended on each other for strength. "The only way you're going to get through this, mister, is with the help of your classmates." The prisoners of war weren't all academy grads, but they all gave a new meaning to the words *honor* and *service* and *pride* and caring for your comrade. We would do well to study them any time we wish to learn about bravery.

After survival at Fairchild, we went to Miami. In Miami, the subject was water survival training. This training consisted of a day of academics followed by two days of water exercises in Biscayne Bay, Miami, Florida. A large flight deck had been welded to the top of what appeared to be an old Higgins Boat (the landing craft that GIs and Marines came ashore in during the Second World War) and the pilots and aircrew that were there for training used that deck to launch in parasails into the wind. We were towed behind an outboard motor boat with two three-hundred-horsepower Chrysler inboard/outboard motors.

The noncom giving the training was specific about the procedures:

"When the safety officer in the back of the boat waves the big white flag the first time, you are to prepare for launch. When you are ready, you are to wave your hand at the deck safety officer standing off to your side. He will then wave a large safety flag at the boat, and the boat will start to move forward into the wind. You will start running toward the towboat the minute that you feel the slightest tug on the line. The towboat will accelerate faster than you can run and lift you into the air by the end of the deck.

"When you get to a height of approximately two hundred feet, you will note the boat slowing down. The safety officer in the back of the boat will then wave the flag three separate times. On the first wave, you are to disconnect the towline. On the second wave, you will open the parachute harness connector covers. This will expose the rings by which you jettison the parachute. Just before hitting the water, you will see the safety officer wave the flag the third time. This is just a reminder that you are about to hit the water and at the exact instant you do, you will release the parachute."

I looked at Jerry Becker and smiled.

"I don't think Herr Schmidt got that all straight."

I was referring to one of the allied German students who was taking the training with us. His English was good, but not good enough to pick up all the inflections and innuendos that the old sarge was putting out.

I was right.

The German was first, and he got off the deck of the boat just fine, but as the boat came to a stop, trouble began. Our group on the old LST saw the towrope fall from the airman as he was slowly drifting down in his parachute. He did this before the safety officer waved his flag the first time.

"He's one step ahead of the guy in the boat. I hope he doesn't wave the flag twice."

He did.

On the first wave, the group could see the pilot's hands go up for the riser connecter covers on his parachute.

"Don't wave the flag."

But that's just what the safety officer did, not having caught on that the pilot was a step ahead of him. When the safety officer waved the flag the second time, the German, considering that he was still a hundred feet in the air and that he had already exposed his riser connections, must have had to take a deep breath. He thought and then did what he thought he had been told to do. He released the parachute and fell into the warm waters of Biscayne Bay. He probably cut his feet on the bottom of the bay before the life preservers under his arms started him back up toward the surface. When he bobbed to the top and waved that he was okay, a cheer went up from the rest of the troops.

"He's probably thinking that we're a bunch of tough sons-a-bitches."

"Well," said Beck, "I've got no mercy for him. He's gonna go back to Germany and all that good beer and fly F-104s when he gets there. Walk around the officers' club with the damn spurs on his feet chinking like an Arizona cowboy and be shittin' in high cotton." That was a reference to the "spurs" that F-104 pilots had on their flight boots. These spurs were attached to cables on the Martin Baker ejection seat when they climbed aboard their "Starfighters." The little cable, upon ejection, pulled tight and kept the pilots legs from flailing when he jumped out of the airplane. The spurs that they attached to were considered cool by those of us who didn't have them.

The training ended, and the gang broke up. Now it was time to go home and be with the wife or family for a little while before going off to the war.

It's a difficult time for the family and friends on a soldier's last furlough before going to combat. Everyone he sees wonders if they'll ever see him again. And everyone he sees wants to sit and recall the good times they had way back when. It's as if they're afraid they won't have told the guy that they liked him and they're afraid he'll get killed. This leads to many long silences or just "take care of yourself" wishes. The neighbor across the road stated to me that he felt the whole thing would be over before I got there. All that had to be done was decide if the negotiation table would be rectangular or round. I wished him right, but in a way was looking forward to it not being over.

There's a funny thing about training for combat. When the time comes that you're trained and ready to go for your first tour and all the good-byes have been said and all the relative visits have been made and a youngster is caught up in the swirl of events that will take him to one end or another of a smoking gun, he actually would be let down if he didn't go. His buddies are going, thousands of others have gone, thousands of others have come back.

Every day, hundreds returned home. They made it. They did it. With skill, luck, and bravery, they got through it all. Now it was our turn.

We were all volunteers. We all finished high enough in our classes to get whatever type of assignment we wanted. It was a curious fact that of those of us who had finished high enough in our class at pilot training to get whatever assignment we wanted, we all chose the F-100 Super Sabre. Flying a single-seat, single-engine fighter was the epitome of what we had dreamed of and worked for all those years.

CHAPTER 15
Off to "the Nam"

Fighter pilots chose their line of work. That's what we did.

W E CHOSE TO FLY F-100S—A line of work that, at that time, meant
better odds of dying at twenty-five years of age than smoking
three packs of cigarettes a day did at age seventy. There were pictures
readily available that showed an F-100 in a strange back and forth sort of
wing wave inches off the ground. The plane continued through about three
of these oscillations before crashing in a huge ball of fire.

It was said that the definition of an optimist is a fighter pilot (usually
this referred to an F-105 fighter pilot at the time) who quits smoking
because he doesn't want to die of lung cancer.

We wouldn't have missed it for anything. For us, if you were a pilot,
you wanted to be a military pilot. If you were a military pilot, you wanted
to be a fighter pilot. If you were a fighter pilot, you wanted to be a single-
seat fighter pilot, and if you were a single-seat fighter pilot, you wanted
combat. If you flew combat, you wanted "downtown"—Hanoi, the big
show. Anything else was not the first string. Anything else was "here,
pussy pussy pussy." Ah, the bravado of young men who haven't yet been
shot at.

We headed out on the long trip that would bring us to Hickam Air
Force Base in Honolulu, Anderson Air Field in Guam, and Clark Air Base
in the Philippine Islands for the jungle-survival school. Travis Air Force
Base, just north of San Francisco, gave us our first taste of our overseas
assignment. All day long, we had worked our way across country to the
passenger terminal where the friendly porters took your bags before you

107

could say anything and stuck an orange sticker with a big "25cents" sign on each of the bags. "You guys are great. Here, gimme the bags."

Some of us had arrived in San Francisco a day or two before with wives, but for the most part, we were young kids—all fresh from our families, mothers, fathers, girlfriends, brothers, and sisters. And we came together at the bar at the officers' club at Travis, and we drank. We drank with the enthusiasm of young warriors who hadn't yet seen combat.

I remember talking to Tom Kiser months later at Bien Hoa. He told me that his father-in-law had flown him and Bernie down to Dallas in the old man's Bonanza for Tom to catch the plane for San Francisco. Bernie just cried and held on and then kissed him good-bye and it was over. He was off. He would come back. But that wasn't a given at that time.

I again ran into the "combat rumor" club. The same club that had known the three different versions of what would happen to us the first day we rode the bus out to the academy. These rumors are "truths" that spread just before any outfit or person goes into a new assignment, a deployment, a battle, or any one of the many unknown adventures that await military folks. It seems that everyone has heard that this is going to be tough ... that "they" haven't planned for this or that, that the equipment wasn't up to par ... or that Lieutenant So-and-So has a father who is in headquarters, and he cried when they saw what they were planning for the boys in the front end of the Super Sabre.

Again, it's the combat rumor, and it's been around since Cain plotted against Abel and heard, from somewhere, afterward that God was coming after him and was really pissed.

There were four bases in Vietnam at the time that were homes to the F-100: Bien Hoa, just north of Saigon; Phan Rang, further up the coast; Tuy Hoa, right on the coast near the center part of the country; and Phu Cat, just north of Tuy Hoa but inland, near the central highlands. We talked about the fact that those guys going to Phu Cat (Greg Parker and I) were flying into the southern parts of North Vietnam on a regular basis and taking a lot greater losses than the rest of the F-100 guys. This, with the exception of the Misty FACs, would prove to be completely false, but it was my first "combat" rumor associated with combat. At any rate, I decided it would be at least a week until I even got into Vietnam, and it would take another week or so to get familiarized with the local procedures. I still had two weeks of "normal living" and would worry more about the rumors in ten days or so.

Eat drink and be merry ...

"Trans International Airlines, flight to Saigon now boarding through gate 1 ... All personnel with reservations on this flight should be in the departure area."

The fuselage of the DC-8 was one long tube full of seats. There were no classes of passengers going to Southeast Asia.

This was not a commercial flight, with the well-to-do sitting in the front of the plane and receiving special and individual treatment. This was the military. Everyone was a GI. We were all going to try to survive for a year. How long a year seems on the first evening. How many bridges had to be crossed in the next 365 days. How many of us would be coming back? How many of us would lose our nerve or, worst of all, let one of our buddies down? That was the worst sin. Everything up to this point was done for the purpose of being a member of an elite outfit, US Air Force Fighter Pilots. We came for flag-waving reasons, for patriotic reasons, for the adrenalin rush of doing something beyond the pale of normal living, for a true belief that the country was trying to do something worthwhile, for professional satisfaction.

The flight took off about one-thirty a.m. Everything in the air force moved at one-thirty in the morning, it seemed. These commercial carriers were chartered under programs set up by the Military Air Transport Command. People said that MATS (Military Air Transport System) actually stood for Midnight Air Transport System. The transport eased into the black sky, making a slow climbing turn from a northeast heading on takeoff to a southwest heading for Hawaii. It was the first of many times that I would think how different lives were for the civilians flying this plane and the men in the back who were going to combat. Those up front were going on the first leg of a really cushy job. They'd be in Honolulu for crew rest on the beach with the girls in the back, and then on to Guam. From there, they'd head out for a turn at Clark Air Base in the Philippines and be back to Honolulu in two or three days. The guys in the back would be going to, in some cases, struggle for their lives for the next year.

San Francisco blinked in the darkness off the left side of the airplane. All the young soldiers and airmen were in a good mood. They laughed, joked, ate box lunches, smoked, slept and talked … all the way to Hawaii. The girls who worked the MAC charter flights said that one of the biggest contrasts they saw was the laughter and frivolity on the way to Vietnam and the nearly dead silence on the way home. Men went over in groups, with the comrades they had trained with, and then split to separate bases. They came home as individuals, some with nightmares about what they had seen during the previous year that would play through their brains for the rest of their lives.

For now, there was mostly laughter and talk.

Five hours and ten minutes later, the plane floated onto Runway 4 at Honolulu International Airport. The time changes on the westbound leg left us still in the middle of the night as we off-loaded and milled around the small pond with the huge goldfish, and then got back on the plane and headed for Guam.

In Guam, it was late morning. We got out, walked around, and smoked a cigarette or two, while another guy and I tried to get close to a couple of the stewardesses. The girls were like kids in a candy store. They had more men ogling them and trying to get in their pants on any given day of their lives than most women would have in a lifetime. Many of the girls were "ready." All the guys were ready.

I heard of a little old lady on one of the flights that mixed GIs with regular passengers who went to the rear lav and found a pair of tiny little bikini panties, forgotten and left behind. She brought them to the stewardess she had seen go back there and said with a little smirk, "I believe you forgot these." Those stewardesses were the fighter pilots of the female world. But they were also a touch of home, a touch of tenderness, a touch of kindness, warmth, even love in a world that for the most part was devoid of females.

In Guam, refueling completed, we were off to Clark Air Base near Manila, Philippines. Clark was the main support base for logistics and personnel going into and out of the Southeast Asia Theater of Operations.

We were flying the route of the Pan American Airways flying Clipper Ships. The famous China Clipper used to go from San Francisco to Honolulu, and then to Guam (after Midway and Wake Islands) and on to Manila Bay. Now, only thirty years after Captain Edwin Musick had done those first flights in an old Martin, some of the same pilots were still doing it in Boeing 707 aircraft. Pan Am had charter flights out here also. Some of the grizzled old captains on those routes knew virtually every wave-top and island in the Pacific. And there was talk that in a year or two more, they'd be doing this route in a giant four-engine plane called the 747 that was nearly twice the size of the 707 or DC-8 and traveled even faster. All this in thirty-three years. These captains had seen it all, and now they were carrying the fruit of America's youth to a far-off war.

But we had drawn Trans International Airlines and a DC-8. No matter, except for the fact that sometimes the 300 series Boeings could make Honolulu to Clark Air Base nonstop. The DC-8 was just as comfortable. "Just as comfortable" is to say that both types of airplanes, in the MAC seating configuration, were torture chambers for comfort. Six seats abreast, one cabin, just over two hundred guys.

We came into Clark Air Base in the Philippines. The first thing that I saw as I got down off the boarding ramp was Mount Pinatubo to the West. The same mountain that had stood there twenty-seven years earlier when, to the GIs on this field, it seemed like every airplane in the Japanese Air Force came over the hill and started bombing and strafing the field.

In 1968, Clark Air Base was the shining jewel of the US military in Asia. This was the base through which everything that was based in or going to the Asian theaters seemed to pass. Even the flights that came in through Yokota in Japan often came down to Clark before going in-country. But that would change. In 1968, the US had plans for three beautiful new bases in South Vietnam: Cam Ranh, Phu Cat, and Tuy Hua. Schools, movie theaters, clubs, pools, firehouses, and BXs would be built. It was the American way. It was going to be worth all this effort to establish bases on the "belly of the beast" of China. There was a lot more at stake in this conflict than just South Vietnam. We were implementing a blocking pattern to Dulles's line of dominos. We were containing Communism by stopping "wars of liberation."

From the fifties, the US policy on Communism had been containment, and moving from Clark to the main continent of Asia would choke that ring of containment down.

We arrived on a Friday and spent the weekend in Angeles City, just outside the main gate. It was a bustling little place, with the hotel where they put us up just across a small stream on the west side of town. Some of the guys I was with had been dependents of military personnel assigned to Clark and had grown up in the area. Those guys were familiar with the friendly locals and the not-so-friendly local problems.

There was constant petty and not-so-petty thievery. The story of the man who had a watch stolen from his arm as he waited in traffic served the purpose of preparing people to be careful. The gang of thieves who stole a base fire truck and blatantly turned on all the sirens and lights and drove out the front gate, being signaled through that gate by the MPs, also made the rounds. But in general, there was a friendly relationship with the locals, and we were able to walk around the town freely.

The night before training was to begin, a card game broke out in the hotel room. Art Suro rallied us to the Hearts table, and while some took shifts sleeping, the diehards played on through the night, finally settling in to sleep about four-thirty in the morning. This wound up giving us about two hours sleep before jungle-survival class began.

The first day class of our survival course was held in a non-air-conditioned building on the east side of the base. Buses came to pick us up at six forty-five in the morning and delivered us to class by seven. The class was taught by survivor instructors, paramedics, pararescue men, and survivalists in general. The heat combined with the lack of sleep made the morning almost unbearable. By the afternoon, though, we'd settled into the routine, had sorted our gear, and were ready to begin the next day in the jungle.

It's interesting how all the preparation on the way to war sort of blended into a foggy background of voices and lectures, of people telling you "the most important piece of information you would need to know" and of friends, of laughter, of joking to cover up the nervousness as the inevitable day drew closer and closer, the day that we would be inserted into the cauldron that was Vietnam.

Jungle-survival school began with all of us being airlifted by ancient helicopter back into the jungle of the Philippines around Clark Air Base. We were left there for a week.

The guides for the campout in the jungle were the black natives of the area. They were called Negritos by the Filipinos. These were the friendlies. The combat-rumor club ratcheted up fear a notch with the stories of the bad guys, the Huks, the tribes that lived in the jungle—although not that near to this location—who hated the US and the Philippines.

A story went around of the group of pilots on their way to Vietnam who wandered from the "safe" area of the jungle and set up camp in Huk territory. They were all killed. No one could give the actual details of this foray, but the rumor spread through our class. This was the "advanced" rumor club. From the academy to pilot training, to survival training to the checkout in-country, there was always the extra easy way you could die if you weren't careful.

From our childhood, it had been that way. From the nuclear bomb that could go off while you sat in a small country school in northwest New Jersey to the Huks in the jungles of the Philippines. You could always die, easily, if you weren't careful.

We were given one survival tin of food to make it through the week. Setting up camp near a small stream deep in the jungle, I made a cot out of branches and parachute cloth, made it into a swing and placed rest of the parachute cloth over the top for a mosquito net. This was survival with a guide.

As the week wore on, survival hikes (always on the lookout for Huks), war stories from folks who had not yet been to war, and college stories ground down to one overriding concern: food. I remember how it had been on our survival trek during our first summer at the academy. We used to sit around a campfire and talk about our favorite dishes. Jan Jaeger and I were consummate chefs by the time that week was done. We had also been given a live rabbit on the first day, which we carried with us for about three days. We were allowed to do anything we wanted with the rabbit, including keep it as a pet. We ate it.

Now, in the Philippines, by the second day, most of the survival tins were gone. We were down to rationing out the five or six cigarettes as "meals" while we waited for the Wednesday afternoon feast to be prepared by the guide. The meal of roots and fruits, berries and grasses was a gourmand delight. It was worth waiting for and worth talking about after for another day.

The night of the "survival challenge" came.

This was to be our last night in the school. We would be dispersed in an area of about five to eight acres to hide from a group of friendly natives who would search for us. When they found us, they would say "Hell-o, sir," and we'd give them a little blank metal dog tag that acted as a chit. This they would turn in to the US government in order to receive food. We said, later, that the natives had a giant IBM computer in one of their hootches that had feeds to it from sensors in all the good hiding spots. They found every one of us within an hour or so and then settled in for a good night's sleep.

Tom Kiser and I crawled into a bramble thicket thinking we had outfoxed the natives who were seeking us out for the rice chits we had.

Tom and I had become close during the week. I remember confessing to him that I thought he was greedy holding on to his cigarettes when everyone knew he didn't smoke. He just smiled and said, "I'll give you a cigarette for a sandwich, Rosie." Actually, he was so hungry he smoked a cigarette or two that week. He claimed they made him so dizzy, he was able to stop thinking about food for a while.

Anyway, after Tom and I cut ourselves all over spending nearly half an hour climbing into the middle of a huge bramble thicket, we settled in, feeling we had to be "safe" here. Within a minute, there was a little voice, "Sir ... sir ... have chit, please?"

After a half-hour, half the little metal chits were gone. Shortly thereafter, we just hung them on one of the bramble branches and when we heard the quiet little, "Sir, I seeeeee you," we would just point the light at the chit and tell them to help themselves. We figured these guys were so well-coordinated that once we ran out of chits, the word would get passed, and we'd be left alone the rest of the night.

About midnight, it started to rain. It rained like hell the rest of the night. At dawn, we were soaked.

Wheels took the offer that we all thought was stupid. He gave all of his chits to one of the Negritos from the little village near the camp. He did this before the exercise even began. In return, that guy built him a fire, made him a dinner, constructed a shelter, and brought him cigarettes. Lesson learned. Next time, stick with Wheels.

Camp Jungle ended with a helicopter "rescue ride" back to Clark. We assembled in a clearing and popped smoke canisters or signaled the helicopter with mirrors or waved or fired little pen-gun flares, just as a downed pilot would when signaling for rescue in Vietnam. As I recall, it was only about ten miles back in the jungle, but that helicopter was sure a welcome bit of transportation. We were dismissed and all spent the rest of the afternoon at the club getting "the works," which consisted of a haircut, neck and scalp massage, leg and foot message, manicure, pedicure, and shoeshine. The cost was about four bucks.

The Clark Air Base club was an oasis in a war zone. There were single women , stewardesses from the charter flights, nurses, teenagers who were dependents of assigned personnel, wives and babies, and GIs there from the war for one reason or another. Around the pool, these folks all gathered as they would at the local country club in the States.

CHAPTER 16
Last Leg

Next day, the lineup at the passenger terminal in Clark ... "All personnel going to Ton San Nhut Air Base aboard Mac Flight 2389, please report to Gate 3 at this time."

THE DC-8 STOOD AT THE other side of the gate. What a beautiful airplane. Its lines were so sleek and beautiful. The plane was massive yet delicate, strong yet beautiful in its lines. This would be a short flight. The last taste of civilization for a year. About seven or eight of us F-100 pilots boarded the plane and settled in for the final two-hour flight over the South China Sea for delivery into the mouth of the war.

As we idled down over Saigon, the view out the windows was serene. It looked like any other international city in any other underdeveloped country. Dark green colors around the outskirts. The remnants of European influence seen in the large and tree-lined boulevards leading to the center of town. Old stone buildings looking like any old Western capital. "The Paris of the East." The whole of the city sitting in a huge flat flood basin surrounded by thousands of rice paddies and the little levees that ran through them to aid with the irrigation of the crops. With the aid of conditioned air, it was a beautiful place to behold in the late spring of 1968.

"Ladies and gentlemen, please check that your seatbelts are fastened and that your tray tables and seatbacks are returned to their fully upright and stowed position."

"How many ladies do you see?"

"Just you, sweetheart, and the lovelies who are running around this big beautiful airplane."

The laughing and joking and loud talking subsided. It was time to put up and/or shut up. There were no more friends to listen to bravado. There were no more veterans, parents, relatives, or classmates to egg you on and encourage you in what you were about to do. Now you were alone with your thoughts, your hopes, and soon, your sweat and fears. There was nothing else to do but keep putting one foot in front of the other until the fear subsided and you could fall into whatever sort of routine the future held.

The terminal at Saigon was full of GIs, passengers from commercial flights, baggage handlers, thieves, kid thieves, people peddling cigarettes, phony watches. "Can you believe that stupid little kid sold me this Rolex for fifteen dollars?" I remember a guy arriving at Phu Cat making that statement. His watch literally exploded into about twenty pieces within a day or two.

The heat on the tarmac was unbelievable. There was no such thing as a jetway. In the walk down the airplane steps and across the ramp, we newbies soaked our shirts through and most of our pants. By the time we mustered in the terminal, it was two o'clock in the afternoon—heat of the day, lucky us. We headed for a C-130 dispatch area. These were the commuter jets of the Vietnam War. Actually, not jets at all, but huge four-engine turboprops that would carry us to our various in-country bases.

We mustered around a tall, black aerial-port worker who was directing the men to their various in-theater bases.

Finally, after a long list of call-outs came, "Phu Cat, Qui Nhon, and Chu Lai will load on Mac flight 124 . Proceed through the doors behind me, gentlemen. Bring your own bags to the airplane. The loadmaster will tie them down when you board. Let him know which base you are going to as all the luggage for each base will be loaded on individual cargo pallets."

We dragged our gear across the ramp. Most of us had, among other things,one huge B-4 bag. This was a sort of zippered double-sized laundry bag that had literally all the clothes and personal effects we would need for a year. After a year in-country, most people came home with about three sets of underwear, work uniforms, and uniform items only. All their personal clothes were too worn and beaten by constant hand-washing to be used anymore. Good clothes were sent directly home from whatever R&R port they were purchased in.

Our personnel and financial records were carried in a rolled cardboard tube that we turned in when we arrived at out new base. Most who weren't going into the field but to a base position, such as the noncombatants or the fighter pilots in this case, also carried a small suitcase of our personal effects. We carried pictures of the family or the most recent girlfriend, such as I had left in Phoenix. Nobody wants to go to a combat theater without someone of the opposite sex waiting for their return. I just never wrote her again. This was getting to be cowardly habit. Some guys took pictures of their most recent affair and let themselves believe they had something in that person to go home to … someday.

The ride in the C-130 began. I was the only one of the group going to Phu Cat, so I was alone. All my buds were gone. Greg Parker would join me within a day or two, but for some reason we didn't arrive together.

Nope. I was alone. Jeez.

It seems the C-130 has been around forever in the military. It is the in-theater workhorse of the air force as well as the other combat arms. The high wing and four turboprop engines are the hallmark of this plane. Its power and fuel economy make it capable of short hauls to short runways and great distance nonstop flights both.

We climbed up the ramp into the back in the heat and the exhaust of the left outboard engine, which was running to supply power to the ship. It was one of about six or seven C-130s timed to be here at the arrival of the two "freedom birds" that enveloped the troops in carbon monoxide exhaust and heat as they climbed up the extended ramp in the rear of the plane, threw their bags on the appropriate pallet, and found their seats on the web benches that line both sides and the middle of the big transport. There is no sense worrying about how you look. At this stage, you're soaked through and through, and every newbie just took his place on a web seat, put his head down, and dripped onto the floor. Average Americans have never seen or experience heat like that unless they live in the deep South. I'll bet there are few US cities with the heat and humidity of Saigon.

Heat, heat, heat.

The loadmaster said something about taking our seats and strapping in, and the engines began as the ramp closed in the back. It was amazing how the voice of one person could be changed into a tone and broadcast at such a volume as to be heard in that din, but the C-130s system somehow did just that for the loadmaster assigned to watch us in the back of the plane. I looked at the guy and noticed that even with all the work he was doing, his flight suit was only slightly stained under the arms and down the middle of his back. Maybe there was some hope yet that I'd adapt to this heat.

The plane rolled down the runway and lifted off into the afternoon heat, vapor contrails coming off the wingtips as the transports squeezed the moisture-laden air for lift.

We climbed to about fifteen thousand feet and started the trip north. Still above the fray, still too high to be affected by the bloodlust occurring below. The Vietcong and the North Vietnamese had no weapons that could reach us in this part of the war, but the pilots headed out over the South China Sea just for an added measure of safety. The C-130 was "feet wet"; it proceeded up the coast. The vast majority of north-south traffic in the theater did all or part of their routes visibly flying over the ocean away from any potential ground-to-air threat. The C-130 droned on for over an hour. By that time, the wet casual uniform I was wearing was beginning to get darned cold in the conditioned, humidity-free air of the C-130.

During this ride to our combat bases, each person was alone in his own thoughts. It was the resolve that built in some men slowly and in some quickly, versus the never committing to the fray in others, that separated the combatants from those that stay home.

And I'm not talking about the wealthy and famous who make their fortunes portraying brave men but have never been to the war. I mean the Audie Murphys, the Jimmy Stewarts, the little skinny kids from Iowa and from Brooklyn, from down east Maine and from Portland, Oregon, who came, dug in, and vowed, somehow, not to let this thing run over them. They arrived committed to doing what was right for their families and countries and left judging themselves by how well they held up for the fifteen or twenty men who stood closest to them in battle. This is the time when scared men hunkered down and set their jaw and became determined men. It was determination more than bravery that moved people along. It was determination that kept people coming back when all was lost. It was the determination to care for, support, fight next to, laugh with, and help your buddy that started to build in the hearts when they first were introduced to the scene of battle. Not bravery, determination.

We passed Tuy Hoa, one of the four show spot bases built to mark a continuing commitment to the people of South Vietnam by the people of America. Tuy Hoa, Cam Ranh Bay, Phu Cat, and Phan Rang seem a concrete way to say, "We'll be here to help you forever, friends. Count on us." The engines continue at the same drone, but the power behind the propellers lessened and the plane started down. As we began our descent, the loadmaster announced a change in plan. "Men, we've begun our descent into the army base at Qui Nhon. All those of you bound for Qui Nhon will off-load at this destination. Also those of you going to Phu Cat will off-load here and have to find your own transportation up to the base. Because of priority cargo onboard, we will not be making the extra stop at Phu Cat."

"FUBAR"—fucked up beyond all recognition. Now I know where that saying we had to learn at the academy came from. Nothing goes as you think it will in the field, I guess.

How was I going to get up to Phu Cat?

I was pretty sure I wouldn't be spending the war in Qui Nhon; something would turn up. But until that point, I had been the prima donna, the man who had volunteered to go to Vietnam. All the training, all the travel, all the extra training posts, all the lectures and special training sorties had been set up and ready for me when I arrived. If I showed up, the work of training went on. This was not training—merely showing up didn't get the job done. You had to pick up the pieces that were dumped on the ground in front of you and make your way up to the next spot.

I thought of "Muckrock" at this time and wondered how he was getting along on his way to his first assignment in an F-4 squadron in Thailand.

The plane glided down, and I looked out the small porthole window on the left rear door. Below was a long highway, Route 1, that wound from Saigon to the DMZ and from there on up to Hanoi. It was the "street without joy," the "trail of tears," the Hanoi Highway, and on that afternoon, it had been the location of an ambush against a small army convoy. I could see the bright, bright red flames coming off of the lead truck in that convoy as it burned. There was something about that color of fire. It seemed that whenever there were human deaths, the fire around the scene was different from other fires. The flames were seemingly more severe, more violent, a dark red mixed with orange and a seeming touch of purple, almost black in the red … I could just tell that someone had died in that fire. It gave me an uneasy feeling. Welcome to the war, jerkoff.

"Keep your heads down," I muttered to the loadmaster watching next to me.

"Yeah."

The C-130 came into Qui Nhon and arrived exactly on schedule. I say arrived because, as I remember, the runway at that location was only about four thousand feet long. The pilot had no room to finesse the big bird to a smooth landing. He came over the end of the runway, flared, and if the wheels didn't go on smoothly on the first attempt (they didn't), he just eased forward and plopped the bird down quickly. This allowed him to get the propellers into reverse pitch. Early C-130s in reverse pitch, with high power applied, slow down very quickly. We were taxiing by the time three thousand feet of runway had been used..

We off-loaded into the heat and humidity of the port city of Qui Nhon. I won't ever forget the feeling of being at an outpost. It was as if somehow the first place we'd been to, Tan San Nhut, was a safe, large, indestructible place where the enemy wouldn't dare be found. In fact, that was the case at most of the big air bases in Vietnam.

But this little location at Qui Nhon seemed to me to be a fort, out in the wilderness, open to attack. Actually, guys who spent time out in the field, nose to nose with the enemy, would laugh at that description. To them, Qui Nhon probably seemed as safe as the big bases did to me.

But this was my first day. I'd learn, along with the rest of the military and the rest of the world, that these little buggers didn't hesitate to attack Saigon, Phu Cat, Qui Nhon, or any other place they could. We got out, got our bags, poked around, and were headed for the club for a cold one when two grunts spotted us. "Hey, sir, you going to Phu Cat?"

"Yeah, how'd you know?"

"Not a lot of air-force guys arriving in Qui Nhon for a year of fun. Hop in."

I remember looking over at the driver as we drove out the gate of Qui Nhon and headed through the crowded town in the open jeep.

People had been saying it for a year, but that moment was when I learned how vulnerable and how easy it was to get hammered if you happened to be in the wrong place at the wrong time. We drove through the crowded streets around the town before getting out into the countryside. Hundreds of Vietnamese were within reach of our open jeep. Anyone of them could've, if they so desired, flipped a grenade into the jeep. What a mess that would've been.

"Don't you guys worry about these people flipping something into the jeep?"

"Nope, Qui Nhon's a safe city … don't sweat it."

If he says so, I thought.

We pulled into the main gate at Phu Cat about thirty minutes later. It had been a very pretty ride through the countryside to the south and southwest and then west side of the Phu Cat Mountains. It would amaze me in later months that in these hills would be fought some horrendous battles, and the wounded and the couriers and the liaisons would hop in a helicopter and be at the relative safety of the big air base in less than five minutes. They were fighting for their lives up in those hills and could look down and see a safe place.. The bases were one of the big enterprises in Vietnam, and I felt as safe on any of them as I would in the United States. Yeah, there were the occasional rocket or mortar attacks, but what were the odds, on one of these huge pieces of real estate, of you getting hit? We used to sit on top of the hootches and watch the mortars hit. The gomers who launched the rockets usually had so little time to do so that they just aimed in the general direction of the base. They were not very accurate. Da Nang, Tan Son Nhut, Bien Hoan, Long Binh, Phu Cat, Tuy Hoa, and Cam Ranh were all safe. There was no "safe" place in this war, but the air bases, while the US was in Vietnam in force, were as safe as any city in the US. There was literally more chance of being killed as a clerk typist working late hours in a major city than a clerk typist working 24/7 at a job in administration on one of the big bases in Vietnam while the American military was in-country.

The "homes" were safe. As I've said before, they were kept that way through the efforts of air police, military police. and infantry units assigned the detail. The military police—air police in the air force—were usually detailed to guard gates and do traffic work at bases in the land of the big BX (U.S.). Over there, these guys, the "sky cops," were in daily combat, protecting the assets on the base. They sweat and struggled and fought so that we could be comfortable at our home. Everything and everyone in the air force was there to see to it that I was ready and able and had the equipment to take that machine into the air and take the war to the enemy. I may have been the tip of the spear, and I liked that position, but I have always been aware of how many men labored and fought to make sure I was capable of doing my job. And that job, as I've also said before, was to try to help the grunts.

Phu Cat was guarded by the 1st Korean Army Division, the Tiger division. These guys took their job very seriously. I remember once running into a young Korean private who had somehow wandered onto part of the base at Phu Cat and become disoriented and lost. He was as afraid to go back to his unit as most were of the enemy. Discipline and duty were highly respected by these guys, and a poor young grunt lost in an American air base brought neither to his unit. As I came to realize how tough they were, I was awfully glad they were there.

I never knew what the relationship was between the Koreans and the Vietnamese, but the prisoners I often saw in the custody of the Koreans seemed pretty well convinced they had screwed with the wrong pooches.

CHAPTER 17
Moving in with Chris

"Here's to the bee that stung the bull and started the bull a-bucking.
Same old bee stung Adam and Eve and started the world a-f_____g."
Birds do it and fly.
Bees do it and die.
Kings and Queens do it and sigh.
But I don't do it, and I'll tell you why.
Because I'm true. But I'll tell you what I will do.
If we lie down together and I don't move, I'm not cheating."
—Quoted by Chris Kellum on numerous occasions 1968–1969.

THAT AFTERNOON, THE BASE ADMINISTRATION had closed by the time I got there, so I checked into transient housing and got a room in the barracks on the top of the hill on the east side of the base. I took a shower, jumped into a clean flight suit, had a couple of beers in the club, and came back to the tiny little room that would be my home for the first night in country. What a day it had been.

I was in Vietnam.

I have been amazed as I put this story together at how many times different folks' paths crossed mine. That is one of the wonderful advantages of a military career. You're never far from a very close friend.

On or about that first night in Phu Cat, I met Bill Bowen, a guy who had gone through pilot training just ahead of me. He married a girl from Selma, Alabama. It was tough for a northern bachelor to get out of Selma unattached.

When I finished the F-100 tour in Vietnam, I returned to the states for an assignment as a T-37 instructor pilot at Craig Air Force Base in Selma. During that time I met the woman who I would, after many delays and false starts, marry in 1974. During the time that Bill's outfit (Sioux City, Iowa Air Guard, F-100s-Bats) was at Phu Cat, they only lost one man. The man they lost had been the best friend of my wife's first husband. That first husband was killed in a fighter accident in Japan. Those were the times. Those were paths that crossed.

I again ran into Bill Bowen years later when I joined the New York Air National Guard. I married my wife in 1974 after my second tour. She had been childhood friends with Bill's wife. And they live about five miles from us. Small world. I wish all these guys in this story lived as close as Bill and Jackie.

Anyway, the next day, after administration sent me to the 416th squadron, I went down and checked in with the commander, Rupert Scott, and his deputy, Elmer Follis. In the whole year that I would be in Vietnam, I would only have two commanders. In those days, a commander served his entire tour as a commander. In the later years of the war, the period of command became shorter and shorter as more and more men were trying to get their "tickets punched." Scott was the first, and a man named Paul Davis was the second, both outstanding leaders. Davis knew a lot of the younger "old heads" who showed up from European squadrons while I was at Phu Cat. His deputy, as I remember, was a great guy named Red McKeon. Red had a heart attack and died about halfway through the year.

I was told I would live in the fighter-pilot hootches in a porta-camp trailer. These were little, green, air-conditioned trailers with a small room on each end and a shared bathroom in the middle. There were two junior officers or one senior officer (major or higher) in each end of the trailer.

I was to room with Chris Kellum, and it was a wonderful draw for a roomie. Chris was like an older, just slightly older, brother to me, and we have stayed close in the years that have passed. We originally shared our space with a crusty old major named Jake Neely in the other end of the trailer. I don't know it to be a fact, but I'd be willing to bet that Jake had been a fighter pilot from the day he graduated school until the present. At that time, I would guess that covered a period of about twenty years. He was a great guy, and Chris and I spent hours talking to him.

One of the funniest events I remember in my first tour was a strike mission that Chris and I did together in March of 1969 that was pretty typical of missions flown in the south of Vietnam. I happened to be Lead that day by chance. Chris was every bit as qualified as me, but we headed out, Detwiler in charge.

We had dropped on a troops-in-contact up near Da Nang somewhere and been requested to stay and put in the 20-mm in about a half hour. I informed Panama control that we would need a tanker to come back and help the FAC. They complied with a strange-sounding call sign that turned out to be a Marine C-130 off the coast of Da Nang. The KC-135s that we were used to using had a long, fixed boom with about five feet of hose on the end, with a basket on that hose. It was fairly easy to get the refueling probe into the basket, and Chris and I each had logged over 125 hours connected to that hose during our tours in Misty.

When we saw the tanker, the hoses on the C-130 were about sixty feet long, and the basket on the end, into which you had to fly the F-100s refueling probe to take fuel, was going up and down about twelve feet.

"This should be good," I said.

"Fucking Marine could do it," said Chris. He said this on a frequency with only the tanker and us on it. The guys in the tanker laughed.

"C'mon up, we'll watch."

I went first, hit the basket by complete luck, and took on the fuel I needed. Chris came second and eased into position. His closure rate was such that when he missed the basket, it slowly continued over the top of the wing and back to about the tail of Chris's plane.

"Missed, pal," said I.

Then the fun began. As Chris started to back away, the basket slowly worked its way up the top of his fuselage. Then it bounced over the canopy and down the nose in front of him. Before I could say "Watch it!" the basket got stuck sideways in his air intake for a brief second, causing a compressor stall, a sort of engine back fire. As he said later that night, "I figured at that point it was all over but the hand-clapping."

"Jesus!"

Old Chris calmed down. On his second attempt, he got into a little oscillation as he approached the end of the long hose, but settled it out on his own without having to start over. He missed the basket, stopped immediately, backed out, hit it the next time, and took his fuel.

On the way home, he started feeling a vibration in his airplane. Vibrations could be extremely dangerous in the F-100, as it had a huge piece of machinery, an AC generator as I remember, that hung down for cooling just in front of the engine itself. If that generator were to let go, you lost your engine.

We felt that Chris might have taken a hit on the bottom or just behind the cockpit of his plane. I looked him over as carefully as I could and saw nothing. Nevertheless, he decided he'd rather get it on the ground, so we diverted to closest runway—the giant Marine base at Chu Lai—and landed in a rain shower. I went in first, as he was under complete control and would foul the runway if for any reason he took the barrier.

I was waiting in the de-arming area when I saw Chris, slowed to about forty-five knots with about fifteen hundred feet to go before the turnoff. His plane turned sixty degrees to the runway and slid sideways for about three hundred feet before straightening out. He taxied into the de-arm area with the drag chute cable caught in one of the little pieces of metal under which it was normally tucked in flight. It hung out the back of the airplane fluttering madly in the exhaust..

"That should impress the Marines," said I.

"All over now but the hand-clapping,"

They looked over his plane and never found a thing. They unwrapped the chute and repacked it, and we pressed on for the twenty-minute flight back to Phu Cat.

Chris said later that night that the next time he landed at a Marine base with a declared emergency, he was going to open the canopy on the way in and "reach about with my .38 and put about four holes in the son of a bitch."

We would spend the last few months of our tours flying regular close air support missions like that, in the southern part of Vietnam. We never ventured once across the border into North Vietnam as that area had been closed since we'd last flown there in Misty in Nov of '68.

But Chris' problem and our divert to Chu Lai took place in early 1969, after we had finished our tours in Misty. Let's go back to mid 1968, before Chris and I joined Misty.

In our trailer, Jake was replaced by another senior major, Dick Durant, who would play a big part in our joining the Misty FACs. Dick would spend hours talking to us, sitting in the big living-room easy chair that Jake had left, sucking on Pall Malls and drinking bourbon.

Dick Durant was a good guy, and his words wore into us.

"You fucking guys don't realize there's a war going on up there. You don't know shit about what's going on up north. There are targets up there that blow up when you hit them, and there are people dying trying to get those targets. This stuff in the south is necessary, but not like up there. That's where it's at. If you want to be a fighter pilot, you belong there."

The first time we heard this, Chris and I came back to our side of the trailer and just shook our heads.

"That guy's got quite a story to tell."

"Yeah."

Chris and I spent many hours on many nights just sitting in the trailer and quietly drinking coffee or booze (depending on when we were flying the next day), talking about what we'd been up to that day, about families, or girlfriends in my case, back home. As I've shown, Chris's favorite saying was, "it's all over but the hand-clapping." He'd use that about once an hour as I recall. "Boy, when that fucking bomb hits, I'm telling you, the fighting's all over but the hand-clapping," or "Little Bob Fitzsimmons took old so and so on behind the club over some silly shit. Bob hit him once and it was all over but the hand-clapping, I'm telling you."

I remember an interesting night at Phu Cat when some of the guys were downing brews on one of the party platforms. All of a sudden, I wondered where Chris was, as he had a pretty good snout-ful the last time I saw him. I headed out in the dark on my 90CC Honda motorcycle to see if I could round him up. About one hundred yards down the road, out of the dark, Kellum goes by me about three feet away. He didn't have any lights on and neither did I. We missed each other completely out of luck, and we were both moving pretty fast.

I went back to the party.

About ten minutes later, Chris comes into the party looking like he'd just seen a ghost. When I asked what was the matter, he turned to the other direction and the entire left side of his flight suit had been rubbed off. He had a "Honda rash" from the tip of his left ear down to the top of his left ankle.

Much later, near the end of the tour, old Wheels met his demise in much the same manner down at Bien Hoa. He and another group of his friends in the squadron had made it their routine, when they were all at home, to drive their little Hondas to the club in formation, tight formation. I had sat on the back of Wheels's bike on one of these forays, and these guys were good.

About two weeks before Wheels was scheduled to go home, the "Thunderbirds" were in tight formation, having been approved to make a pass on the revetments down on the flight line and receive the applause of the maintenance troops as they went by. Wheels hooked his handlebar on the flight suit of the leader—I told you they were close—and went over in a pile on the taxiway. In true Fornal fashion, he got up, staggered over to his bike, and rode on to the club. Only when he couldn't walk into the club on his own power did they decide to ride over to the hospital and see what was wrong with their right wingman.

Fornal was in surgery in Japan two days later and home, horizontal, two weeks later.

Fortunately, Chris and I were able to go get his bike out of the ditch he had crashed into the night before, and it started without skipping a beat. No injuries.

CHAPTER 18
Mistys

In the southern panhandle of North Vietnam in 1967, the US was confronting a big problem. This was a major transshipment area for supplies to the South, but the Forward Air Controllers sent there in light airplanes to find those targets were facing withering gunfire from large caliber antiaircraft guns that were not found in South Vietnam. There had to be a way to accomplish the Forward Air Control mission with a better chance of survival than those slow airplanes experienced. Enter the Commando Sabre unit, call sign "Misty."

MISTY FACs HAD A DIFFERENT mission than the rest of the F-100s in Vietnam. We were not deployed as strike fighters. We were an intelligence-gathering, reconnaissance, and target-finding mission all rolled into one. While many of the strikes in the south did the vital job of hitting in close to support troops in contact with the enemy, the Mistys weren't supposed to hit anything. We were to find targets and bring others into the area, mark the targets with white phosphorous marking rockets, and let the others strike.

All of North Vietnam was divided into geographical areas called "Route Packages." Misty's missions were in the southernmost of these packages, Paks 1 and 2. The navy had Pak 3. No one was hitting further north during the summer and fall of 1968. Most strike flights would come into an area, hit their target, and be out in less than five minutes if no one was hit. We patrolled the area for four to six hours without heavy ordnance to slow us down. Our only firepower was two pods of marking rockets and several hundred rounds of 20-mm ammunition for the two guns. We'd constantly jink back and forth across the road and highway network, pulling four to five gs while turning, easing off those gs and flying across the road, banking in the opposite direction and again setting in four to five gs as we banked back in the other direction to recross the road. When we'd find targets, we'd guide other ships in there to quickly hit them and leave. If one of the strike fighters was hit and ejected in the area, we'd manage the rescue. This was done by first marking and having other fighters take out high-caliber guns that may be in the area, and then dropping antipersonnel weapons around the downed airman but not near him. Finally, the slower, propeller-driven A-1 "Sandy" and "Jolly Green" helicopters were brought in for the pickup.

This Misty unit was actually designated Detachment 1 of the 416th Tactical Fighter Squadron, my squadron at Phu Cat. Because of that fact, I had been close to Misty from the day I got to Phu Cat.

Misty was a volunteer organization. It attracted a certain type of fighter pilot. Major George "Bud" Day was chosen as its first leader. At the time, Bud was one of the most experienced fighter pilots in the entire air force.

The type of pilot that came to Misty didn't mind the higher aspect of danger inherent in the mission because that Misty mission went in alone, flew wide open at the peak of performance of the airplane, answered to no one for the decisions made in the area of operations, and sought out and destroyed the enemy face to face in his territory. There were many times when a lucrative target was found that the Misty would use his strafe ("you carry those goddamn bullets for marking purposes only") to destroy the target, one on one. I believe it was Clyde Seiler, who you'll meet later, that said, "just keep marking that truck until it blows up". When a strike flight would show, the Misty would give the credit for the destroyed target to that flight. We weren't strike fighters … har har.

I JOINED MISTY IN LATE August 1968. As I stated before, Chris and I had been sharing our trailer with a senior major named Dick Durant. In those porta-camp trailers, there was room for two junior officers in a bunk on one end and one or two more senior guys on the other. All shared the bathroom. Dick was a Misty, and the first time we listened to Dick we came out of his end of the trailer shaking our heads.

"Yeah, let's go to North Vietnam. There's just not enough risk flying around here in the South. Let's go up where the action is. Is he kidding?" We laughed, went to dinner, and forgot all about it.

But, as I've said before, Dick began to wear into us with the stories he told. I began hanging around with some of the Mistys when I'd see them at the club. I met a brand new guy named Kelly S.F.D.D. (short-fat-dumb-dumb) Irving the night he came up from Bien Hoa to join.

When you first met Kelly, you'd think of a lot of different occupations that this man's appearance would fit. He could be a school teacher. He could be an accountant. He could be a computer geek. I assure you that fighter pilot is not the occupation to which SF's appearance leads you. Remember, the "S" stands for short, and he is that. But he is, or was, healthy, never fat. Curly hair, large glasses, round face, sort of talking out of the side of his mouth. He looked like the last thing he'd want to do is get in a fight. But he's not "dumb dumb," and he sure can fly a jet airplane. He actually completed a circling engine out approach in an F-100 at night into Tan San Nhut Airport. In the F-100, you start with only one engine, and if it quits, you become a glider with the flight characteristics of an anvil.

One of Kelly's favorite sayings is, "never let the truth stand in the way of a good story." But that night, dead stick, circling approach into Tan San Nhut is not just a story. He's got the "Order of the Able Aeronaut" award to prove it. Kelly and I would go on to Selma as T-37 instructor pilots.

He became my supervisor when he moved to academics, where I had been a platform instructor for nearly a year.

Talking about coming to Misty, he said, "Why not? It's here. It sounds like a challenge. I had to give it a shot."

About two weeks later, when Dick Rutan finished his tour, I joined Misty. It was early September of 1968. You didn't have to wait long to be taken in after you volunteered. Chris joined about three weeks later. The Mistys were losing about one plane a month and being hit two or three times a week. Although many of them got back, we each had our doubts. As is always the case in combat, "My buddy did it, and I sure as shit couldn't leave him there alone." We were in the Mistys.

HERE'S A STORY ABOUT A Misty flight.

As I stepped out of the trailer, the "bread truck" was already waiting. I'd arranged a four-thirty pickup the night before with the admin sergeant from the 416th, and he picked us up right on time.

"Good morning, Sunshine."

"Hey, Wells. Sleep well?"

"Like a baby."

Wells probably had slept like a baby. As I said in the introduction, I use the term "warrior" carefully. Wells was emblazoned with the spirit by which men not only survive, but endure and lead others to success in combat that would not otherwise be possible. Many men like that are quiet loners, great in combat but not socially able to put it aside and just talk and communicate with people. Wells and Clyde Seiler, whom you'll meet later, were not only unbelievably aggressive in the air, but real "people folk" back at home.

Wells knew what he was doing was right. He was convinced he would win and he would take the fight to the North Vietnamese every chance he had, with whatever means he had at his disposal, until he either beat them or they killed him. It was as simple as that. There were no second thoughts about how poor these people were, if they had a reason to want us out of their country, if we were being an international bully, or if we were fighting and taking sides in a civil war. He was ordered to seek out, find, and destroy the enemy, and by God that was what he would do until the goddamn war was over or he was dead. Simple proposition to Wells.

Wells had previously rescued a fighter pilot who had been downed in a very hostile area of North Vietnam. I think it was Dick Rutan that had been running the rescue before he "timed out" and Wells came on the scene. Dick had been told to call off the rescue after a number of the helicopters had taken severe damage in the area and an A-1 sent in as part of the rescue package(group of planes) had been lost. Dick's transmission was "please ask the commanding officer the exact words he wants me to give this pilot I'm talking to as we all leave him". The rescue continued.

After Wells expended all his ordnance on the enemy, he came around again and strafed them with 20-mm cannon fire from the two barrels in the front of his ship. The F-100F that the Misty FACs flew was a two-place airplane. The pilot in the back did the paperwork and the pilot in the front flew and worked the fighters. Because of the space that the extra seat took up, the F model could not carry as much ammunition as the C and D model single-seat versions. Wells had quickly expended all his ammunition keeping the heads of the enemy down as the helicopters tried to make a pickup. When this failed, Wells made a pass or two at the enemy, dropping empty wing tanks on them. This in itself was dangerous, as the tanks, with high g loadings on them or in the twisting jinking world of evading ground fire, could easily have hit his own airplane. Wells hadn't cared. He had a comrade on the ground. He was going to save him.

When he ran out of gas tanks to drop on the enemy, he marked the position of heavy guns firing at the rescue attempt by telling the flight leads to watch in front of his nose for the muzzle flashes of the guns that would be shooting at him. When the guns caught onto that act and stopped firing each time Wells rolled in, he flew over the top of the guns and lit his afterburner over them using the flash as a marker. He and one or two other Mistys and some really big-balled helicopter pilots got the guy out. This was after three or four attempts. To Wells, only one thing mattered, and that was the mission at hand: destroying the enemy and saving your comrade.

The wing headquarters of the 37th TAC Fighter Wing, as I remember, was a two-story sort of plywood monster erected, probably in less than two weeks, as Phu Cat had become a functioning air base. It had the basic necessities. That was all. The Misty FACs used the upstairs of the building but entered and exited via a long outside stairway that led directly to our operations section. As you entered the unit area, there was a picture of "Bud" Day hanging on the wall. Although many men would lead the Misty group during the years of war, there was never a day that any of us doubted that we were working for Bud. He'd started the Misty program and took the call sign after his and his wife Doris's favorite song.

By the way, Doris's nickname is Viking, and it is a moniker that she easily fits into. Although Bud says in his book that it was because of her blue eyes and light features, I think it fits her spirit to a T. Think of what it took to go on, to raise four kids, to wait for years for a husband you knew was being tortured so badly he could die from it, and to represent that husband's and his comrades' interest to a country that, outside of the military, couldn't care less. A country that, until Richard Nixon was elected, asked the POW wives to keep quiet about their loved ones so as not to disturb delicate negotiations.

Doris worked tirelessly with other wives and people like Ross Perot, never giving up on their husbands. She's as tough as Bud.

Bud had been shot down early in the Misty program in North Vietnam and made his way almost back to the safety of a fire support base after crossing the DMZ into South Vietnam. Badly injured and within sight of the base, he was recaptured and sent to Hanoi. While there, he would earn the Medal of Honor for the bravery he displayed and the leadership he gave to his fellow prisoners. He wrote a stirring book called *Duty, Honor, Country* about his years of captivity. It has been my honor to be associated with this man and his wife even in a very small way. He is a perfect example of a quiet man put in an extreme situation who could not be pushed around by anyone.

We came past the picture of Bud and took the intelligence briefing from Rog VanDyken. Rog has in recent years gone back to North Vietnam many times with money he raised himself or with grants from major corporations. He works to bring programs to the people that improve their lives and helps them set up small capitalist enterprises. He even dabbles in democracy in some of the small towns that used to be on his target sheets. He, like John Haltigan (who has become a virtual historian of our efforts), Ray Bevivino, Bob Guido, a classmate from the academy, and Jim Titus worked tirelessly to support us with intelligence facts and briefings. "Chance of some activity today up around Bat Lake," said Roger. He had added this after the briefing as we were leaving the room.

"I'll keep that in mind, Rog," I said as we walked out of the building and went to the 416th for equipment. We stopped in at the bar area of the squadron building for a cup of coffee before the mission. As I have said, the Mistys were actually Detachment 1 of the 416th's TAC fighter squadron, and therefore, this was " our" building. Most of the pilots from Misty had come from different bases around South Vietnam and merely used the building to hang their flying gear. For me, a member of the 416th before joining the fast FACs, this was my squadron home.

Doc was in the bar area with Ed Osborne, who had been an academic instructor at the Air Force Academy before his tour.

"Hi, Rosie, what's up?"

The four of us talked. Ed was going to be a supervisor of flying that day, which made him sort of the wing commander's representative to all that was going on in the air. It's funny how many times someone says something like, "I remember having a cup of coffee with Rosie and Wells just this morning, down at the squadron, just them and Doc and Ed, and now they're gone." That thought went through my mind, as I had already had just that happen with two friends. Funny.

Dean drove us to the flight line, again in the "bread truck." Love having a doctor to drive you to work.

We usually grabbed at least two frozen bottles of water out of the freezer in the personal-equipment section. While the average F-100 strike flight was in a target area for about ten minutes, the Misty missions lasted at least four to five hours, and even at this time of the year, September, it was hot enough on the ramp to need about a quart of water before a mission even took off. We drank deeply just before leaving the squadron area. We'd put the frozen-solid water bottles in our g suits and drink the cool liquid later in the mission. The water was usually gone before we headed for home.

Dean dropped us off.

"Strap in, Wells," I said. "I'll do the preflight."

"Roger."

Wells made himself comfortable in the backseat and set up his "office" for the mission. The maps were put to the side. His list of places to look went in the box next to the maps. He eased his six feet in under the canopy and settled into the back. It was hot.

"Thanks, chief."

This to the man who owned the airplane and strapped him into the rear seat. It wasn't that a man couldn't do this himself. It just made it so much easier when someone laid the straps over your shoulder and all you had to do was reach down in your lap and put the two shoulder straps into the seatbelt.

Command Post: "Misty 11, mission clearance".

Cleared to start, Misty, go get 'em."

"Roger."

Although in later years, we Mistys took to calling ourselves by the timing with which we joined the organization (I was the 67th out of about 156, so I'm now "Misty 67"), during the war the first Misty of the day was Misty 11, the second 21 and so forth up to Misty 61 when there was night work to be done.

Another aside here. I flew one of the first missions with a new instrument called a starlight scope in the back of a 61 mission at night in North Vietnam. Steve Amdor was the front-seater, and I had the scope in the back and was trying to look through it. It was about eight or nine inches in diameter and about twenty inches long as I remember. They told us "it uses available light energy to let you see a picture in the dark of what's going on below." The "picture" seen through the scope was monochromatic (green) and not very well-focused. We were determined to find the gomers up around the "disappearing river" bridge crossing on Route 101. We knew they brought it out of the giant cave the river ran through, but could never catch it. This would be our chance.

Just moving that scope around the back of the airplane as Steve would jink back and forth was tiring. I finally got to where I would only look through it from one side, as it took too long to move it to the other, find the road, focus in, and then try to see anything. Besides, looking through the small aperture was making me sick. At one point, Steve dropped a flare, and I remember it was like a torch going off on the other end of the scope. NVGs were a long way off.

Back to Wells and I.

A signal to the chief, and the powerful air turbine unit at the side of the jet blew air into the starter turbine of the F-100. Slowly, so slowly, the big J-57 engine started to roll over. Throttle around the horn. The start button glowed red in the center, signifying ignition, and the exhaust-gas temperature showed an ever-so-slight rate of increase. Almost painfully slowly for an airplane that was so capable of such high speeds, the engine came to life. After about fifty seconds it was at idle, and I signaled the crew chief to disconnect the air cart. Flight controls, signal speed brake, speed brake checked, signal flaps, flaps set for takeoff.

"Phu Cat, Misty 11 ready taxi one."

"Misty cleared to Runway 33 altimeter 3009."

"3009."

As the throttle came forward, the big J-57 chugged, unable to get enough air in the back of the up-slanted shark inlet. It continued to *chug chug* as the power slowly came up. A tap of the brakes, out of the steel revetment, and we were rolling.

The huge air base was just coming alive as Wells and I went through arming at the end of the runway. The guns were charged, the seven 2.75-inch-in-diameter folding fin rockets in each wing pod were armed, and Misty 11 was number one for takeoff.

"Phu Cat, Misty 11 is number one."

"Cleared for takeoff, Misty."

"Roger."

The extra-long canopy of the F model 100 came down, slid slightly forward, and was locked into position with a snap of my left hand on the shoulder-high knob. The seal inflated, and we felt a push of pressure as the cockpit began pressurizing.

"Showtime." Wells from the back.

Into position and hold as the power comes up to 100 percent and the engine instruments were checked. It was seven-thirty, and to help the base wake up, I released the brakes and eased the throttle outboard. The engine pressure ratio gauge, which gave the ratio of pressure of air going in the front of the engine to air going out, dropped two-thirds of the reading it had been showing as the exhaust pipe on the rear of the jet opened to allow the extra thrust.

Boom.

The sound reverberated all over the base. And as, all over the base, admin officers, doctors, radio men, cooks, electronics gurus, maintenance men, cleaners, civil engineers, and air police lay sleeping, Wells and I headed off to war.

I was newer to the Mistys than Wells but had been in the organization for nearly a month by this time. I was an old hand. You get to be an old hand in combat by surviving. It was not unusual to have a first lieutenant leading a lieutenant colonel into a combat mission if the lieutenant had been in the theater much longer than the colonel. I had arrived in Misty with Chris Kellum and "Short Fat" at about the same time. I was a front-seater Misty, which implied that, as a minimum, I had finished the first five rides, which were always done in the rear seat. Five rides in Misty, in the late summer and early fall of 1968, was a fair amount of fighting.

We climbed into the "cool" air. Outside air temperature at the base was about eighty-two degrees. Autumn in Vietnam.

"Panama Control, Misty 11 with you, climbing to sixteen thousand feet."

We headed out over the water. Panama control was the air-traffic control agency for flights in the central and northern part of South Vietnam. "Feet wet," as I said in the chapter about coming to Phu Cat, was the term used to describe traveling off the coast of Vietnam, North or South, while keeping out of range of any ground fire that might be there. For us there was little threat from ground fire at fifteen to eighteen thousand feet, but we flew over the water anyway. Habit. For the guys in something like a Caribou or even a C-130, the safety of the water had more to offer. The Caribou spent about 90 percent of their approaches, however, going into little tiny fields all over the place, probably being shot as much as anyone.

It was a beautiful clear day, with just a little fog in the valleys. My mind drifted as we headed north. There was very little cockpit chatter in those parts of a mission, mostly just two guys in the same airplane, thinking about the targets and the plan they had hatched with the intel guys and letting their minds drift to pleasant memories.

FOR SOME REASON, MY THOUGHTS initially drifted back to TV shows in the fifties. There was Walter Cronkite and the CBS shows *You Are There*, *The Twentieth Century*, and more importantly *Air Power*. Week after week, Walter had narrated as bombs fell on Nazi Germany and imperial Japan. His stirring voice implanted in us kids admiration for the achievements of our own parents who, knowingly, sat and watched Walter with us. Walter was the cheerleader for the US military. Serial after serial had him extolling the bravery of US airmen in the Second World War, raining their bombs down with "daylight precision bombing" while taking terrible losses. These were the men who kept us free. Theirs were the sacrifices that saved our country. They were to be emulated. They were heroes.

Walter even went to Vietnam and got as close to the combat in Hue as one could be without actually carrying a rifle, closer than some who were.

I don't remember his exact words, but I do remember when Cronkite would later say that he felt the war in Vietnam was unwinnable. It felt like

I'd been kicked in the stomach by an old friend. At the time, I couldn't believe he'd given up on us. I grew up watching this man cheer the US Air Force every week.

We were raised by a generation that had overcome the worst military threat to freedom in the history of the world. Everyone had been in the service.

"Your uncle drove an LST at Iwo Jima."

"Your dad was a pilot during the war."

"Mr. Yannell was a fighter pilot hero who shot down and killed at least five German warplanes. He was an Ace."

"Mom was an instructor at Embry Riddle."

"Uncle Ray was a B-29 aircraft commander at Tinian and he was only 23 years old."

"What brave men ... men who saved our country."

"You'll see what it's like when you go in the service."

Along with Cronkite, kids watched *Victory at Sea*, a series of films made by US Navy documentary crews during the Second World War and set to stirring music by Richard Rogers. The narrator led you through the grief and struggle of so many little islands that kids felt a share of the honor of these men. These films were not a part of the regular weekly fare, but picked up here and there on Saturdays when the kids weren't outside. The films carried into the outside play.

"You be the Jap."

"Got ya, ya dirty Jap."

The show that old Walter put on describing the dropping of the atomic bomb on Hiroshima was met with awe. President Truman's decision to drop the bomb on people was held almost in reverence. In those days, when you went to war, the whole country went and no one was allowed to stop or give quarter until the enemy had unconditionally surrendered. The bomb had saved millions of lives and only from a sixty-year run of peace and prosperity could it be looked at as the wrong move at the time.

We were the progeny of a generation that had lived through the Depression. Success in life was measured by how well you were fed, how healthy you were from work, not exercise, and whether you went to college or not. "If it's the last thing on earth I do, you three will be college graduates."

I saw Chu Lai, the giant Marine base, go by under the left wing, and the F model 100 headed out over the South China Sea. I could see Da Nang further north from our present position.

"Misty, switch to Panama now on 236.6. Good hunting."

"236.6, see you on the flipside."

My mind drifted again, this time to the weekend from which the three of us, Wells, Dave Jenny, and myself, had just returned.. Clyde Seiler was the commander at this time or the ops officer, I can't remember. Clyde hadn't gone with us, but he always commented that he couldn't understand why within three hours of him saying, "Okay, take a couple of days," the guys would be calling from Clark in the Philippines or Kadena Air Base in Okinawa or sometimes even Hong Kong where they got on the base Gooney Bird or a transient C-141. When they were due back, there was always a "problem" with the transportation. But we rarely stayed longer than two or three days. Others were doubling up while we were gone. We'd do it for each other, but when you were the one not flying, you began to feel guilty after about the third day and started working your way back "home" to Phu Cat.

Anyway, I was thinking back to the little hotel we three had picked to stay at in Okinawa. It was a civilian crew layover base, and there was a fresh crew in at least once a day.

Each afternoon at five p.m., we held a "sick call" at the bar in the hotel. This gathered at least four or five, sometimes six to ten, flight attendants together as they came to go out to dinner with the rest of the crew.

The routine was the same each night, and we couldn't have been more obvious if we'd had the word "horny" tattooed across our foreheads in big red letters. We were swimming in money and looking for some women who just wanted to drink, eat, and most importantly, party. In the days after the pill and before herpes and AIDS, there were virtually no threats worth worrying about on the road to sexual satisfaction, and all the girls were on birth control pills "to make my period regular."

I remembered inviting three flight attendants to join us the last night we were on Okinawa. We bought the girls a few rounds and headed for the base and the officers' club at Kadena.

When we got there, the three girls, with half a buzz on courtesy of us Mistys, walked out on us when their captain and copilot showed up.

No problem. In the door walked another crew, and the whole shooting match started all over. I meandered over to a cute little blond from Continental Airlines.

Dave had picked a beauty who was a former high-school mate of mine. When I saw her I figured I was set, but she took a liking to Dave . Ever the gentleman, he asked me if I minded him "playing through." I thought that was gentlemanly of him.

According to later reports, this gal liked sitting on top, and as Chris Kellum used to say, almost with a tear in his eye, "if we lie down together and I don't move, I'm not cheating."

We got back to our rooms about one in the morning. I had talked to Dave and was already packing. He called Wells.

Wells had been just as lucky. His date had been a middle-aged—nearly twenty-seven years old—blonde from the great state of New York. She was beautiful.

There's a song today that goes, "We started in spending my money and she started in calling me honey, we went to every honky-tonk in town."

Well, that night, at Kadena, there had been only one honky-tonk, and it was at the base in the form of a jukebox. After a couple of drinks, Wells asked his date if she'd like to dance. He later told the story using Kellum's favorite line: "We got out on the floor, and it was all over but the hand-clapping."

Wells showed her the "business" card that some of the early Mistys had had printed up:

Get Fac'd by a Superfac
Call:
MISTY

Easy Terms	Specializing in
Flak Free Areas Optional	SAMs, Trucks, Supply Areas
At Extra Cost	and rescaps

After a long paragraph on the back of the card advising how this trained professional killer had been hired by your government to seek out and destroy enemies of the state, had nerves of twisted blue steel, and had to be carefully handled, the card advised that upon this handling he would become very docile. "You are advised to give him the love and care he needs so badly."

She read it and looked at him, smiling. "Don't tell me this works."

"I'm hoping for a first time." Like I said about Wells, he was a warrior at the appropriate time and Mr. Social when that time was right.

Smile.

Out on the dance floor, Connie asked, "What happens if I don't give this trained killer the careful handling he needs?"

Wells could tell by the way she moved in and up against him that this was just foreplay.

"Well, I don't know. I hadn't considered that. I figured that you wouldn't want to let a lonely fighter pilot down."

"I don't. I'm just afraid that you might not like my tender care and attention."

"Well, can there be any doubt about how much I'm enjoying it so far?", said Wells

She moved in even closer. "Did I do that?"."

Wells said, " it sort of has a mind of its own at this point."

Wells told me later, "I couldn't remember, as we left the club, if she walked next to me or just continued doing what she was doing on the dance floor while she jumped up around me and wrapped her legs around my waist. God, it was great."

"What's up, Wells?"

"Just cleaning the saber."

"Had enough?"

"Can you get too much of this stuff?"

"Just talked to Clyde. There's a 141 leaving in about an hour and a half. Let's get back."

"Rog."

We left that night on the C-141 that came through and headed back for Phu Cat. That story would be told many times over the coming weeks.

"Good morning, Misty, you going to want to refuel before you go into the pak?" "Tanker is just coming into the area now."

"No. I think we'll have a look around up there first and then come out for some fuel."

Mistys plied our trade at about four thousand feet and at four hundred knots indicated on the airspeed—more if you could get it. You usually couldn't, and if you did, you didn't keep it for long. Someone had figured that it took about four seconds for a gunner to reach a targeting solution about where a plane would be, to feed that solution into a barrel, fire the shell, and for the shell to get to the point at which it was aimed four thousand feet down-line from the barrel. Therefore, the Mistys went across the roads that they patrolled, jinking back and forth every four seconds or so. A hard right-hand four-g turn traveling up a road until the plane had crossed over the road, relax, reverse to the left, and then set in four g's and make the hard turn back to the left, again crossing the road, all the while looking for signs of trucks and camps and stores that were hiding all along the Ho Chi Minh trail in the jungles and limestone karst regions of the southern end of North Vietnam.

All of this jinking and high-power turning at low altitude used a lot of fuel. I liked to get into the area, take a look around, and then go out and cycle off a tanker. That gave me a chance to see if anything was going on, have a look, and let the area "cool off" before we tried working any fighters on it.

People could get hurt when an FAC spent too much time hanging around what the folks on the ground knew was an obvious target. One of the biggest kills of the summer of 1968 was instigated by a man called Charlie Summers (later to fly a T-28 piston airplane through thunderstorms on the Weather Channel—jeez, Charlie) who just looked down and saw a few too many trails going off into the jungle in one place. Rather than hanging around, circling, and alerting everyone, he just noted the position and went out to a tanker, cycled, and came back and put ordnance on where he thought trucks would be parked. He did a lot of damage that day and, as I recall, no one on our side got tapped.

The gunners got ready when someone had hung around an area for a long time. This was bad for two reasons. One, someone could get hurt, and two, lots of other people could get hurt trying to get the first someone recovered.

We passed the DMZ as the killing began for another day. Off to the right was Tiger Island. Somehow that island was left for the North Vietnamese during the entire war. It was about two miles off the coast and could've been easily captured, but it never was taken.

My reverie was over, and I started the nose down from sixteen thousand feet as we went by the DMZ. Power back as the speed was building rapidly.

"What's the plan, Rose?"

"Going to Bat Lake to see what the intel guys were talking about. If there's something hot there, we'll have a look and head out for gas before we hit it."

"I'm with you."

Down into the area around Bat Lake we came. The lake itself was on the west side of the coastal plain that led from the South China Sea to the limestone karsts and mountains. It sat higher and almost reminded you of a reservoir in a more developed country. That morning, it was shrouded in fog. We could see the fork from Route 101 that fed up into the region around the lake, and we knew we were the first visitor of the day.

Wells suggested, "Let's shoot up the road, in under the overcast, and see what's going on. We can always pull up hard if we start to lose sight of the ground."

Great. Into the fray, wide open at 450 knots. I knew we'd have to get below the overcast to keep the road in sight. That was going to be below four thousand feet. Into the realm of calculated risk.

"Getting a little low, Rosie."

"Got the road in sight, we're below the fog. One pass and haul ass."

"Good." As if I had to talk Wells Jackson into hanging it out for a possible SAM.

Up the north side of the road, headed west, not bothering to jink as I hoped the fact that we were the first ones through and we were going so damn fast under the overcast would let us get away with this.

Looking, looking, looking. The road disappeared about a mile ahead as the fog lowered to the ground. Just a few more seconds. Nothing. Nothing. One last, quick look outside, inside to center attention on the attitude indicator, and then ... pull, pull hard about five g's.

"Shit."

"What?"

"There was something there. Like a missile, big fucking aluminum-looking thing, not camouflaged at all."

We popped out of the top of the overcast into crystal clear sky, one three-shot string of 37-mm shells off to the right. Firing at the noise. They were nowhere near us.

"What was that all about?"

"We got to go back, Rose. Get in there and take another look."

"Now?"

"Yeah, now, get a shot, get this thing on film. Document it and then get some fighters in here and blow it the fuck up."

"Okay, but we're going to make about a thirty-mile circle here and come at them again from the east. Sun in their eyes, give them time to settle in and settle down."

"Great plan. You are a wonderful leader, o great lieutenant."

"Fuck you, captain."

Wells had taken me around the route pak on one of my earliest missions. He had shown, with painstaking clarity, what 37-mm, quad-23, and 57-mm looked like. He did that by flying, at relatively high altitude, over the various sites he knew to exist and then clinically discussing the fire we received. He was smart and aggressive and knew where to find the stuff, how to get it to fire, and how to stay far enough away from it when you could, so that there was very little chance of it hitting you.

Very little, but not none. What a guided tour that had been. I also learned, on that tour, the sound that AAA can make when it gets close enough to the airplane to hear it snap as it goes by.

Anyway, back around we came. Wells had his handheld camera ready. He would watch as we came up the road, have the camera aimed pretty much down the wing line, call for just a little left bank when he saw the "thing," and snap the picture.

The Misty handheld-camera shots were renowned for the information they gathered. Often taken at treetop level, they allowed intel gurus to make out individuals on the ground many times. The shots were amazing testimonials to our work. The ones Wells took that day later proved that we had, indeed, found a surface-to-air missile, a SAM. It should also be added that although the missile or truck or AAA site could usually be seen, it—and especially people around it—were blurred from the speed at which the Misty went by.

"Here we go."

"I'm ready."

I could see the road disappearing into the fog ahead. This time they knew we were coming. This time I started down from about seven thousand feet with the throttle full forward all the way. I was going to be going about as fast as I could possibly get this old sled going.

Tracers arced across the road, and I instinctively jinked. Shit, that wasn't going to work. If I jinked, Wells might not get the shot. More tracers. The rocket pods were shaking now, we were moving so fast.

The rising sun had lifted the fog just a little.

"Wells, I can see the bend in the road, which was the last thing I saw before I started the pull. I'll bring it down the left side."

"Rog."

Ten seconds … five …

"I see it."

"I see it too."

"Tracers. Just one more second …"

"Got it. Pull. Pull hard."

We rocketed back into the overcast, tracers seemingly punching at us out of the fog. *Up,* up hard, on top. Clear.

"Misty 11, Hillsboro here, what's up? I have a flight of F-105s checking in with Mk82."

"Send 'em to alpha freq."

The tactical frequencies in Vietnam were changed every day to try to keep the enemy from jamming them. Sometimes it worked, and sometimes you could hear all sorts of shit in Vietnamese on the frequencies. Whatever code was given to the frequencies, there were only about ten of them. It wasn't hard to get jammed. Alpha was just one of many frequencies that were used for the point control of fighters.

The Thuds (nickname given to the big Republic F-105 Thunderchiefs) came up.

"Misty, Hatchet Flight here with a flight of two Thuds, twelve Mark 82s and 20-mm."

"Here's what we're going to do. I want you to follow me up a road and keep me in sight. When I say so, the target will be on the ground, right below my left wing, put your ordnance there. You're going to be low, so just let one or two of them go and then pull, hard, so you don't blow yourself up."

"What's there?"

"We think it's a SAM."

"Shit hot, let's go."

"Fucking Thuds. I love 'em."

"Let's get some gas."

"Hatchet, can you hold ten minutes while we cycle out for some fuel?"

"We've got to do it now, Misty."

"Shit, three times over that fucking target in ten minutes. This is pushing it."

"Hold on."

"Hillsboro, Misty needs some fuel. Can you spare a few thousand for each of these 'Hatchet' guys?"

"Sure can. You're on Apple tanker. He's been listening to you. He's fifty miles east of you over the gulf."

"Want some fuel, Hatchet?"

"Sure, let's go."

We went out to the tank. The tanker guys often listened on the tactical frequency and were a big part of the team. Apple 22 started toward where he knew we'd be coming out of the north. He started the turn just outside of a potential SAM ring if one had been located at Dong Hoi. He heard us call "tanker in sight" and began a turn back to the east and rolled out on a north heading to get the sun out of everyone's eyes.

We topped off and the Thuds took about six thousand pounds each. Wells and I had been down to about three thousand after the ride up the coast from Phu Cat and all the low altitude and burner work I'd been doing.

Back into the area; the fog was about up to about fifteen hundred feet this time.

"Lead, you follow me. I'll talk you in."

"Rog, Misty."

"Two. You stay up here and scatter your bombs in two passes where you see Lead's go off. You'll have perfect cover from the fog and a perfect target from the explosions."

"We hope."

"Rog."

"Good thinking. Let's not spend the day digging one of these guys out of here."

I knew what Wells was talking about. The third pass was pushing it. Trying to get three planes through there would be next to impossible.

"Here we go, leader. Follow me."

"Half-mile back, Misty, let's go."

"This is the road below me. About two miles to go."

"Rog."

"About here you'll see the road start a gradual turn to the right. When it comes back hard to the left, the target is just on the inside of that left-hand turn." Wells was doing the talking.

"Rog."

"Okay, it's there. Right off my left wing. Right there."

"I got it. I got it."

I looked forward and, as I started to pull out of the grayness, the fog was broken with red arcs, seemingly all over the place.

"Oh, man, they're on us now." I pulled up hard through the overcast. Lead let his bombs go and pulled up through the overcast behind us.

"Got two off."

I just pulled. On the gauges now, I saw the attitude go through about thirty degrees nose up, still coming.

"Jeez."

"C'mon, c'mon."

Daylight—made it.

"Wow."

"Holy cow."

I banked hard to the right and looked over my right shoulder as the nose of the F-100 came back down through the horizon.

"You sure as hell hit something explosive."

"Two, scatter yours in that area. Keep it moving. The heat from the explosions has burned some of the fog off. They'll see you."

The two Thuds worked the area.

We called that long cylindrical thing that Wells had seen a SAM because it looked like one and was heavily defended, and because all hell broke loose when the bombs hit it. The picture confirmed it.

"Want us to strafe the area, Misty?"

"No, I don't. You did enough damage. Great work. On at twenty-five past the hour and off at fifty past the hour. Hundred percent on target and one SAM and associated launch equipment destroyed."

There was no percentage in letting a couple of these guys go strafing at low altitude after this encounter. Not all the guys on the ground who were shooters had been hit. They'd be ready and they'd be mad, and the darn Thuds would strafe right down to the treetops. At that point in the war, the 105s were still manned by some guys who had been downtown. They thought the southern part of North Vietnam to be an uncontrolled gun range where they couldn't get hit.

"We piss on that kind of shit, Misty."

Compared to Pak 6, it was a lot less dangerous, but still dangerous. We sent them home.

"Head home, Hatchet. Nice work."

"Roger, Misty. Nice target."

And so Wells and I lived through a fairly tight situation without a scratch. We hit a valuable target to the North, blew up an awful lot of something awfully explosive—a SAM, as the photos later showed—disrupted a lot of the enemy's plans, and finished the rest of the mission that morning completely unscathed. In fact, after that, we'd hardly broke a sweat. There was no rhyme or reason to this, but that's the way it worked.

Earlier that month, Dave Jenny had gone into the area with a high-ranking officer from the wing in the backseat. I forget the man's name, but he had the balls to fly with us. Anyway, they took a hit around Bat Lake and came staggering out over the coast and were heading for Da Nang. Dave didn't think the plane would make it, but he was going to give it a try. They passed Tiger Island. Now over the ocean, Dave knew that at least there would be no escape and evasion on the ground in North Vietnam if they had to bail out.

"Well, sir. We're on the way to Da Nang. I don't know if we'll make it or not, so be thinking of maybe bailing out ..."

Bam, bam.

Dave was flying solo in an airplane with the canopy and the rear seat gone.

There had been so much noise in the airplane that the only two words the officer in back heard were, "bail out." He did.

Dave told us the story saying, he circled the other man once or twice in his chute, and then he jumped. He regaled us with his story of "skydiving" from sixteen thousand feet. Dave was a great storyteller, and we laughed at that one for days. We also teased Dave about the photo that came out in the "Stars and Stripes" a few days later. "Stars and Stripes" was the military newspaper. There was a Vietnam Edition. As I remember the story, there was the senior officer, safe onboard the Navy ship that had picked them up. Dave and the ship's Captain were also there. The caption listed the names of the ship's Captain and Dave's senior officer crewmate. Dave was listed as "an unidentified Navy corpsman."

ON NOVEMBER 1, 1968, PRESIDENT Johnson and our leaders in Washington again decided that the way to win the war was to stop beating up the enemy. This was a "cagy, sly," unsuccessful tactic they had tried two or three times in the past, and it would be left in place for nearly four more long years of the war. It never worked.

I cannot write of my times in Misty without more mention of Clyde Seiler. Clyde was a Colorado Air National Guard pilot and an airline captain for Continental Airlines. He walked with a sort of loping gait, and I never saw him that he didn't smile at me, even during the times when he was mad at me, and there were a few of those also.

He was tall, about six-two as I remember, thin but strong-looking, like a defensive end. He had long reddish hair, barely meeting air-force standards, as if we cared, and a giant handlebar moustache that he had to bunch in behind his oxygen mask and talk through on the radio. We teased him that he sounded like he was talking through the "thatch" between a woman's legs. He liked that.

Clyde showed up in the early part of late September 1968, as I recall, and flew for a month with us in the southern part of North Vietnam. He was aggressive with an airplane, and in the war heart and soul. He missed home and family and his cushy job at Continental, but he was the first to say, "This is what I signed up for. This is what I've trained for. I'm fucking ready."

He and I were flying a Misty mission one day along the trail in Laos when we saw little puffs of smoke coming out of a thicket of bushes. Clyde asked me if I saw them.

"Sure do, little gomer is trying to put a hole in your jet, Major."

"I'm going to circle around and strafe the little bastard. That all right with you, Rosie?"

"Clyde, why don't we go up the road for about ten minutes and then come back. We'll ease off to the west and then hit him out of the sun. He's in the clump of bushes just to the west of that big karst. Should be easy to find."

"Rog."

And that's what we did. We came back and laid a line of bullets right through the area that the little puffs had been coming out of at the time we first flew over. On that pass, we saw nothing, but if that little guy hadn't moved, we had him. Clyde was practically growling in the mask as we strafed.

I often thought about that. I had done things like that myself. We were not supposed to use the strafe for anything but helping to mark targets, but you put aggressive young fighter pilots in an area alone, and they get shot at or find a target that is moving or is openly vulnerable and they can't get ordnance through the command structure to put in on that target, those pilots are going to strafe.

FACs were lone hunters. They went out alone and often disappeared with no one to witness their demise. In the Mistys at that time, we often referred to them and the guys in the Hanoi Hilton as "Missing Mistys." They were airplanes that just vanished from the face of the earth. It happened in the Misty and it happened in the Laredo, Storme, Wolf, Owl, and Tiger FAC programs. The planes got hit while they were nose to nose with a gun that they hadn't told anyone they were strafing.

At one point, because of the unfound losses, people tried to put a wingman in with each FAC mission, but it just didn't work. They got in the way of each other. So there they'd be alone, working a road like they were supposed to, they'd see something, maybe try to get ordnance or maybe just think they'd tap it themselves. They'd take a serious hit, try to pull out, level off just enough to smash into the jungle at a low angle, and disappear under the trees. No mayday call, no nothing. They were gone, hidden in the jungle. That thought ran through my mind that day with Clyde as we came back and strafed, but again, no hits at all.

Clyde became the commander of Misty during my last month there. He was a great boss but just didn't care for the politics. This is not to say that all high-ranking officers in the service have to be politicians only. Some outstanding examples of fighters who went on to lead came out of Vietnam— McPeak and Fogleman to name two I had the privilege of knowing.

McPeak had been a solo on the Thunderbirds and was an extraordinary pilot. His rendition of "Phu Cat Star—That's What I Are" was a country-and-western favorite at Phu Cat and showed the natural good humor of the man. His willingness to show younger pilots techniques he had learned in years of flying the 100 and his willingness to jump into any fight that was presented to him marked him as a great leader in my book, even in 1968. He was not above turning around and helping those behind him in the grand scheme of things. He wrote four or five letters for me, recommending me for the Thunderbirds, but even his endorsement couldn't put me over the top.

Fogleman was an in-your-face, tough, hard-fighting fighter pilot—a man's man, to use an old phrase. Remember, at the time we knew him, he was a captain. Folks liked him because he was one of us. For all we knew, he'd wind up selling insurance after the war. Well, that probably never would have happened, but becoming chief of staff was not a viable reason to like Ron in 1968. Ron was the reason you liked Ron.

But Clyde was *only* a wartime leader. We loved him. One of the biggest celebrations we had was the night he was named "Misty Commander 7."

One night, after I had finished my tour in Misty and on the night that Bob Konopka was having his going-away party, the Mistys partied late in the club. I was still hanging with them, as I had only been out of the outfit for about two weeks. We came down to the Misty area in the fighter-pilot trailer area and continued. At about eleven that night, the next morning's first two sorties went to bed, and those of us not flying started really getting obnoxious. Without going into the details, suffice it to say that Clyde, myself, and an intel Misty (name withheld) wound up in jail, mostly due to a pretty stupid act I had pushed Clyde into doing. Cass Cassero, from the New Mexico Guard, tells about that night in the Misty anthology.

"If you're going to do it anyway, I'd better be there," Clyde had said.

The act didn't turn out well, and in jail, Clyde whistled one of the MP sergeants over to our holding cell to bum a pack of cigarettes.

The old noncom smiled broadly. "Major, you want to bum a whole pack."

"Sarge, you know I'm good for it." (Clyde had been here before. The MPs even had joked that it looked like the Mistys had been partying again.) "There is nobody coming out here to fetch our bony asses out of this place at one o'clock in the ..."

"Atten-hut!"

It was Ron Fogleman. We thought it a little pretentious of Ron to have the room called to attention. Behind him was the real reason. It was Colonel Bill Creech. Creech was a hardnose, hardass son of a bitch. An outstanding pilot, a good leader, but a real "Don't fuck with me" kind of guy.

Creech had flown missions with us. As a matter of fact, he and I had flown a Misty mission together about a week before the end of my tour in Misty. We (Mistys) had fucked with him before and got away with it because of that closeness with him, but this would be the last time. He drove us back to our trailers. We thought maybe we'd just get a mean look.

"Be outside my office at eight tomorrow morning."

"Yessir."

We showed. Clyde told me he'd go in first. When he came out, he told me, "Creech is gone. Go back to your trailer. Everything is okay. I just called my ops officer down at Phan Rang Air Base [South Vietnam]. He told me he knew I'd screw up sooner or later. He said come on back. They'd always take me." That was the guard.

"Clyde, I did this. You came along to take care of me."

"I'm a fucking guard puke, Rosie. I've got no career in the air force when this war is over. I was going to go anyway. Why hang on to you and take two of us down?"

"That's bullshit."

But Seiler knew. He knew, and he was right about his life in the peacetime air force. He had loved the Mistys and loved leading us as much as it wore on his nerves, but he was heading back to be a line pilot with his outfit at Phan Rang Air Base further to the south.

But being right didn't make it right. He took the hit for me.

Creech knew it, too. He refused to speak to me on at least two occasions when I tried to engage him about the incident face on. He didn't get mad, he didn't yell at me. He refused to acknowledge me and walked off. Seiler had stepped up for me, and Creech had let it stand, even when I tried to tell him that. Clyde went home to Phan Rang. I felt like shit.

Three weeks later, Clyde pulled out of a low-angle bomb pass and the wing of his plane came off. There wasn't time to eject and Clyde went in with the airplane. Would he have been there anyway if I hadn't screwed up? Who knows, but don't think that thought doesn't enter my mind. What a great guy Clyde was to work with and for.

In Misty, I hung a lot with a guy named Rog Rice. Rog was a big guy with a handlebar moustache that rivaled Clyde's, a ready laugh, and always, always a story that would lead you to believe he had just spent the week with some girl in a hotel in New York. We hung out a lot because we were about the same age, with the same interests, and we wound up flying together many times. Rog and I played a lot of pool at the club and became king of the "long green shots," while "Folsom Prison Blues" played on the jukebox. I remember Christmas 1968, as our tour was ending, Rog talked me into watching *Miracle on 34th Street*.

"I watch it every year for luck, Rosie. I've watched it as long as I can remember, and it will be my good luck." He made such a point out of it that I watched it with him. Sort of a sentimental show, but nice for Christmas. We watched into the night on Christmas Eve in the little TV room off the bar at the Phu Cat officers' club. There was no one else in there with us. The bartender left about eleven and told us to shut the place up. I remember helping ourselves to a couple of brews and just leaving the MPC on the register. It was a nice movie.

Rog died in a range accident in Spain the following summer. He released a rocket in an F-100 and, as I heard, he had some sort of camera, either on his helmet or on the plane to watch the rockets fire forward. I was told that Rog just tracked the rockets too long for the picture. Too late, he attempted to pull out of the attack and flew into the ground. I was also told by another friend that Rog had shot a rocket, pulled up hard, and rudder rolled the plane to the right and then left to see the missile impact. We did this all the time in the FAC business. He must have pulled too hard because in that story, the plane stalled and crashed. Either way, Rog was gone.

I have been afraid to watch *Miracle on 34th Street* ever since.

One last Misty story, and I'll wind this chapter up. It happened years later, long after the war.

As I've said before, Greg Parker, with whom Tom and I roomed while in pilot training, went to Luke and also came to Phu Cat with me. Greg was in the 612th while I was in the 416th, but we all flew Misty together. Years later, Greg had been reported as "deceased" in the Misty records.

As often happens, Greg had dropped off the line for about twenty years, just too busy with life to keep up on all the goings on. Doc Echenberg had his own family practice in San Francisco and, around 2005, in walks Greg's mom. They eventually put their histories together, and Dean winds up sending Greg a copy of the Misty anthology that Don Shepperd had put together, or maybe Don's great book about the Mistys, *Bury Us Upside Down*. Greg starts in reading one night, while relaxing on the john, and finds out he's been reported dead.

"Jesus, I'm dead."

He showed up at the next Misty reunion. Bud said he looked remarkably good for a dead man. We later teased him about the very first thing he did after reading his "obituary." I think, but can't confirm, that Doc was the person who reported to Don Shepperd that Greg was dead.

Tom Pre-flighting a T-38, Summer of 67

Thomas A. Mravak

"The Great Muckrock"
-Summer of 67

Hugh Gommel, Jerry Becker, Ken Boone on second story
porch of barracks we lived in at Reese AFB .. Fall of 1966

Pilot Training: At the table with "Ali", Terry Schmidt,
"Sam," George Gates, instructor and Tom.

Wells Jackson circa 1968

Tip Galer- F4's- 13th Tac
Fighter Squadron Udorn 1972

Misty Facs, Fall '68
Kneeling : Unknown, Frank Kimball, me, Al Winkelman,
Bob Fitzsimmons , Dean Echenberg, Clyde Seiler
Standing: Bob Konopka, John "Abe" Kretz, Jerry Edwards, Matt
Hussen, Rog Rice, Bob Bryan, Dick Durant, Jim Perry, Kelly Irving,
unknown, Chuck Holden, Unknown, Greg Parker, Don Harlan(hat)

Dr. Dean Echenberg, fighter pilot.

Wells Jackson, after his final Misty Flight, with some of the guys.
Kneeling Left to Right: Roy Bridges, Jerry Edwards, Chris Kellum
Standing: Unknown, Bob Lynch, Chuck Holden,
Clyde Seiler, unknown, John "Abe" Kretz, Wells,
Rog Rice, Bob Konopka, Frank Kimball

Chris Kellum in our Trailer 1968

Finishing my Misty Tour with Whitey
Thompson pouring the bubbly.

"'Rev' Gommel talks to the troops . L/R
Terry Schmidt, Dan Heitz (unknown behind Dan),
Bucky Jones, Frank Wrublewski, Jay Thompson,
Standing in rear unknown,Jan Jaeger, Larry Broadhead,
Jerry Becker, Muckrock (in rear) "Rev" Gommel, Larry
Morris, Clyde Thompson,) unknown in rear)."

The line up for final flight at Udorn in F-4's.
John Broom, Preston Duke, Buf Tibbets,
Myself, Tom Lampley, Wheels

Wheels and a Winston.

Kelly Irving gets ready to fly-
1968 Bien Hoa, Vietnam

Dave Jenny 1968

Gerry Becker debriefing an instructor pilot-1967

F-100 gun school-Luke Fall of 1967- all 66 grads except Greg Parker
Kneeling L-R Tom Kiser, Wendell Cook, Don Kilgus, (Misty-IP-
credited with only air to air F-100 kill in Vietnam), Dale Fowler,
Wheels, Me, Dan Cecil, Standing Art Suro, Greg Parker, IP
Bert??, IP Gene?? Tom Meshko (65) Lacy Veach, Gene Sexton, IP

Bill Bowen, Phu Cat Air Base, 1968

CHAPTER 19
Walking Home from One

"Rosie, did you ever notice how nice and quiet things seem when we arrive in a target area? Looks so peaceful down there and all. Then we go and kick the bees' nest and stir the shit up. We're the ones that stir the fucking pot each day to get it going. That's what fighter pilots do." —Chris Kellum

IT'S FUNNY WHEN I THINK back on the day. It seemed to have been characterized by things that went wrong right from the start, but none of them seemed so far out of the ordinary to me that I gave them a second thought.

These were things that weren't necessarily related to flying, but were indicators of a bad day.

First, there had been a rocket attack on the base at about three or four in the morning. We didn't sweat those much and often didn't even go to the bunkers. Remember what I said earlier about how safe life on those big bases could be. The guys out on the perimeter were at war, and we slept comfortably. God bless them.

Waking up early in the morning and sitting there talking to Chris for an hour or so as we determined first that the rockets were not hitting near us, that a cup of coffee would hit the spot, and that we'd have to get together at the club after our two missions that day. This killed enough time that getting back to sleep and getting up again at seven didn't leave much room for restful sleep. No sweat.

Then there was the ride to the squadron briefing room. In Misty, there had been a truck to come and pick up the individual crews at their quarters and take them. But there were only about twelve or fourteen guys in the Misty detachment at any one time. There was no problem for one of the intel guys, one of the admin guys, or one of the other pilots to man the van and go pick up guys at their trailers. With a squadron of twenty-some pilots, that was impossible. People had to get to the squadron on their own. That was accomplished through bumming a ride with a senior officer who had a jeep, grabbing a shuttle bus or any other truck or van going the mile or so to the building, walking, or as I had done, buying a small motorcycle.

That motorcycle was a laugh. There were probably thirty or forty of them on base. They were all small 90cc Hondas or the like. You merely found a guy getting ready to DEROS (date of expected return from overseas—go home) and offered to buy his bike. It was a very gentlemanly deal. The going price was fifty bucks. You paid fifty for it when you got it and you took fifty for it when you left.

One guy had a prospective purchaser ask for the title and insurance papers. "There's no title. There's no insurance papers. There's no contract, but I'll tell you what there is. There's a line of guys standing behind you, willing to pay the money today. Ya want to ride or you want to walk. Makes no difference to me. Fifty bucks."

Sold.

Anyway, that bike was a cold starter. You had to jump on the starter thirty or forty times to get it going, or you had to do what I usually did, which was to start down the long hill before the BX and hope that it kicked into life before the bottom of it. It always did. Not that day. I had to walk it up the hill beyond the BX and all the way to the squadron. Another problem.

We briefed. I was the leader of Elect 21 flight. Four F-100 Sabres going to Laos to hit targets found for us by a Misty FAC. Our scheduled takeoff time was about noon, as I recall.

The second element (Ships 3 and 4) was led by Al Winkelman in the Number 3 position. Al was a friend, a bachelor to this day, a health nut ("I run a mile and smoke a pack a day—that should be about right") and most importantly for this mission, an ex-Misty like myself. The two wingmen were Dick Halick, I believe and Lee Gourley, a fellow classmate from the academy who would later be killed on a Misty mission himself.

Although a fellow classmate, Lee had gone on to some other program after graduation and arrived about six months behind me at Phu Cat. These two had arrived at about the same time in the 416th and were coming along real fine. In fact, I had been sitting in Mobile one day when an old European F-100 guy and Dick had been caught out and came back to Phu Cat with fairly low fuel and very low weather in heavy rain. We watched the big oval noses come out of the clouds at about 250 feet. Because of his lack of experience, the squadron commander and the supervisor of flying had come out to the mobile unit to watch Dick make his approach. There he was, right on the button. Dead on. That was an accomplishment for a new lieutenant with about two hundred hours total in the F-100.

So we briefed.

I remember to this day giving the statement about what we would do if Al or I got shot down. How the other would act as the first on-scene commander for the rescue that would begin at the shoot-down. How we would turn it over to the Misty FAC when Al or I left. I got the names (Al and the FAC and me) wrong and backed up and started over and got the names wrong again. I knew what I would expect to happen, as did the other three because the rescue briefing was the same every time. I finally left it as "whichever one of us is left after the bullets stop flying will be the on-scene commander." That got Al laughing, and his laugh was infectious. We all left the briefing feeling pretty good.

Little did I know.

After the briefing, we went to the personal-equipment area that was right next to the two briefing rooms in center of the 416th area. The guys in the personal-equipment area spent their entire working time in-country looking out for our emergency needs. The parachutes were lined up on stanchions, each with our number or name on them.

Also hanging on the peg was our individual g-suit, a set of bladders that went around your waist and upper leg, like a girdle, and then zipped tight all the way down your legs. The g-suit bladders filled with high-pressure air when the airplane was making high-g turns. The bladders would keep blood from pooling in the stomach and big arteries of the legs. They served to give you about two g's more tolerance.

Also on our individual pegs was the survival vest. This was made of a strong mesh material with pockets that contained two survival radios down by the waists, signal flares in the breast pockets, and various other devices, such as a holster to carry the issued .38 and some extra ammunition. There was also a hundred feet or so of lanyard that you were supposed to use to let yourself down to the ground if you wound up hanging in a tree.

The pistol, for some reason, was said to be carried as a "signaling device." There were various brags around the squadron that ran the gamut from "I'll never be captured alive" to "Probably the safest thing you can do with that thing is throw it at the enemy so he'd know when he captured you that you never intended to start a war with an entire platoon." As it turned out, some of the most successful escape-and-evasions were done by guys who did neither of the above, but just dug into the area where they were and laid low until all the troops that were looking for them went back wherever they came from. Each rescue was different. And the discussion of "What I would do?" was never-ending.

We got the gear on and reached into the freezer for a frozen bottle of water. As I said in a previous story, these rubber canteens went out as a block of ice and were normally not consumed until after the flight had departed the target area. By that time, they were usually ice water, and they always tasted fantastic.

The same personal-equipment guys who took such good care of us also manned the step van or "bread truck," as it was known, and took us around the flight line. The planes that were assigned to the flight were posted on the schedule board that was the first thing one saw when arriving in the semi-dark squadron area. Across a little aisle from the scheduling board and ops desk was an office for the CO and an office for the squadron operations officer. The commander at that time was a guy named Paul Davis, and he was a great guy, an ex-European F-100 guy who seemed to know all the more experienced (prior to Phu Cat) guys. Everyone liked him and respected him. Davis had a bad back, but rather than tell the flight surgeon and risk being grounded, he suffered in silence. I remember walking down the hall in the PE section one day past one of the briefing rooms and seeing him laying on the floor.

"Holy shit, sir, you okay?"

"Relax, Rosie. This isn't another McKeon ordeal." He was referring to Jim McKeon, another old-head European guy and a great friend of his who had died of a sudden heart attack one morning after finishing a briefing. "My back hurts so bad that I just had to lay down and straighten it out." He laid there, smoking a cigar.

We walked through that area and out into the heat. Takeoff was scheduled for just after noon. The planes all had a parking spot next to them on the schedule board, and the NCO from the personal-equipment section knew the ramp well enough to get us all to our planes with only one pass-through.

Talk in the bread truck on the way to a mission is always falsely lighthearted, always about something other than the war it seemed, and always completely unremarkable, except that it killed the time.

I stepped out of the truck and shook hands with the crew chief. A guy named Papenfuhs—Pappy to everyone else. The plane he was crew chief on was "my" airplane. On that particular day, Pappy had come over to help launch me on another airplane. I always liked working with Pappy and the rest of the guys on the line. A preflight usually consisted of merely checking that the bombs were on secure. When Pappy said it was ready to fly, it was ready. I trusted him with my life.

I climbed up the ladder, slung the chute into place, and clipped it to the survival kit that was in the seat pan with the two metal clips on the bottom of the chute harness. Flight cap went into the bottom pocket on the g suit, gloves up on the glare shield, helmet on the top of the canopy bow, and helmet bag tucked into the left rear of the cockpit. There was a routine, and that routine was followed every day.

After a few words with Pappy and the maintenance guys who gathered around, it was time. Up the ladder, leg over the side, right foot in the middle of the seat, left foot up and over and onto the floor, grab the canopy bow to support your weight and down onto the seat. The crew chief came up the ladder when you pulled the second leg in and helped you by throwing the shoulder straps over the top and down the sides of you. Four-point seatbelt connected, g suit plugged in, helmet on, mike cord plugged in, and you were ready.

"Go get 'em, sir."

"Thanks, Pap, see ya in a couple hours."

Engine start was routine. I checked in with the command post before I checked the guys in on the ground-control frequency. When you talked to the command post, you were basically asking permission to do the mission. Missions were seldom canceled, but you could get a delay at that point depending on weather or the availability of a FAC or something else "brewing" where they might need the ordnance somewhere else.

These missions were generally pretty routine, even the ones to Laos. By the time these missions got to the target area, the drop tanks were usually just going empty. You were not allowed to drop with fuel in the drops, so the timing worked out just fine. You arrived, met the FAC, dropped, and went home. They were a lot easier time-wise compared to the amount of time that you spent flying a Misty four- to six-hour mission, but not in the location to which you were directed.

"Elect 21 flight check.

Al and I had both come from Misty, where the missions went a lot further north and lasted a lot longer. A strike flight like the one today barely lasted two hours, seldom even needed to refuel, and was pretty simple. I'd become complacent.

BECAUSE PRESIDENT JOHNSON STOPPED THE bombing of the north in November of 1968, the last two months we had spent in Misty had been flown in the panhandle of Laos. We were both very familiar with the area we'd be going to. Most of the targets that the F-100s hit in South Vietnam had nothing more than small-arms counterfire at that time. Big threats to the slow-moving FAC airplanes and to guys on the ground, but pretty boring moving at over four hundred knots.

In Laos, they were beginning to get quad-mounted 23-mm guns that could throw a lot of lead out and bring down a fighter. Also, there were 37-mm guns. As I said, when the war first turned to Laos in November 1968, there was little to scare an F-100. That had begun to change as the enemy knew that all of North Vietnam was once again "safe." By early spring of 1969, things were getting a little dicey, and the Misty FACs would soon face some horrible losses in that area of operation.

As ex-Misty FACs, familiar with the area, Al and I had volunteered for and flown several night missions. These were in escort of giant C-130 gunships. Although we didn't know it at the time, these airplanes were just becoming equipped with new night-vision equipment and the ability to hit moving targets (trucks) with stunning accuracy. Our job on those missions had been to loiter in the area when the gunship was shooting and roll in on any ground fire that appeared as flashes in and around the gunship's target area. Those gunships flew high enough that they were usually out of the threat, but if a 23-mm or 37-mm got their bead, they were playing a pretty deadly game.

For those of us in the fighters, the ground guys had no radar, so they fired at the noise. Most of the airbursts we'd see at night were well behind us. It was exciting for us, though, and much more so for the guys in the gunships.

Today we were going to an area south of the giant bend that a river made in Central Laos. The target areas were defined by what we called "Delta Points." We were due to be bombing in the area of Delta 87. Al and I, because of our experience, knew this was, or could be, a pretty hot area.

"Two, three, four."

"Let's go, button three [pre-set channel three or ground control]."

"Elect check."

"Two, three, four."

"Phu Cat, Elect 21. Taxi with four Fox 100s."

"Elect, cleared to taxi to Runway 30, wind-calm altimeter 29.98."

There wasn't much need to give any more information. The sky was clear, the temperature about ninety with the humidity close. Another fine day in South Vietnam was well underway.

We taxied down the hill to the arming area, and the munitions guys came out and pulled the pins on the bombs. The old F-100 could only carry four munitions. The 750-pound bombs and the napalms were the heaviest, both just over eight hundred pounds. In the arming area, the pylon locking pins were checked closed for a final time; the arming wires were checked to be attached at the proper place. As I said before, a general-purpose bomb was armed by the air acting on a little propeller in the front of the weapon. Before the bomb was dropped, that little propeller was held in place by a wire that ran from the pylon, up along the side of the bomb, and through a little bracket on the front of the bomb. This wire kept the propeller from spinning. If necessary—for instance, if you had to drop the weapon on takeoff because of a mechanical malfunction—you could drop the bomb safe. Once in the target area, the solenoid that held on to that little arming wire was activated, and it pulled the wire off the bomb when it left the pylon, allowing the little propeller to spin, thus arming it.

The final check was a stray voltage check before the little cartridges that fired the "pushers" on the pylon were armed. The bomb wasn't just released from the pylon. It was fired off by two pushers activated by these cartridges. The goal was to not have that action happen before reaching the target area. We were ready.

"Elect, go button [preset channel] four."

"Two, three, four."

"Elect 21 flight check."

"Two, three, four."

"Phu Cat. Elect 21 and flight ready for takeoff."

"Elect, you're cleared on and off Runway 30. Winds light and variable. Altimeter 29.98."

We dropped the canopies together. It's good to get the flight thinking as a group as much as possible. You may have to count on them being active participants in your struggles, and it's good to have everyone on the same page at the same times. For this reason, we line up the helmets in the arming area, make the check-ins crisp and quick, and bring the bottom of the canopies to the top of the canopy bow when we have completed all the parking and pre-taxi checks. From that point, we're one flight.

The canopies come down the final ten inches or so together, slide forward an inch, and as the seal inflates, lock into position. We go onto the runway for engine run-ups and checks. When Four is ready, he signals by looking at number three. When number three looks at me, I know he and Four are ready. Looking over my left shoulder, I see number two looking at me, nod, and release the brakes.

On takeoff, we move individually. It's all the old D-model can do to get this load off the ground in this heat without having to give power to a wingman to maintain formation. There is an engine-pressure-ratio gauge in the lower left. Throttles are at the 100 percent position when the engine checks are complete. Then, the throttle is eased outboard for afterburner and pulled to the minimum afterburner range. The EPR gauge drops as the fuel control sends high-pressure fuel to the actuators on the afterburner nozzle ring and the nozzle swings open. When the burner lights, the EPR gauge swings back up to the top of the little marker that we use to show that the old Pratt is pushing all the air it was designed to push.

Takeoff in a fully loaded F-100 at ninety degrees requires a great deal of concrete. The roll begins, and by the time the plane goes past the mobile control, about a thousand feet down the runway, the airspeed indicator is barely moving. There is a tremendous amount of noise at this point but not much speed. At about the halfway point of the ten-thousand-foot runway, the speed is up to one hundred knots, but it takes 185 knots to get this load off the runway. The rotation comes at 170 knots, and the liftoff generally occurs just in front of the cable that serves as a last-ditch abort barrier, about nine thousand feet down the runway. There are a couple of very grim stories of friends who aborted at very high speeds, dropped the tail hook to catch this barrier, and had the hook skip over the barrier. The abort procedure called for the pilot to drop the ordnance (safe) and deploy the drag chute before taking the barrier, but that all took time. The tail hook was on the end of what was really nothing more than a giant spring. When it hit the ground, it often did what springs do, and skipped over the wire. The F-100 would go off the end of the runway at well over 150 knots, and the results were usually catastrophic.

I lifted off just ahead of the wire and snapped the long gear handle to the up position. The plane was very wobbly for the first four or five hundred feet of altitude.

The leader usually went straight ahead until the speed got fast enough to bring up the flaps, and then he climbed at that speed, starting a turn to give his wingmen a cutoff angle to use to catch up. The others caught up by turning to the inside of the turn and staying low, letting their airspeed build until it was fifty to seventy knots greater than Lead had briefed he would fly. Then, trading altitude for airspeed, they pulled up next to the leader. Two always came up on the inside of the turn, and Three and Four went to the outside of the turn.

The old F-100s were heavy at this time, and it took a lot of room to get them going and a lot of room to slow them down when they got in close to the leader. By giving a cutoff angle, they didn't have to fly at nearly as high an airspeed. I settled in at three hundred knots as briefed, and the three wingmen joined. Lee, the number two, came up first, and then Al and Dick respectively passed under Lee and I and joined on the right side. We continued in a tight fingertip formation as we rolled out of the left-hand turn and headed for the target.

As soon as we rolled out on a heading toward Laos, I spread the formation. This was done, without a radio call, by easing back and forth on the rudders. When the members of the flight saw the yaw, they moved out and put about three ship-widths between each of the planes in the flight. This gave more room to maneuver than the fingertip and allowed the guys to clear for other traffic more easily.

"Panama Control, Elect 21 and flight are off Phu Cat heading 330 to work with Hillsboro."

"Radar contact 21, say altitude climbing to."

"We'll be heading to the target at sixteen thousand."

"Roger."

The Hun wasn't good for much above that altitude with this much weight onboard. We settled in for the twenty minute or so ride up to southern Laos.

It had been a rough period of time. Cass Casero had bailed out and been picked up. Bullet Bob Bryan had been shot down twice. Lacy Veach and Ron Standerfer jumped and were picked up after some terrifying moments. Guys told Ron he had something to talk about now besides the famous Marion the Librarian New Year's ass-prints on the ceiling. Ron was a Jersey guard puke (common term—I referred to myself that way when I joined the Guard) who later wrote a great book called *The Eagle's Last Flight* about his life in the air force. He was a guard guy, a weekend warrior who, when called, not only willingly went, but went and volunteered for the toughest mission, Misty. Abe Kretz (Abe's real name was John, but we all called him Abe because Wells thought he looked like Abe Lincoln) and Cass Cassero were New Mexico Guard pukes (Tacos).

Clyde Seiler came from the Colorado Guard and Jerry Edwards from Iowa.. These guys didn't flinch for a minute when called.

Other recent shoot-downs included Noel Duncan, who had jumped out, and another relatively senior major named Rod in our squadron who had jumped.. I think Tom Purcell also took a hit, but made it back without jumping out. Things were getting a little tense, and I was two weeks from going homeThere was a CIA post on top of a hill overlooking the river, just to the north of where we would be dropping. I often wondered how these guys got away with what looked like a campsite so close to the most heavily trafficked enemy route in Southeast Asia, but they did, and their doing so helped us immensely. I tuned in to the nav aide that was located near there and started to proceed directly to the location. I knew, as did Al, that our target would be just to the south of that camp, and we would recognize it as we got into the area. We went over to Hillsboro, the airborne command post, in a C-130 orbiting over Thailand and then checked in on the tactical frequency.

"Misty 41, this is Elect 21 with four. We have sixteen 750s for your control with about thirty minutes of play time. Mission number as fragged."

"Rog, Elect. Misty 41 here." It was Bob Wilson, with Jack Dickey in his backseat. They had joined Misty about the time Al and I left.

"We have a 37-mm gun site for you today. Some ZPU out of the sight and also 23-mm. Random run-ins approved. Nearest safe area is to the east. NKP to the northwest about fifty miles."

When I think back to how to describe anti-antiaircraft fire, I would say 37-mm gunfire was characterized by bursts of three shells that traced and then detonated, whereas 57-mm was characterized by long red flashes from the guns themselves and a little less tracing but much bigger airbursts. The ZSU and 23-mm, as I remember, was hard to see if you didn't see the white puffs of smoke from the actual barrels as they fired.

"Okay 41, we're in the area of the target now, coming down to ten thousand. What's your position?"

"Misty is over the river just west of the target point at six thousand. I'll give you a wing rock."

The sun caused a flash off Misty's wing, and I picked him up.

"Okay, Elect, the FAC is at my two o'clock low. Let's go trail and call the FAC in sight please."

"Two has the FAC. Three. Four."

"Good."

I wasn't big on attacking gun sites. There was little upside and a lot of potential trouble in so doing. If you killed the target, the enemy hadn't lost any ability to wage war on the ground. When I was in Misty, I used gunfire to indicate something that the enemy wanted to protect and tried to attack that instead of the guns. But the Mistys were on to an awful lot of the supplies coming down the trail at that time, and they had taken a tremendous amount of fire in so doing. If Bob was putting me in on a gun site, there were probably supplies very close that would be hit later. .

"Misty is in to mark the target."

I watched Misty roll in and saw the stream of smoke out the back of his left wing as he let the smoke rocket go. His wing disappeared in contrails as he pulled off the target, jinked hard to the right, and then came back to the left.

"Smoke is good. Hit the smoke."

We loved to be able to say that when we were FACs. That meant that you had hit the target with your marking rocket and that there was no need to give corrections from the plume of white smoke. Wilson was good.

I remember working with a FAC in a slow-moving O-2 way up north in the Mu Gia pass. This guy had a lot of nerve even sticking his nose in that area, but he was smart also. He let the smoke rocket go way out over the west edge of the line of cliffs that formed the side of the pass and then dove back down to the top of the trees on the higher ground to the west. The rocket eased up in a long arcing flight out over the edge of the pass and then down, hitting the ground about a mile from where he wanted us to bomb. He then talked us in to the target from there by easing up to the edge and calling the corrections from where the smoke rocket had hit.

Misty was fast enough that he could come right into the heavily defended target and hit it on the first pass, as he had done.

"Check bombs armed. Leader is in on the smoke."

I came around to the east side of the target and rolled in, pulling the plane up hard to slow the forward speed, rolling to the left until upside down and pulling the nose of the plane toward the target smoke inverted. This was just like old MacCathun had showed me about eleven months earlier.

Rolling back out, the bomb sight was just below the target. Starting the roll in from ten thousand feet, I knew the speed would build rapidly, so I pulled the power about halfway back and felt the first enemy shell hit the airplane.

"Lead, they shot part of your right wing tank off, it looks like."

I didn't respond. All I did was continue tracking until I reached the release altitude and pickled the two outboard 750s off.

"Lead's coming off to the right and then back to the left."

I felt the plane jar as the second round hit it just at the release point. The hard jink to the right destroyed the tracking solution the guns had, but it was too late. I looked at the warning lights at the lower right of the instrument panel. There were about four lights on, but I zeroed in on the hydraulic failure light. The 100 wouldn't fly well without hydraulics. I checked the number-two system and it was at zero psi. That was the smaller system that controlled only flight controls. That was some relief, and I remember thinking that it was good that I still had the big system left. The big system worked the landing gear, flaps, *and* the flight controls. I checked it and saw that it was at twenty-two hundred psi instead of three thousand and declining fast. It hit zero about the time that my nose pulled through the horizon in a steep climb. Funny how I remember thinking that something had to be wrong. If there were no hydraulics, I wouldn't be able to move the controls, but they were still moving. They froze about three seconds later.

"Lead, you're on fire. Bail out."

By this time, I was in a steep left turn on the west side of the target with the left wing looking down at the ground. I saw my bombs hit fairly close to the smoke and thought that it would be difficult to explain myself to the folks down there who I had just bombed. The disposition of other fighter pilots who had jumped out in this area was not good.

At about eleven thousand feet, I had to do something. Although the flight controls had mostly seized, the rudder on the F-100 was designed to work manually when all hydraulic power was lost, and the tail plane would move to and seize in a position that would give a slight climb, I forget how much, if the pilot held about 280 knots of airspeed. I pushed the left rudder in until the airplane was in a ninety-degree left bank. This brought the nose of the airplane down through the horizon, and then I rudder-rolled the plane to a wings-level position and "cleaned the wing." This meant that I jettisoned the two remaining bombs, the two fuel tanks, and the four weapons pylons onto which the bombs had been loaded. The airplane was now clean-winged, and I was headed due east. It was about ninety miles to the South China Sea. I decided to go for it rather than try another turn, at minimum control, back over the target.

Al came up on my right wing. The other three had dropped their bombs on a high pass through the target area and we were now flying along with Al on my wing and the other two in wingtip formation off to Al and my four o'clock position. All was as it should have been briefed, had I not been tongue-tied at the briefing.

"It looks like the fire's gone out. The right wing has a couple of holes in it, and so does the fuselage. You can see a red streak where the hydraulic fluid ran out down there. There was a lot of damage to the right tank, but that's gone. How's she flying?"

"Seems okay. Going to try to make it to the water. Someone out of Da Nang should be able to get me there. Maybe I can land this thing."

"Right." Al was kind enough not to tell me at that time what a stupid idea that was. Instead, he pointed out, "You're on fire again."

I remember looking up and seeing Al bank away from me and take up a position about four hundred feet off my right wing. Probably didn't want to be caught in the blast.

I've always thought that it was interesting the way movies portray a person in a life-threatening situation to be moving in slow motion. I found out that day, and I remember to this one, that there is a reason for that. Your mind speeds up to such an extent that the rest of the world seems to be in slow motion. Another explanation is that your mind takes all the information in, but there is so much that it has to review it at slow speed to absorb all of it.

That phenomenon kicked in for me at the point of the second call of fire. I claim that I said to Al that I would probably have to jump out soon. I can remember looking at a line of thunderstorms about twenty miles ahead that I didn't want to fly through on fire. I claim I heard his acknowledgement and then carefully took off my clipboard and stowed it in the left side of the cockpit, sat up straight, and prepared for ejection. I gave it a little thought, as by this time I had climbed to twenty-three thousand feet and wished I hadn't climbed so high.

I remembered the old gag about how the five steps of an ejection from an F-100 were on a decal on the bottom of the canopy. The first was to sit up straight and put your feet in the "stirrups" as you prepared for ejection. The second was to pull the ejection seat handles up. This blew the canopy, and the remaining three steps in the ejection procedure went with it. You'd better have them memorized. I did.

Al claims to this day that I said "I better jump out" and before he could acknowledge, the canopy came off and I came out of the airplane.

Back to slow speed. The canopy fired and scared the heck out of me. I remember thinking that right there was the air at twenty-three thousand feet. I was basically sitting in an open cockpit twenty-three thousand feet up in the air.

"No turning back now."

I initiated step three: pull the trigger levers. I pulled the trigger levers in the handle grips. Nothing.

I distinctly remember squeezing the triggers at least two more times, but nothing happened.

Then the seat slowly, and I mean very slowly, started moving up the tracks and out of the airplane. I saw the instrument panel go by. I saw the top of the canopy rail go by, slowly, very slowly. I saw the empty cockpit as I looked down, and I saw the big silver luminescent 13 on the side of the airplane. The airplane was Mike Peloquin's, and I think he named it "Luck." I remember thinking that, for tempting the gods of fate, I was going to put a finger in his eye if I ever saw him again.

Then I was just sitting about ten feet above the canopy, flying along with the airplane. I remember a conversation with Bullet Bob Bryan at the Phu Cat club where he said that he tumbled very violently right after the seat cleared the canopy. Bob had jumped out twice and was considered our expert on the experience. I was thinking that the tumbling hadn't happened yet.

Then it did happen. I tumbled so hard that I thought I would pass out. When it stopped, I was now sitting twenty-three thousand feet in the air on a chair, just falling. The lap belt was supposed to have opened automatically, but it hadn't.

I thought to myself that maybe it was lucky I had jumped out so high, as the seat didn't seem to be functioning correctly. I waited for the lap belt.

Nothing.

I waited some more, and still nothing happened. I started to go for step four: open the lap belt manually. I reached down to do so and saw a small puff of smoke right in front of my belly button, and the two sides of the lap belt and the shoulder straps floated away from the middle of my stomach, very slowly.

If that belt opens at all, it opens one second after the seat triggers are pulled. It takes that long for the residual charge to work through the tubing that connects it to the seat. It takes one second. All that I've described since pulling the triggers takes one second, or it doesn't happen at all.

It's funny, but at that instant an unrelated thought went through my mind. I had had three days in Hong Kong the week before with a beautiful Pan Am stewardess. She was a Swedish blonde who I first saw walking down the street in Taiwan in a miniskirt with that sort of "can't touch this" gait, and I, as Vince had described his thoughts about Linda, damn near passed out. She was that sexy. Legs like that and a miniskirt would open the hormone gate on any man who's breathing. Like many good-looking European women, she had her blouse unbuttoned all the way down to between her breasts, and it looked like one or the other would fall out at any minute, but they never did.

I walked up to her figuring I'd think of what to say when I got there, but I knew I had to say something. I had been looking for Dave Jenny. He was ferrying an F-100 to Taiwan, and we were going to hook up and have a couple of drinks talking about old times. I said to myself, "Wherever you are, Dave, good luck." He never entered my mind for the next three days.

"Do you have any qualms about drinking with strangers?"

Great line, out of nowhere. I congratulated myself.

She looked at me and complimented me on a great pickup line and then walked off. I thought I had detected a smile, so I reengaged.

She kept complimenting me and then walking off. I kept coming after her like a hound with a nosefull of something that smelled awfully good.

The next day, she was doing a Saigon turn, flying from Taiwan to Saigon and returning to Hong Kong for a two-night layover. How in the hell would I get to Hong Kong? The answer to that was simple: swim if I had to. I caught a Cathay Pacific flight, no orders, no passport, no nothing but horny determination and a verbal okay to be away from the base for a few days.

I was waiting at the Kowloon Sheraton Hotel when she checked in and just sat there and watched her read the note I had left for her. She smiled. I went up to the room and waited, giving her time to check in.

We spent two of the most romantic nights in my early life alone in Hong Kong. The first night, when we got back to her room, she sat down on the bed. When a woman sat in the short short skirts they wore at that time, the skirt generally pulled up high enough that there wasn't much left to the imagination. I was virtually hypnotized. Remember, there were no women at Phu Cat, and I'd been there for almost four months since returning from R&R.

I sat down next to her, leaned over to kiss her. She moaned quietly and leaned into me. I quickly got around to touching her on one of those beautiful legs. I slowly slid my hand up that appendage. I thought my head would explode.

All of a sudden, she stood up and said, "Let's not do this."

"Oh. Let's not do what?"

"Let's not wrestle for fifteen minutes getting our clothes off. Let's just take them off and get in bed."

God bless Sweden.

We dined one night in the Hong Kong Hilton, which had a restaurant on the top floor called the Eagle's Nest or something like that. We ate there with about twenty violins playing, and I thought I was in heaven. Two days later, she and her crew left.

We continued the romance as soon as I got back stateside, spending more time in a little berg, just north of San Francisco, each time "leaving on a jet plane" after about two or three days together. I went on to my next assignment in Selma, Alabama. When she came down there to visit, she was a big hit with all the student pilots.

Eventually the charm of our meeting location and the initial response to San Francisco wore off. Besides, there were a couple of other nice gals I knew, one from Texas and the other from upstate New York. After a year with virtually no women around, I was like a kid in a candy store. The whole deal got pretty jammed up. As is the case when a man tries to have it all, I wound up with nothing from the three of them but pleasant memories.

We broke up on mutual agreement, but what a weekend that was in Hong Kong.

As I sat in that seat at twenty-three thousand feet, convinced I'd never see her again, my only thought was, "What a waste."

So there I was, no lap belt or shoulder harness buckled around me anymore, just sitting in the seat still. I remember thinking that the seat kicker wasn't working either. The kicker is a strap that is connected to an inertial reel behind the pilots head and then runs down the back of the seat, under the pilot's rear end, and connects to the front of the seat between his legs. When that inertial reel is fired, it winds up the strap and separates the pilot from the seat.

Figuring that the seat kicker wasn't working, I thought about pushing away from the seat and started to do so when I felt the seat peel off my butt and fly away. It didn't kick me out. It peeled the seat off me.

The air charge that fires that kicker is the same one that opened the lap belt and shoulder harness. It had continued through the tubing and fired the kicker half a second after the belt opened. It happened half a second later, or it wouldn't have happened at all. Every thought that I described about my romance in Hong Kong and all the thoughts from when I looked down and saw that puff of smoke as the lap belt opened happened in half a second.

Falling down over Laos now, shoulders low, with only the parachute on my back, I remembered the story Dave Jenning had told us, and I previously mentioned, about how he jumped out over the ocean on aMisty flight. He had been hit while working in North Vietnam and decided to head for Da Nang as an emergency divert. .

Dave punched out. But he had been a skydiver, and he regaled us with his story of the sixteen-thousand-foot skydive he accomplished.

Why not try skydiving? I thought now.

I tried to roll over on my stomach and do the normal picture of skydiving, and all hell broke loose. I tumbled so violently that I remember seeing red. I said, "Dear God, get me out of this and I promise I won't fuck with it again." I immediately found myself in the same position as before, falling with my head low and feet high, on my back.

I didn't fuck with it.

Another point worth reviewing here is that when you jump out above fourteen thousand feet, you're supposed to pull the lanyard on an emergency cylinder of oxygen that is strapped to the side of your survival vest. This feeds oxygen through an auxiliary line to the oxygen mask and lets you breath while you're falling from such a great height. If you don't pull it, not only do you not get the supplemental oxygen, but a valve on the mask never opens to let you breath at all. I never pulled it. I breathed ambient air, against the closed valve, the entire way down. No problem.

The next thought was that somewhere around twelve thousand to fourteen thousand feet, the chute was supposed to open automatically. This was important, as the terrain in the safe area over which I thought I had jumped was at about forty-five hundred feet. I wanted this to work, obviously. I found the ripcord handle on the chute and put my hand on it. I thought that when I could see squirrels jumping around in the trees, I would pull it.

That would have been cute. Pull, crash, dead. It would have been way too late. Anyway, the chute opened automatically at about twelve thousand feet, and I was swinging like a pendulum below a huge canopy. All had worked as advertised.

We had a procedure for cutting the four rear risers of the canopy (two on each side) if all the rest were okay. Risers were the little ropes that came out of the ends of the four harness strapes, two in front and two in back of the pilot and led up to the canopy. This was to let the air flow out the rear of the canopy instead of bubbling out first on one side and then on the other as the chute would swing back and forth. The four-line cut went perfectly. I stowed the knife used to make the cut and reached down and deployed the life raft in the seat pack under my rear end. It fell to the end of a twenty-five-foot lanyard and inflated. Later, the procedure was changed to maintain this raft in the seat if it looked like you were going into the trees. You'll see why shortly.

So with the chute working, the seat pack deployed, and me drifting down into a "safe" area, I thought, why not do the cool thing and talk to Al on the survival radio? I pulled it out and made several comments to him. I heard him say that the Sandys (other A-1s out of Nakhon Phanom where Vince would later be killed) and the Jollies (Rescue CH-53 helicopters out of Da Nang) were on the way. I thanked him and stowed the radio.

How cool could I be?

This is a dividing point in the story, because from here on I stopped doing everything right and started doing everything wrong. At about four thousand feet, I began to notice that the "safe" area was covered with trails into and out of the jungle and into and out of lots of clearings that were evidently being worked. I drifted over a small settlement at about three thousand feet and continued in toward the jungle. The deployed life raft caught in the trees, stopped my forward movement, dumped me into the triple canopy, and let go when I hit.

When I sort of bounced up off the tree canopy, the chute came in on top of me and wrapped around me, and I was cocooned upside down in the branches, about twenty feet off the ground.

Panic set in.

I struggled to get my first radio out of the upper left vest pocket and make a call. I did that and pushed down on the transmit button so hard that when I released it, it flew off the side of the radio. I stowed that radio and pulled out the second radio. I pulled at the antenna to extend it to transmit and pulled the antenna out of the radio. My gun fell out of the holster to the ground below.

Easy, big guy. I fought myself for composure. *Slow down.*

I heard and saw Al fly right over the top of me, no higher than fifty feet. That felt good. I knew he knew where I was.

I could no longer talk to anyone, but I did have a method of responding. I pulled out the first radio again and, when anyone asked for an acknowledgement, I pulled the antenna on the first radio out to the fully extended position. This caused the radio to emit an automatic *beep-beep* sound that could be heard on the guard frequency. I would push the antenna back in to stop it. After about the second time I did this, I heard Al say, "Roger your acknowledgment." Good.

The Sandys checked in and buzzed over my position. That was good. I heard the clattering of those huge radial engines and felt they knew where I was. There was no ground fire in the area. Al and the flight would leave for fuel and be back if needed.

The lead Sandy ran a string of 20-mm down about two hundred yards from my position. It seemed that the friendlies were on the way from the village out to where the chute had landed, and he wanted to find an effective way to keep them away from me without hurting any of them.

He had done just that, and in so doing caused me sheer terror. The sound of 20-mm high-explosive incendiary bullets going off within a few hundred yards is still with me. When I figured out what it was, I again settled down.

I was stuck. I wondered for a second if there could have been many guys who, like me that afternoon, had safely escaped their airplane only to get fouled up and die on the ground. I could literally not move enough to free myself. I remember getting a leg free and down to a branch on the tree below me so that I could get my head higher than my stomach and that felt good, but the leg was cramping badly. I put the dying thought out of my mind and waited for a little brown face to appear below me or a helicopter above me. Fortunately for whoever would show up below, I had nothing I could shoot them with, so they'd be safe.

The helicopter showed first.

I could see the crewman in the door and the pararescue man coming down on a jungle penetrator, a large yellow teardrop-shaped metal object that had three paddle-like arms that could fold down from it and provide seats. The noise of the helicopter was deafening, and the rush of air was blowing all sorts of debris around. I found out later that the elevation of the pickup was so high that the pilot had to pull maximum power to hover. It took so long for the pararescue guy to cut me out of the mess I was in that the pilot ran the engine into the red to complete the pickup. Bless the Jollies. One of the things that always inspired me was the way the leadership would stop the war if necessary to make every effort to pick up a downed airman. Misty FACs had worked many rescaps, and now I was the object of one of those missions. It felt good to be covered.

I was free. I felt the last riser let go and grabbed onto the waist of the pararescuer still upside down. We rode the penetrator to the ground and the first thing to hit was my head.

No pain at all.

I turned around quickly and sat down opposite the rescuer on one of the metal penetrator paddle seats. I lifted my arms as he ran the strap under me, and we held on to each other as the lift started up. We had just cleared the trees when the chopper started moving forward. The pilot had to get moving to cool that baby down (a CH3, as I recall, the smaller of the two commonly used rescue choppers).

We had been trained not to reach for the helicopter. Just sit on the seat and wait for them to pull you into the fuselage of the helo. I did that. In fact, I didn't let go until we were inside the helo and both laying down.

"You can let me go now, Lieutenant. We've got you."

"Oh, oh yeah. Of course."

And so the rescue was over. We were about seventy miles from Da Nang, so the ride would take about forty-five minutes. The medic did a quick once-over to check and reported to the pilot that I was okay.

Good.

I heard one of the pilots say something about "Thank God for the Mistys. Their pickups are usually easy."

That comment made me feel good. It had been easy. But the point to remember is these guys would've have come, in that big cumbersome slow helicopter, wherever I had been shot down. The Jolly Green Giants were the backbone of morale for us. They'd come for you. They'd get you if it were humanly possible, and sometimes they'd die if it were not.

Thanks to Charles Lowry, Bruce Prouse, James E. Jenereaux, and John Eldridge. Eldridge is the man who left the safety of the helicopter and came down on a sling to rescue me. If you enjoyed this book so far, thank him and the rest of that crew.

Someone must have told them I had been a Misty. I know that we had worked a lot of rescues where the pilots had jumped out right in the area where they had been shot down. Sometimes this was due to panic, sometimes it was due to the fact that there were no other options. Nevertheless, those were difficult pickups. I took it as a matter of pride that I had stayed with a bad airplane until I got to a known safe area and caused no casualties in my rescue. Most all of the Mistys who could do so, did the same.

When we landed at Da Nang, I remember the flight engineer and the pararescue men asking me if I wanted to be carried to the ambulance or wanted to walk. My legs and lower body were pretty beat-up from the ejection, and I had a cut on my left arm where it had smacked against something during the episode.

I told them that I intended to walk in. As the door came down on the back of the chopper, I noticed that a crew of girls from Pan Am had stopped by to see the "fighter pilot who had just been rescued."

"Why don't you carry me, fellas."

They did carry me, smiling all the way as they stopped in front of the ladies to let them administer a little appreciation. When we got to the hospital, I walked in.

I had been through a normal mission brief, normal departure, normal egress to the target, normal procedures for bombing, a moment of terror when the plane was hit, ten minutes or so of emergency procedures—executed calmly and perfectly—and then I arrived in the trees. There I demonstrated ten minutes of near panic, thirty more of waiting for rescue in the trees, elation at seeing the helicopter, and now I was back in the land of the big BX and beautiful women. I had made it. I was safe.

I returned to Phu Cat the next afternoon on a Caribou. Doc checked me out. I was fine, but sore from the ejection. Most of us kept the crotch straps on the parachute quite loose during missions in the F-100. The thought was that if we ever bailed out, we would tighten them first. I hadn't tightened them.

So along with the blue crotch that I got from the opening shock and the injury to the arm came a Purple Heart. Sort of a weenie one when you think of how bad some guys get shot up for one, but I took it and took it with pride. Not at the lack of extent of my wounds, but the fact that I had stuck my nose in the enemy's face, taken a shot, and survived.

I made it, and so many good guys didn't. People will tell you that this wears on the psyche of guys and causes them grief. I never felt that way for a minute. I was and am eternally thankful that I made it. I was and always will be eternally sad that others didn't make it. I don't know why. I only know I made it and will forever be grateful for that.

I've told you the story. See if you have a reason. . Think of the sadness as friends and families visit Tom's, Scotty's, Lee's, and Vince's now grassy gravesites at the academy. Think of the sadness that fifty thousand other families, groups of friends, and even acquaintances feel as they visit the black marble wall in Washington.

I went to a recent reunion of my 1962 high-school graduating class. This was the first reunion we'd had in nearly thirty years. One of the girls from the class, who like me had missed the 1967 and 1972 reunions, came up to me and said, "I'm glad you're okay. I heard you were killed in Vietnam in 1969."

I had a very funny feeling when I thought about that comment. For thirty years, she thought I had been killed but had given it no more thought than "too bad." There was no reason for her to feel more, I guess. We had never been close friends. She moved to a distant state, and we lost track of each other. A life or death struggle of one person can be a moment's thought in the afternoon to another.

He went, he got killed, and that's too bad. What's for dinner?

The vast majority of guys don't talk about their "war years" at meetings or in church or at gatherings of friends. They just go on, knowing they gave it their best shot, still disappointed at their performance sometimes and proud of it at others.

But, oh, when they meet one of their comrades after so many years, all that changes. The smile, the "how ya doin'?" the "good to see you" says it all.

Those guys who were with me that day fit in that category.

CHAPTER 20
February of 1971

Tom Mravak on his second tour.

TOM STEPPED OUT OF THE shower and walked, with the towel around him, back to his hootch in the squadron area. The fighter-pilot hootches at Udorn were built above an open concrete drainage ditch. It wasn't raw sewage, but it did contain the wastewater from all the buildings on the south side of the huge Thai Air Force Base. It stank. Some senior officers had quarters in the individual units on the other side of the ditch, and a lot of other personnel were housed in the big concrete quarters on the other side of the senior officers' quarters. Probably anyplace on the base was better than the hootches, or one-room houses, over the ditch.

The hootches were built of wood and, although air-conditioned, had cracks between the boards that formed the floors of the rooms. It took a while to get used to the constant gnawing of mosquitoes that took place in the tiny rooms above the ditch. The ditch was called a klong. I was told that, in Thai, "klong" meant ditch or canal. It also came to mean, more or less, anything that moved on water, such as a ferry, and later with constant use by the GIs it came to mean nearly anything that moved as a conveyance between one point and another. Thus the afternoon Thai Airways flight to Bangkok was also called a klong.

Tom walked along the deck, above the klong, and into his room. He only had six more weeks to go on his tour. It had been a long hard route to follow on the way to a dream of becoming an astronaut. From the first time he sat in high school and watched Alan Shepherd blast off on what was really an artillery shell and "fly" downrange about two hundred miles to splash down in the Atlantic, Tom knew he wanted to be an astronaut. While he believed in the war, it was more a stepping-stone for him. A stepping-stone on the way to a dream.

He was almost done with his second F-4 combat assignment. It had been a long two years away from Sandy and away from any of the gang back home.

He'd soon receive his new assignment, Hopefully he could get an F-4 assignment to the States, so he could fly cross-country once or twice a month and politic at the AF personnel center at Randolph. Politic with a classmate he knew who was assigned there. Politic to get into Edwards, to the test-pilot school and on to the rocket ships. He would make it happen.

TOM'S SQUADRON WAS GEARING UP to fly missions in support of a giant operation in the Xepone (Techepone) area of Laos. The operation would be known as Lam Son 719 and would prove to be a total disaster for the South Vietnamese effort to take over the defense of their own country. In support of that objective, many good Americans would be shot down, and many would die. There was some tough flying ahead.

Tom had just returned to Thailand from a visit back to the states. What a good time that had been. It had been completely unexpected by Sandy. Four of the planes at Udorn were being returned to the States, and he was selected to fly one. After the short hop to the Philippines, the flight had gone to Guam, then seven hours to Honolulu and on to George Air Force Base, the big base in California that he and Sandy had had so many good times at while going through the various F-4 schools. After dropping the fighter, he'd taken a week's leave. He yearned for Sandy and showed up in Houston at six-thirty in the morning. She was just up getting coffee when he hit the front-door speaker button.

"Yes?"

"Is Mrs. Mravak at home?"

He heard her scream through the microphone, felt the buzzer go off in the door, and walked into the hallway. Before he could get to the steps, she came down, wearing a pair of pajamas that she had bought for him but he never wore, and jumped at him from about the third step up. She wrapped herself around him and kissed him, embracing his neck and crying as she hugged him and kissed him and hugged him. All the worry of the previous nine months was gone. All the heartaches, the fears, the anger as she watched the nightly coverage of the war was gone. He was home.

"Oh Tom, you're here. You're here. Oh, I love you, Tom."

Sandy didn't make it to work that day. They came out of the apartment around noon, and she called her mom and told her Tom was home. They would stop in for an hour or so but were going to hop in the car and head for the beach at Galveston to relax for a few days. They'd be back after the next weekend.

They relaxed. They ate, They called friends. They called me. They planned their next move. They'd hope for a place in the US. There were F-4s based at MacDill in Tampa, at Homestead in Miami, at Holloman in New Mexico, and at George AFB in California. Any one of those places would be fine with them. Obviously, Florida would be preferable, but New Mexico would put them closer to Sandy's folks.

They called Tom's mother in upstate New York. She was a single mom. Tom was an only son with an older sister. They were very close. Mom, Rose as I remember, was an artist. She was always talking, always had an opinion on everything, always adored her son, her wonderful son. The son she had raised into a man and seen off to the Air Force Academy after two years of school in a nearby college.

"My darling, why are you going way out to Colorado? You're over halfway through college here in New York now. Almost ready to go out on your own. Why go back to the beginning and start over?"

"I want to be an astronaut, Mom."

"In one of those rockets?"

"Yes," he smiled, "in one of those rockets."

"Don't be crazy."

That had always been the reaction Tom received. When the initial seven astronauts were chosen, the space program was barely known by people in the states. Nobody knew and fewer cared about rocket ships. That was until Sputnik. Tom remembered going out on the back lawn and watching the tiny little ball go by in the nightly heavens. The thinking at the time was that it could have a bomb in it. They could have us if they wanted us.

The whole country united behind the space program. Every failure was a reason for depression. Every success was a cause for celebration. But few would commit to being the part of it that wanted to ride on top of one of those rockets. Then President Kennedy spoke: "I believe that this nation should commit itself achieving the goal, before this decade is out, of landing a man on the Moon and returning him safely to Earth."

Tom was in. His mom had to go along with it. And off he went to Colorado. Then off to Texas for pilot training. Off to Houston when the confirmed and committed bachelor had married Sandy.

But Rose loved him so much. So much she told me she cried herself to sleep each night and cried when she thought of him in the day. He wanted to ride a rocket. "Oh, my son, may God watch you and keep you. That is the only thought that I can bear."

Sandy and Tom had talked to Rose for an hour. They would come east, but only for a day or two. It would be at the end of the following week. Tom would leave from there to return to Thailand, and Sandy would go straight back to Houston. Home stretch.

As I've said before, Jerry Becker and Tom had started a band their first-class year at the academy. As far as I know, this was the first time this had ever been done. They were the Flameouts.

They had even recorded a song. A song that Tom had written called "My Girl." When he first met Sandy, before falling helplessly in love with her, he told her he had written it hoping to find a girl like her one day. She had almost cried then. Tom was just snowing her at the time, or trying to at least. It had taken Tom about a month to realize that Sandy would do anything in the world for him. She was, in fact, the girl he had written the song about.

"How do you not love such a beautiful person who loves you so much? I know I wanted to be a bachelor, but I cannot live without this girl. I can't do it."

During the last quick trip home from Thailand, on the last night in Houston, they called "the buddies." Jerry Becker, me, and I'm sure a bunch of other guys. I mentioned this call in the introduction. How many stories did we have together? How many times since pilot training had we talked into the night of dreams, wishes, women, booze, cars. How do you hold a friendship like this and not be together all the time? We all went about our lives, but always sort of had a "wonder what Jerry's up to" thought every now and then.

When Tom left his mom in tears, he headed straight for Travis Air Force Base, just north of San Francisco. This was about the fourth time that he had gone through that place on the way to Southeast Asia. Now the war was almost over for him. He had done his part. He had stuck it out, stayed with the guys, done a tour as a back-seater and a second tour as a front-seater in the F-4. He was almost ready for the rest of his life. Now he was to be an astronaut. "Everything I want in my professional life revolves around going into space, orbiting the earth, and being in on the space program," he told me.

We later learned that on the day of his last mission, Tom dropped off a letter for Sandy. There was nothing to say that hadn't been covered during his visit to the states, but it felt so much better to let the love out onto a piece of paper, to seal it and send it off and let the object of that devotion read the words. I would imagine he poured himself out about the week they'd just finished in Texas. God, it had been good.

Finishing that, it was off to the club for a bit of lunch before the flight. The club was half bar and night club and half dining room. He went through the front door and turned left into the dining room. There were four or five guys from the squadron sitting at one of the tables, and he joined them and ordered an iced tea from one of the pretty Thai waitresses.

"Getting' short, Muckrock."

Short was a term for not much time left in a tour before you went back to the States.

"Yeah, I'm back to the land of the big BX in about a month-and-a-half."

"Anything come in the way of an assignment yet?"

"No, but I'm hoping for test-pilot school. I did the undergraduate work. I probably won't get it, as I don't have an advanced degree. Second choice is an F-4 stateside and then the Master's program at Purdue. Masters in astronautics.

"Still focused on space, huh?"

"Yeah, but mostly focused on going to bed with my wife every night of my life. God, that will be great."

"Don't do anything stupid out there. This war is just about over for the US, and it would be a shame to bust it on a tree-banger."

"Right."

Tom listened, but disagreed with letting up just because it was getting near the end of the tour. His feeling was that guys on the ground still needed the interdiction that they were doing on the Ho Chi Minh Trail in Laos and the passes coming out of southern North Vietnam. I knew Tom, and if someone did say that to him, it would've had little effect. He wasn't going to let up on the way that he flew. How would you explain that to some grunt who had to face the front end of a rifle loaded with ammunition Tom might have stopped had he just pushed a little harder? But he knew what his friend meant. It would be a shame to get stuffed this close to the end of his second tour. He'd been away so long. He just wanted to be back to normal.

After the club, Tom hopped on the blue shuttle bus that ran in front of the club, circled the cantonment area, and then headed out around the big base to the flight line side of the base. The 555th fighter squadron was down the line from the command post in the wing headquarters, so getting there meant a good fifteen- to twenty-minute ride.

He stopped off at the wing headquarters and went in for his intelligence briefing and met the rest of the guys there. There was a short stop at the weapons shop to talk to another buddy, who had just returned from an R&R to the States also. The two men talked for about ten minutes about the times back in the "land of the big BX," and it was time for Tom to go.

"Hey boss, how about a ride?"

The squadron commander was going through the command post. Tom hooked a ride with him in his six-pack pickup back to the squadron area. That saved waiting in the heat for the shuttle bus and made up for the time that he had spent talking to his friend.

After the briefing in the squadron, he walked out on the porch on the flight line side of the squadron building and smoked a Winston while waiting to go to Personal Equipment. PE, as it was called, was in the building next to the squadron building. Tom walked in and caught his breath. The sarge in the PE department was an old head from Alabama. He knew from years of experience that there was no need to suffer from heat with the advent of air-conditioning.

Night was coming, and Tom picked up his gear and headed out of the PE building and back into the now "cool" moist night air. The bread truck was there waiting to take him and the rest of his flight down the flight line to the revetments. He stowed his gear next to the plane and started a walk-around inspection while the back-seater climbed up the ladder and settled into the back cockpit.

Everything in the air force runs with plenty of time to spare. That way, if something goes wrong during the preflight, there's time to fix it and still make the TOT, "time over target." Tom pre-flighted the giant fighter at a very leisurely pace while the back-seater was using ground power to check out the aircraft systems. Climbing up the yellow boarding ladder, he smiled acknowledgment at the chief as he strapped him into the front seat.

Tom did a quick glance around the cockpit to check that all the switches were in the correct position and plugged his oxygen hose into the receptacle over his heart on his left shoulder strap, plugged the interphone cord into the aircraft cable, and checked in with the back-seater. They were ready.

HE COULD HEAR THE LOWERING sound at the MA-1A starting unit began pumping air into the starter turbine of the big jet. The MA-1A was really just a small jet engine that was on wheels and able to be moved from plane to plane. This small jet was used to produce electrical power and air for the starting of the jets on the big airplanes. A choreographed dance began as hand signals called for the crew chief to direct air ("air on two"), first to the right and then the left engine. As the giant turbines wound to life, the hydraulic systems on the airplane were powered.

Hydraulics are the blood of a jet. When they were powered, the flight-control checks could be accomplished.

Tom was melancholy. He had his mind on Sandy. So close. So close to being with her again. What a beautiful week it had been back in Houston.

Signals for the crew chief to check the flaps and ailerons for security.

How did he ever wind up with her after all the women he had known? She was thinking of him also. His mother was thinking of him. His sister was thinking of him. I, and I'm sure most of his buds, happened to have had many a quick thought about old Muckrock.

Signals for the crew chief to check for bleed air flow out of the back of the leading edge slats. This "bleed air" is actually excess air that is bled from the compressor section of a turbine area and used in a jet wherever high-pressure air may be useful. Uses included the pressurization of the cockpit area, the inflation of the g-suits that the pilots wore around their waists and lower legs, and the blowing over the front of the wing when at slow speeds that actually created lift for takeoff and landing. This allowed the big Phantom to approach at much slower speeds and to lift much bigger loads off the ground.

Beck was talking at a bar in Georgia, telling a friend about the times we'd had at the academy in the band and at pilot training. I was back in Selma, Alabama, teaching a class of student pilots the basics of aeronautics as a platform academic instructor in the air-training command.

Signals for the crew chief to unplug the cart, pull the chocks.

A warrior goes to battle with the hearts of his friends and family in his pocket.

Cadillac flight took the runway and blasted into the night. At the giant airbase, the routine continued. This was just another night in the war. There would be a smattering of flights like Cadillac taking off and returning. Air America would come and go through the night. Maybe an airlift command C-141 or even the new C-5 would arrive. It was a normal night.

They worked with Brigham first. Brigham was the local sector of US Air Force radar control for this part of Thailand. Brigham followed toward the tactical area to which they were assigned and turned them over to the tactical area controller circling over eastern Thailand in the back of a C-130.

"Cadillac flight, go to tactical frequency."

"Two."

"Hell-o, Moonbeam, this is Cadillac. Two F-4s, mission number 2301 for control with Owl 22."

"Roger, Cadillac. Right on time. Contact Owl on 236.4."

"236.4. Go, Cadillac."

"Two."

Moonbeam was the ABCCC or airborne command and control center. This was a communication center that was in the back of a C-130 cargo plane. They monitored flights coming into and out of their area of responsibility and forwarded messages to the various command posts and, when needed, rescue components. They "bored holes" in the atmosphere for most of the night while the men in the rear of the plane continued the vital communications necessary to run the war at the tip of the spear.

They would be replaced in the wee hours of the morning by another Moonbeam. The call sign was the same, the mission the same, the frequencies the same. Moonbeam stayed up until replaced by Hillsborough the following morning.

Owl was a nighttime FAC mission out of Ubon Air Base. Owl was an F-4 also.

"Owl, this is Cadillac 21 with two F-4s for your control. We're about twenty miles out."

"Roger, Cadillac. Putting you in on Ban Phan Nop. Pass tonight. Echo sensors picked up a lot of activity there an hour or so ago and looks like you got a chance of catching some of them coming out the south end of Mu Gia."

"That's what we came for."

"Cadillac, go radar trail, five miles. Owl, we're in your area."

"Okay. I'm not going to mark for you. Just put your load in along the pass between and to the South Vietnam side of the two giant mountains. Spread them along the road, just off the road, and we'll see what happens.

"Got it. Two, you go in first."

They worked the target. It was a routine mission. After dropping the bombs, they turned for home.

Who knows what happened. Had he taken a hit on the target? Did fatigue get to him and he had a lapse of consciousness without being aware of it? Did something go terribly wrong with the airplane for reasons unknown? It doesn't matter, because on the way back to Udorn that night, Tom crashed while turning final to "home." He died with the lights of the big base in sight, suddenly, without warning, without a radio call.

I remember the funeral at the academy. It was a freezing cold late winter day at seven thousand feet altitude, at the place we'd all come to as kids just nine years earlier and worked so hard to get through. At the gravesite, Sandy bravely took the flag. She had to be supported when she stood to get the flag. A lonely T-33 flew by and pulled up, and I can remember Tom's mom saying, "There goes Tom now." It was absolutely heartbreaking. The sacrifice made by Tom was magnified by the suffering that Sandy and Tom's mom and sister endured that day and for the rest of their lives.

Sandy's mom and dad were there, and I remember drinking with them in one of the quarters on the academy. We talked about old times and memories. It had been just over four years since Tom and Sandy had met. Sandy was determined to visit Tom one last time, and I believe Jerry went with her. I would've gone if no one volunteered, but I wanted to remember Tom as I'd last seen him. Sandy's mom died about a month later, probably because of her personal breathing problems and the cold, high, very dry air.

Probably the most influential friend I ever had in my life was gone. Again we carried on with the work. Not enough life had gone by at that time to realize the rarity of finding a friend like Tom. He and the guys from the first and second tour and one or two others since then are about all that is allotted to a man in this life. There has never been a day of my life since that cold February day in 1971 that I haven't thought of Tom. That's my "Post Traumatic Stress Reaction," I guess.

I came back through Houston about two years later, after my second tour, and went out to dinner with Sandy and her new husband-to-be.

Life goes on. I'm surefor every lonely thought that I have of Tom, she has many more. You never get over it, but she did pick up the pieces and move on with life, somehow. I remember, after we'd gone out that night in Houston, sitting down on the couch. She came over to me, sat down next to me and we just embraced for about twenty minutes. We were both crying a little, just trying to be closer to Tom, and then we fell asleep. She woke up a little later, said, "Oh, this is great, Rosie," and smacked me on the head, acting like I had tried to make out. We laughed about it the next day.

The Great Muckrock was gone.

CHAPTER 21
A Couple of Years Later

"What the hell are you thinking? You made it. You did what you were supposed to do and lived through it, and now you volunteer to go back again? That's just not using your head." That comment came from an old master sergeant who worked with me at the aerial application business I spent my spare time flying with in Selma, Alabama. For some reason, I had never given a thought to the whole proposition being stupid. I just knew that I wanted to get back into fighters, and the only way to do so was to go back to Vietnam. The comment gave me a little pause, but what the hell. It's what's going on, and it's where I should be.

FORNAL AND GALER AND ANOTHER guy who I would meet, Preston Duke, went to Williams Air Force Base in Phoenix after our first tours. Pres had done his tour in F-105s and had a ton of great stories to tell about flying that airplane. Tip and Wheels had an apartment together, and Wheels spent much time at Pres and Emilee's place as they tried to take care of Wheels. But as Wheels told me, he was "un-take-care-of-able." Hugh Gommel went to Luke to fly F-104s in a program where the USAF trained the German Air Force fighter pilots (remember the story of the German unhooking his parachute several hundred feet in the air?). I had a great dinner with he and Kathy there when I passed through on my F-4 checkout. Beck wound up in Moody Air Force Base in Valdosta, Georgia, flying T-38s, and Chris Kellum and I wound up in T-37s. Other than flying T-37s, life was good. We were home safe.

The "we made it" syndrome was strong when I first came home. I had hoped to fly T-38s, a hot little training airplane, as an instructor in the training command. There were virtually no domestic F-100 assignments, and I wanted to stay in the States. Mentioning the training command was all it took. I wound up in T-37s at Craig Air Force Base in Selma. It was, to me, the end of the earth, and pretty much the end of my life as a fighter pilot, as I saw it.

I remember telling the admin guy when I checked into Selma that I had to do something to get out of this place. He told me that the only way I could get out of there was to volunteer to go back to Southeast Asia again. I signed the papers that day, figuring that I'd at least get a head start on getting out of that place.

I stepped into a town that had been the center of the civil-rights movement two or three years before I got there.. There was still a tremendous amount of stress in the local population that would last for years to come. Flying aerial application with some "good old boys" at a local two-thousand-foot airstrip, I got to listen to their impressions of the civil-rights movement. Their general thought was that most of the trouble in town had been caused by outsiders, and that most folks got along just fine. Like viewing an iceberg, they had only seen the tip of what was happening.

I met the woman I have been married to for thirty-eight great years while at Craig, so the two-and-a-half years there was not a loss. She and I split when I got the F-4 assignment to my second tour, and got back together and got married in early 1974.

Our wedding ceremony is an interesting story. It all started to unfold on one January Sunday in early 1974. My younger brother, Alan, a Navy instructor pilot at Pensacola, later to be an A-7 fighter pilot assigned to the USS Ranger, called and asked, "Are you guys married yet?" I told him that we weren't. He said, "Well, Sandy and I are coming down to see you this weekend, why don't you get married then?" I told him to hold on and asked Sharon if she wanted to get married that weekend.

She looked up from her book and said, "Sure, why not?" So we did, thirty-eight years ago. My brother and his wife and Sharon, me, and my new daughter, Bonnie. We were married at a place called the "Gene Measles Wee Chapel of Love."in Tampa. After the ceremony, we went to the club for a magnum of champagne and on to the Rat Skellar for dinner.

The girls turned in early and Alan and I watched "Shock Theater" before going to bed. Monday morning, I had the seven a.m. brief.

Sharon's first husband had been killed overseas in a fighter crash while they were based in Japan. ... Bonnie had been born within days of Bernie's death and I figured any woman that could hold it together and function on her own after a tragedy like that was a pretty tough girl. Now I had a new, adoring little daughter, a beautiful wife, a new home in Tampa, and I was flying F-4Es. It couldn't have been better. Marrying Sharon was about the best move I made during the entire time of this book's story.

But there had been some tough flying in between, and I'll tell you a little about that.

Kelly Irving (SFDD), former Misty, was also assigned to Craig and kept a light airplane that he had purchased at the same little field from which I was learning to fly aerial application. He had an old Stinson and I had a Piper Super Cub, and later a 220-horsepower Stearman that I bought for the spray work. When Jake Jewell, the owner of the spray service, tried to fly my airplane with a load of chemical on it, he determined it was too dangerous for the job and allowed me to fly the 450 Ag Cat that they had. He flew the 600-horsepower model of the same airplane.

I worked many months learning the art of application, with Jake watching me spray water first on the runway at the strip and later on the field to the east of the runway. The field had trees on each end and was a better primer for the type of flying we'd be doing.

I went along on several application jobs with Jake but got out of the business after only one or two flights out to an actual field where Jake was working. It was time to go back to SEA.

Kelly got his assignment to F-4s for his second tour about six weeks ahead of me. Kelly went back just in time to get a chance at the April 16, 1972, resumption of bombing in the deep north. I got there about the end of May.

After nearly three years in the T-37, I returned to Vietnam in an F-4 assignment after a twenty-nine-hour checkout at Luke, again in Phoenix. During this tour, based this time in Udorn, Thailand, I was to meet some new "friends of Rosie." Among them was Press Duke. Mike Rhodes

The Great Muckrock and Rosie

showed up. Mike had been the flight commander of the T-37 flight I instructed with at Craig and was back for his second tour. Dave Parker was there on his second tour, his first having been in Thuds while they were going downtown. He'd been an instructor at Reese in my T-38 flight. Dale Crane was a friend there, as was "Clayboy" Lewis. Clay and his wonderful wife, Ginger, became very close friends when we were all assigned back to MacDill together. I talked a few times with Steve Richie, both as a fellow Laredo and in admiration of the air-to-air work he did. He was in the Triple Nickel, though, and I didn't fly with him. Mike Francisco was there in the 555th also and was always ready to talk and laugh and joke. Ron Henry showed up, and we also flew together back at MacDill. Bart Crews, Ed Allen, Gip McGill, Bill Ridge, Jerry Lochman, Gene Fudala, Bob Connelly (Captain Nasty), and Pete Cleary, who was lost with Lennie Lenor on a Laredo mission. Steve Cuthbert, lost the day he was shot down with Tony Marshal. Guy Mitchell was there. I believe he later went on to be an astronaut. I remember he had a really cool wife that came over and actually spent some time with him while he was flying combat.

The first night I arrived at Udorn, there was no room for me to get a bunk in the fighter pilot hootches. The squadron temporarily put me up in the huge concrete BOQ that was up the hill until they could find me a room. About the third day I was there an Army Major named Tom Kirkham moved in.

Tom was a Mormon. He was in special operations or intelligence or on special assignment, I never really found out. He was assigned to Air America.

Let me say this about Tom. If you ever wanted to keep a secret, tell Tom. He'd spend hours telling me about how his work was going and how much he was enjoying the job and some of the places he'd been. When it was all over, I couldn't tell you any more about the Air America mission than the average guy on base knew.

Additionally Tom brought the perspective of a man of God in a hostile area doing what he thought necessary to fulfill an obligation to his family and his country. He somehow brought a ray of peace into my life when we talked. About six weeks later, when a clerk at the squadron asked me if I was ready to move down to the hootches, I said I was good where I was living. The subject wasn't brought up again and I never asked.

I have seen Tom only two or three times since Thailand. I could call him on the phone tomorrow and say, "I need you." When he got here, he'd ask, "what's up?"

Fred Olmsted was there. I called and re-connected with Fred when I told him he was the "lead off hitter" in this book. That is a reference to the minor league ball that Fred played while he was flying F-4's in Tucson. He was a pitcher, I believe.

A great story about Fred. He used to walk around in pair of big sunglasses that hid half his upper face. He had a wild head of hair and a big moustache. People would ask the wing commander, Col Charles Gabriel, when he was going to make Fred look the way an Air Force office should look. Col.Gabriel's answer was that "Olmsted will be cutting his hair and shaping up when I get my second mig, (Fred had two) count on it." Actually, although he never got a North Vietnamese Mig, Gabriel had a couple of Migs from his tour in Korea. He wound up being a chief of staff. Another great war time and peace time leader.

As on the first tour, it was a wonderful group of friends. Too many to remember them all.

When I got there, we were in the middle of another invasion from North Vietnam. Fortunately, this time, Nixon was in charge, and the North Vietnamese were to pay a much higher price than they had anticipated. All of the US fighters had been taken out of South Vietnam, and we were flying support of the South Vietnamese Army in the An Loch area just north of Saigon. Those were fairly long missions. We'd leave Udorn, hit a tanker on the way to the south, drop on targets in An Loch, and divert to Bien Hoa. There the American ground personnel who were still there would rearm us. We'd launch, hit An Loch again, head north, hit a second tanker, and return to Udorn.

Captain Tip Galer, Net Jets, via
USAF, United Airlines

Picture of myself and plane I currently fly.

Chris at the 2011 Misty Re-union....

Hugh Gommel-Northwest
Airlines DC-9 Captain

Wells Jackson and Roger Van Dyken
at the 2011 Misty Re-Union.

Doc Dean Echenberg at the 2011 Misty Re-union.

Bob Wilson, Misty Fac on
the day I was shot down.

Preston Duke-
Southern Gentleman

Kelly Irving relaxed at his
Colorado home...2012

Dave Jenny at his "modest" Texas Ranch

Jerry Becker at a recent
party with his family.

Bill Bowen in Connecticut 2012

ON ABOUT MY FIFTH MISSION, I took a bullet in the left outer slat while supporting the South Vietnamese Army at An Loc, just northwest of Saigon. I'd been delivering high drags and not moving the plane around enough. That meant I'd been hit in two out of my last five missions, but luck was with my back-seater and I. There was an F-4 at Bien Hoa that had previously been hit and fixed, and was ready to be ferried back to Thailand. We flew a mission in that one on the way home, splitting from Lead after attacking An Loc again, and returning the plane to Korat Air Base where it belonged. The afternoon Caribou transport flight took us to Udorn by dusk.

The squadron was doing new high-speed, high-energy air-to-air formations at the time when the flights went to North Vietnam. It's one thing to fly into an area, roll in, drop bombs, and fly out, but the air-to-air missions required much more diligence to keep position. I flew with the squadron commander, Jack Rollins, on one of them and managed to hold position okay, but called bingo fuel so early that I could tell he was really pissed.

The day after the mission with Rollins, I started flying in the Laredo Fast FAC program. I had volunteered for Laredo during the first week I was at Udorn. Although I didn't look forward to the long, long missions again, I knew that program and knew the area in which it would be flying like the back of my hand. I had flown the same area as a Misty FAC.

I figured I would jump right in, pick up a lot of time, and be a frontline member of the outfit instead of "blue 4," which I hadn't done very well. The North had just been opened again to bombing, and the targets were good; there was plenty of action

I knew what I was doing there. I flew over 150 hours in the southern panhandle of North Vietnam during July, August, and September of 1972. I worked under the command of Bart Crews and Gary Sipple. We lost Steve Cuthbert on the day of my third Laredo mission. I'd been flying with a guy named Nordie, as I recall. My first three missions were in the backseat to acclimate me to the mission. Nordie and I found a group of huge camouflaged slit trenches to the northwest of where the Ron River came down out of the mountains. We put a flight of two in on the targets just to see what would happen. When the lead ship dropped a five-hundred-pounder in the middle of one of the trenches, it looked like a small nuclear bomb had gone off. We worked several flights on the same target with the same type of spectacular results.

Steve and Tony Marshal came into the area as the next Laredo. We showed them the target and cycled out to hit a tanker in the gulf. By this time, there was a lineup of strikes waiting to hit the target, and Steve and Tony went to work.

While on the tanker, we monitored the strike frequency and heard, "Laredo 41, are you okay? I've got two chutes."

Shit.

They were shot down. Tony made it back. I talked to him on the phone the day he was released but haven't seen him since. He was a remarkably capable man and an amateur photographer. I heard he convinced his captures he was a combat photographer who just happened to come along on that mission. If true, that showed some amazing composure and wouldn't surprise me at all.

Steve didn't make it. He and I had a beer together the night before in the club. He told me he'd never be captured if he was shot down.

The day that Bart turned the Laredo program over to Gary, we lost Pete Cleary and Lennie Lenor. They were both members of the 523rd Squadron at Clark Air Base in the Philippines, and the men in that outfit were scattered to various F-4 assignments all over Thailand. Lennie had been a Laredo back-seater, and I had flown several missions with him. He was a short, dark-complected, quiet man and very good as a back-seater. He had finished his temporary duty tour and actually returned "home" to Clark Air Base. He came back to fly Pete's last mission with him, as they were friends. They did the famous "Missing Misty" that I talked about earlier. Pete was a very good, very aggressive pilot, and I'd be willing to bet that, on his last mission, he saw something that just had to be taken out by him. They probably got hit down low and went into the trees at very low angle. There was no sign of them around the area they last reported being in, but that was no surprise, as that report had been long before they went missing. I can remember searching for the crash site for several days. I don't think it was found for nearly thirty years.

Scary.

It wasn't until around mid September of that tour that I felt I was actually a contributing member of the regular squadron and started flying air to air missions again. I flew three of the Linebacker II missions during the Christmas Linebacker II campaign. While that was good for a command post weenie, there were guys that flew three missions in one night during that time.

One other thing I would like to mention was that in the F-4, we were not alone. There was a WSO or Weapons' Systems Operator who flew in the back of the airplane. These guys were unbelievably good and strongly motivated. Dan Petkunas "dug a MiG out of the weeds" for me on a December mission when it was thought to have been impossible to get a radar lock on a plane that much lower than you. Gerry Becker (different one), Chuck Debellvue (who flew with Steve Richie and eventually got six MiGs), Jim Korpi, Rog Locher, who was rescued after spending over three weeks on the ground in North Vietnam and with whom I only had a couple of casual conversations as I had only been on base a few days when he was shot down, and Jack Trimble, who was in Carl Jeffcoat's backseat and spent about three months in the Hanoi Hilton. I've previously described his gutsy exploits while a prisoner. Jeff Feinstein was there and Jeff got five migs during his tour. I flew with him in Laredo also. Jeff went on to pilot training from the Udorn assignment.

I especially remember a man named Tom Lampley, who I grew to really like.

Tom, a West Point grad in the middle of two back-to-back tours of duty when I met him, looked like a "surfer dude" who had been grabbed off a California beach, sheared, put into a flight suit, and plunked into the back of an F-4. You had to wonder how this seeming dichotomy ever happened, but man, was he good.

He also had an interesting take on women. "Rosie, keep in mind this one thing. There are just two kinds of women: them that want to love you, and them that are dead. Now go with my blessing."

In the back of an airplane, he made the dials talk. He, like all these guys I just mentioned, could fly formation as well as any of us.

CHAPTER 22
Udorn—Late 1972

Tip Galer had finished a combat tour in the F-100 and had had enough excitement for a while. But his interest in the T-38, which he flew as a training-command instructor pilot, had worn thin after about two years, and he volunteered to go back to the war, this time in F-4s. There were number of his classmates who had done the same thing, me among them. Throughout our career at the academy, we had been imbued with the idea that it was our duty to be where the fighting was underway. That is not to say that is the reason for the existence of the academy, but we felt we belonged where the war was being prosecuted.

If you were lucky enough to qualify to fly fighters and there was a war going on, you belonged in that war, at the front, flying combat. Tom had gone back and been lost on his second assignment. Tip had come back, along with Wheels, me, Jeff Egge, who probably flew more combat than any other member of the Class of 66, Neil Crist, who had done an F-105 tour, Bill Berry in the big Bufs, and a bunch of others. Over half the guys I flew with on my second tour were back there for their second tour. Academy grads or not, there was a war, and we all saw the job as being there. We went back. It was that simple.

Tip and I were friends from the academy, and I stopped in to visit him and Wheels when I got the F-4 assignment. Tip had already received his, and he was about five weeks ahead of me in the pipeline. Tip and I became good friends during this second tour and continue to this day to stay in touch.

Wheels would get his F-4 return assignment about five weeks after mine.

Tip climbed up the ladder and put his gear into the front seat of the F-4E Phantom. It was late October, nearing what would be the end of the Linebacker I campaign against the North. Whatever had gone on in Paris, Henry Kissinger felt he had a deal in the bag. It was almost time to stop.

Tonight was a combat air patrol of the area just to the west of Hanoi. An earlier F-111 strike had lost a plane, and the search-and-rescue operation to recover the crew had been going on for most of the day. Tip and his wingman were going to ensure that no fighters came after the rescue force from the west while it did its job to the north of the city.

Tip put his gear in the plane and started around the ship for a quick preflight. A pilot's preflight on an F-4 was pretty much just a quick glance to make sure the damn thing was there. There was nothing on the airplane more fragile than a steel bar, so if nothing was obviously hanging off, preflight was complete. Everything on the plane had already been checked and double-checked by the crew chief and the armament guys. It looked like the "McDonnell Ironworks," it was so big. The guys at Udorn called them Rhinos.

Tonight's load was four Sparrow air-to-air missiles and two heat-seeking Sidewinders, one on each inboard pylon. The four Sparrows were carried in recesses in the fuselage and each inboard pylon was capable of carrying two Sidewinders. There were only a total of two Sidewinders, and Tip smiled at this. Of course there was no shortage of munitions, but just not the need to load the max number of missiles capable on this particular mission.

Outboard of the Sidewinders on the second wing station were two 370-gallon drop tanks. These would be dropped if the fighters engaged MiGs. The big "bathtub" or center-line tank held six hundred gallons of jet fuel and was usually jettisoned the moment it looked like contact with an enemy fighter might be made. This tank allowed the fighters to arrive in the area of potential combat full of fuel. There had been a brief period during the summer Linebacker I campaign where the tanks were dropped as soon as they went empty. The wing at Udorn had gone through a huge stockpile of tanks with this procedure in about two weeks time. The tanks were now retained unless it looked like they could be in the way.

Preflight complete, Tom Lampley was already up in the backseat while Tip strapped into the airplane. Tom had been a Laredo FAC with me for the better part of the year and was one of a group of young gurus with the weapons systems in the F-4s. Most of these navigators had chosen to become weapons-systems operators as a backdoor way of getting into pilot training. For one reason or another, they had not been able to get into pilot training—usually eyesight—and they knew that with an F-4 combat tour under their belt the AF would ease the eyesight restriction. Most of the pilots let them fly the airplane to and from the combat area and sometimes even let them make the takeoffs and landings. The Laredo FACs had taught their GIBs ("guy in back") to refuel.

One of them made a "save" when the front-seater of his airplane became disabled, and he landed the plane at Udorn from the backseat.. The landing was made under extreme duress, but made well, probably saving the front-seater's life.

When these backseat guys went to pilot training, they did very very well. In fact, they often came back as front-seaters in the F-4.

"Hell-o."

"Hell-o."

"That completed the interphone check."

"Ready."

"Yep."

Tip was strapped in, and the crew chief had taken away the ladder. He said, "Air on two" into the microphone and the crew chief responded with, "Roger, air on two."

"Okay, chief, air on one."

With that, the crew chief laughed and said, "Yes sir, air on one" and turned the valve in the ground power card so that the air again flowed from the big yellow machine into the F-4, slowly starting the number-one or left engine rotating.

In the close-in steel revetments that were common to all the fighter bases, starting the engines with a ground power cart was a little more pleasant than the alternative. That alternative was to use a huge eight-inch in diameter canister filled loosely with cordite. When the canister was ignited by an electrical spark, the cordite burned at a controlled rate, and the expanding gases were channeled to turn the starter turbine. This was the way an airplane on alert was started in a hurry. It required only moving the start selector switch to the side and then holding the ignition button. It was fast, but the burning cordite smoke hung in the air, often enveloping the entire airplane and filling the revetment, and it would nearly suffocate any crew member who didn't have his oxygen mask on before initiating the start.

They completed the rest of the checks of the electrics, hydraulics, and flight controls. Tom would do more radar checks during the taxi out.

"Ford flight check."

"Two."

"Stagerider, Ford with two for mission clearance."

Tip and I had had been planning two weeks of leave. At that time, the United States had taken Australia off the R&R list of places where a serviceman could go under the sponsorship of the US government. But Tip had been there on his first tour as had I, and we were two bachelors determined to go again.

The squadron commander at the time was a great guy named Curt Westphal—MiG Killer, I might add. We talked to Col. Westphal earlier, but the "convincer" came after Linebacker I ended..

"I don't know, guys. If I let you two jokers go down there, I'll probably never see you again."

Tip jumped in. "Sir, we're here on a volunteer second tour, and we're over halfway through that tour. We've flown Laredo and Linebacker for the last four months, and it's time for a break. Besides, there's nothing going on here anyway. We promise, if we hear anything, we'll get back here."

We headed off to New Zealand and Australia for a great time at Coolangata and Surfers Paradise. Just Tip, Woody Cox, me, and about a fifty of our closest Australian friends. We met up with a group of them and partied for two weeks straight.

But this night, Tip was in the cockpit, and I was in the command post. Jeez.

"Roger, Ford, cleared to ground. Have a good one ... hump."

Fuckin' Rosie. I could tell by his tone of voice he was thinking that.

About four months ago, the squadron commander, at a squadron briefing, had asked if anyone would like an extra assignment to the command post. He stated that it was a major's slot, but that they would take a captain. Like a dope, I had asked one question about it, and then decided I wasn't interested. Too bad. One question was one question more interest than anyone else had shown. I was it and went under protest. I'd been flying Laredo and pulling regular shifts in the command post. That taught me not to speak up when the subject was nonflying jobs.

"See ya, Rose."

"Let's go to button 2."

"Two."

"Buttons" were preset channels on the UHF radio. By using the radio selector in the channel mode, the radio could be tuned to the proper frequency by moving only one knob instead of all four of a four-digit radio frequency. In the F-4, the guy in the back ran the radios; the guy in the front usually did the talking.

The buttons were set up in the chronological order they would be needed. One was the command post, two ground control, three the tower, four departure radar, and so forth.

So Tip was ready.

"Udorn, Ford, taxi two Phantoms."

"Runway 30 Ford, altimeter 29.95."

"Roger, 2995."

"Two."

The Phantoms powered out of the concrete and steel revetments. The thrust of the engines and the whine as the nozzles on the rear of the engines closed to pinch the airflow and create thrust was eerie in the setting sun. The name Phantom probably came from the sound of those engines.

The fighters taxied to the far end of Runway 30 at the huge complex in northeastern Thailand. The arming procedures were accomplished with the aircraft facing away from the center of the airport, safety pins pulled, tanks checked for security, thumbs up to the crews. Tip waited for the wingman to look over at him, looked up at the canopy, nodded his head, and all four of the plexiglass covers—two on each Phantom—came down, powered by air.

When the canopy was down, the big jets were cleared into position. "Ford, cleared for takeoff.

"Roger, cleared," and Tip brought the left engine in a snap acceleration to 100 percent power.

The brakes were unable to hold the plane with both engines at full military power, so only one engine was checked at a time. The massive engines were supposed to "snap" accelerate from idle to 100 percent in less than three seconds. They did. Each time an engine came forward, the nose of the Phantom bobbed down as the fourteen thousand pounds of thrust dug in.

Barely visible in the twilight, the wingman nodded that he was ready. Because of the heavy load, they would roll individually, rather than in formation.

Power up to 85 percent on both engines, check with the wingman, release the brakes, and start to roll, easing in the afterburner and increasing the thrust by 30 percent to 17,500 pounds.

"Yeah baby."

The sound in the cockpit was muffled through the headsets. Tom called both nozzles were open. That meant that the afterburners were creating so much thrust that the nozzles on the rear of the engines had to go to full open to keep the temperature under control. There was plenty of push. Outside the plane the roar shook the entire base, indeed was heard all the way downtown.

Into the night.

Two came off twenty seconds later. Tip pulled the throttles out of burner, trading airspeed for altitude. Two would leave the plane in burner, stay below the leader's flight path, and then kill the overtake speed by pulling up into position as the flight turned out of traffic and climbed to fifteen thousand feet.

"Brigham, Ford Flight with two, off Udorn, climbing to fifteen thousand."

"Radar contact, Ford. Your tanker is Peach 23. Steer a heading of 030 now for the rendezvous."

Two joined on the left wing. Tip still felt awe at the skills of his comrades to be able to take such a powerful machine and make it float in formation, inches from his own wingtip. He could literally look in the other cockpit and see his comrade moving his hands from throttles to lower the nighttime clear visor, back to the throttles, and then pick up a checklist and look at it, all the while staying in formation on his wingtip.

He yawed the aircraft back and forth to tell the wingman to go to a route formation, some thousand feet to the left.

"Ford, your tanker is at eleven thirty ten miles, twenty thousand feet. This will be vectors for the rendezvous."

"Roger that."

"Turn now to a heading of 190."

"190 roger."

The huge four-engine tanker was in a shallow left bank, and Tip saw immediately that the tanker was going to turn outside of him, forcing an overshoot that would take another ten minutes to correct. It wasn't the controller's fault. It was just the position the tanker was in when the fighters arrived on the scene.

"Brigham, Ford has the tanker, we'll take over the rejoin, sir."

"Roger, Ford, Tanker is on frequency 231.4. Contact him now on that frequency. You're cleared to join."

Tip brought his flight over to the frequency. "Peach 23, this is Ford. We've got you in sight."

"Roger, Ford, cleared into refueling position at your control. Current altimeter is 29.92. Call the ready position."

Rock the wingman into a fingertip position. If he was going to be maneuvering, he wanted the rest of his flight close. Bringing the nose of the fighters up, he shot through the altitude of the tanker with the airspeed rapidly decreasing. At about three thousand feet above the tanker, he eased off the stick, rolled right, and held zero g's as the tanker flew past below. Bringing his flight back down behind the tanker, he quickly regained airspeed and closed rapidly from behind. He leveled about a thousand feet below the tanker, three to four miles back with 150 knots of overtake. Closing on the tanker, he eased the flight up and into position, killing off the excess airspeed as he came up behind the tanker.

"Beautiful, sir." It was the boomer. He'd been in the front of the tanker when the fighters first started maneuvering and walked to the back of the big gas truck in time to lie down, actuate the boom, and watch the two Phantoms come into position behind the tank.

"Peach 23 is ready."

"Two, take the right wing."

"Roger."

They cycled through the tanker. The kind of maneuvering that they had accomplished was allowable on a night like this where there were few airplanes hitting the tanker. In a large "heavy" mission to the north, each flight of fighters would have to take instructions from the radar controller as there were just too many airplanes to duck visually.

The tanker rolled out and headed north.

The planes dropped off the tanker and turned toward their orbit point in the middle of the jagged limestone karst mountains that dominated the area. The sun made a final spot of light on the western horizon as they checked in with the controlling agency in a C-130 aircraft.

"Alley Cat, this is Ford, Mission 2356 taking up orbit."

"Roger, you're into the area at this time, Ford. All is on time."

"Roger that."

This mission was pretty far north for a rescue.

Ford rolled into orbit.

"Red Crown, this is Ford, two for your control. Orbit as assigned." Red Crown was a Navy ship, cruiser we were told, that ran the radar intercepts in the North from its position in the South China Sea.

"Roger, radar contact, Ford. No other targets."

"What the fuck was that?"

"Ford, unidentified target, your area, pop up."

An airplane went by so close that Tip had that brief feeling that he was in slow motion, awaiting impact. Then something else.

"There's another one behind him."

"Drop all the tanks, Two, now."

First he put a gentle two g's on the airplane to unload the center-line

600-gallon bathtub. He relaxed the g load slightly and let the wing tanks go.

The second MiG pulled up hard as it went by the flight. Tip went up after it. Fortunately, anticipating trouble, Ford had a lot more energy than the MiG and Tip started to over take the MiG while both were climbing straight up. Tip flipped the switch on the outboard of his throttle and moved the weapons-control system from radar missiles to heat-seekers. He fired a Sidewinder at the MiG, hoping to get him to break hard and lose a lot of energy.

It didn't work.

Now closing on the MiG with way too much overtake, Ford pulled off to the left, trying to conserve energy. The MiG pulled after Ford and crossed abeam Tip. With plenty of remaining energy, Tip rolled back toward the MiG. A vertical rolling scissors developed, both aircraft rolling back and forth trying to get behind the other, Tip using just enough energy to get behind the MiG by going away from it, rather than pulling hard into the MiG and losing his advantage. Finally, the MiG, out of speed, rolled off its climb and headed back down. Tip used his remaining energy to continue upward a little further, figuring he'd dive longer and have more energy when they came back together the next time.

When the F-4s started down, the MiG could not be seen in the dusk. Tom couldn't pick him up on the radar either. He most likely continued the dive to a very low level and headed for home over familiar territory and so advised his wingman.

Now, with the brief fight over, the four men started to breathe a little easier. With no belly or wing tanks, they'd soon have to recycle to a tanker.

"You dirty little son of a bitch."

The two F-4s continued in their orbit.

"Shit. Is that him going below us, headed west?"

"Don't know why he'd be headed west, but let's go after him."

"Yeah."

Ford watched the fighter go by with seeming indifference, straight and level about five thousand feet below them. They rolled in and pulled hard to close on the guy from his seven-o'clock-high position.

"Red Crown, do you have any other bandits in our vicinity?"

"We see nothing at all except the two of you."

That gave Tip an uneasy feeling, but he continued the dive with plenty of overtake as he settled in behind the bandit. As he was about to squeeze off the Sidewinder, Tip thought he saw two engines on the plane in front of him.

"Ford, hold fire."

"Two."

They closed close enough to the target to make out a Marine F-4. He could clearly see the markings on the side of the airplane.

"Alley Cat, this is Ford. We thought we'd found our first MiG, but it appears to have been a Marine F-4."

"Two confirms F-4."

"Ford, come left and back to orbit."

"Two."

The Seventh Air Force canceled the strike by the bombers that was due into the Southern panhandle of North Vietnam that night if the rescap succeeded. They had to get the details ironed out. They didn't know of any Marine F-4s that were supposed to be in the area at that time.

The rescap finished, with the downed airman radioing that he was about to be taken prisoner. Tip and the wingman returned to Udorn, coming down initial at 325 knots and breaking to the north in the night. Touchdown and a good parachute. The fight was over. In forty minutes Tip, Tom, and their two comrades had gone from calm routine to screaming into the microphone, maximum performance maneuvering, yelling commands at each other, and querying the control functions as to what was going on, to imminent disaster, to calm routine, back to attack mode again, to quiet departure, to return to home.

The canopy popped open as Tip flipped the little lever under the canopy rail on the left side of the cockpit.

Fresh air, cool, home ... alive.

Tip Galer's father was still alive at that time. He had won the Congressional Medal of Honor while serving as a Marine fighter pilot during Guadalcanal. I'll bet he was proud when he heard that story. The apple doesn't fall far from the tree in the Galer family. Tip's son is a Marine officer. His son-in-law is an Air Force pilot.

CHAPTER 23
My Chance at a MiG

I wrote this piece for a "Pilot Log" article for Business and Commercial Aviation *magazine. It was one of the final big missions of the war for me and fitting that I flew it with Wheels. As I stated, by the time the Christmas raids came around, I was feeling pretty comfortable in the airplane. Although working the command post, I was still able to fly three missions during Linebacker II. We started hitting Cambodia shortly after this, and I flew some long Laredo missions again in that theater, but the NVN had settled down by then. Ever patient, they knew we'd be leaving soon and they could continue after we were gone.*

"UDORN, BUICK TAXI WITH FOUR Phantoms."
Christmas Season 1972 continued. Udorn, Thailand. We of "Buick" flight begin to roll. Despite our broadcast, Buick is actually a flight of two Phantoms. Linebacker 2, the ongoing bombardment of North Vietnam, has been tough on our fighter wing, and we've got too many F-4s in maintenance to field four ships for this flight.

Today, I'm Lead, nickname "Rosie"; my good friend "Wheels" is Two; my back-seater, Danny, is answering as Three; and Buf Tibbets in the back of Wheels's airplane is Four.

We hope our subterfuge will fool the commies.

Brakes off, ease into burner, and fifty feet of fire shoots out the back end. At the end of the runway, I come out of burner and start a steep climb. Wheels slides up into position. Buick's off Udorn.

"Radar Contact, Buick, left to 280, climb to eight thousand. Your tanker is Peach 33. Number three in a cell of five."

The tankers are flying a huge orbit. Above us in the orbit is a group of fighters out of one of the other bases. One group had already hit the tankers and gone on into the Hanoi area, laying a corridor of chaff, metal reflectors that jam the radar, for the bombers.

Like a giant python, the strike force coils. Shimmering on that snake's smooth skin, our lights blink and flash in the night. The coil climbs.

"Buicks got Peach 33 in sight."

"Buick, go refuel."

"Two, three, four," I smile in the night.

Cycling on and off, the tanker takes little time. With only two of us, it's a pretty simple drill. The lead tanker rolls out and starts heading north.

Showtime.

Off the tanker, we head for a pre-assigned orbit point. We are to provide MiG CAP (combat air patrol) for a force of B-52s. The Phantoms come into the area in the mid-teens. The bombers are much higher.

"SAM ten o'clock."

Four sets of eyeballs watch as the under-cast glows brighter and brighter. Then the surface-to-air missile bursts out of the clouds. The flight path is unbending. It's moving like a space shot, going straight for the heavies (B-52 bombers) high above us.

"Good luck, guys."

It blows, apparently hitting nothing as there's no secondary explosion.

"SAM nine o'clock." This missile comes out of the clouds and starts arching over at us.

"Aw shit."

Easy ... now's not the time to rush the next move.

"Take it down, Buick."

Push to 3.5 negative g's. All eyes on the SAM. Since a missile leads its target, aiming for where we will be when it arrives, we push over to make the point of predicted impact below the SAM's current altitude. The missile arcs over like a giant fiery roller coaster coming over the top of a hill in the night. As it starts to head down, we hold the dive a little longer. We're moving now. The big belly tank is starting to shake. Just a second more.

"Up and left, Buick."

A three to four g pull-up into the missile is made. This means the point of impact it must calculate is way above and behind where it's going. It's been accelerating downhill all this while, and the required turn is too much for its small-tail planes.

The missile tries and goes under us in a skid. Doppler shift, explosion, no hits.

We win.

Climbing now. Roll inverted in place. Pull through level. Roll upright. Wheels follows the moves without a word. A touch of burner to keep moving. Keep the "smash" up. Speed is life. We near the end of the orbit and start to turn back to the east, toward Hanoi.

"Blue (MiG 21) bandit. Bullseye (Hanoi) 240 for 35 (35 miles Southwest of Hanoi) climbing."

I ease forward, accelerate a little, and come back in with about two g's. A thump as the six-hundred-gallon center line tanks come off. We complete the turn and are accelerating when Danny says, "I've got him, Rosie."

I see the attack symbology. We're locked on. Out of good range, but locked on and closing. Looking up, the afterburner of the MiG is clearly visible.

Full burner. "C'mon baby, move, move, move." We are arching up to our left. Out of the corner of my eye, I see Wheels pull up, cross high, and then dive back to stay up with me. Two Phantoms in formation in the night, four burners, fangs out.

"Red Crown, Buick is in position. Clearance to fire."

"Stand by."

"What? Clearance to fire?"

"Buick, break it off, break it off. This is Red Crown. Acknowledge."

On the interphone, Danny yells, "You've got to be shitting me."

The Mig arcs over and his burner goes out, abandoning his attack. I roll inverted and keep the steering dot as close to center as I can until the radar locks onto the ground. Danny tries again, but can't regain lock. Gone.

Later, we'll find out that the attack was aborted because of fear our radar would jump from the MiG to one of the huge B-52s downrange of him to our fire-control systems. There was fear of shooting down one of our own, and apparently Red Crown could hear that the MiG had already been called off the attack.

We continue for two more orbits and head home.

Back at base, I hear Wheels tell the maintenance guys he lost his primary altitude indicator while on the tanker and flew the rest of the mission with only a tiny "peanut" gauge for altitude. That means he had no missile fire control. He was there just to watch my tail.

"Wheels, why didn't you say something?"

"Fuck, Rose, you were having so much fun."

I look at him, long. He sits there with the oxygen-mask line creased into his face and just smiles. A pilot circling at night near downtown Hanoi, SAMs rising, MiGs attacking, and no primary altitude. If he had aborted, Buick might have aborted, since we were not supposed to go in alone. His decision to "hang it out" with us might have saved the lives of the men in whatever B-52 that MiG was after.

Historian Stephen Ambrose summed it up with this exchange:

"Were you a hero in the war, Dad?"

"No, son, but I fought with men who were."

CHAPTER 24
Thoughts After the Years Go By

I told you at the beginning of this that these guys I flew with didn't consider themselves extraordinary men. For them, their participation in the Vietnam War was not the end-all and be-all of their life. They went on from there..

I came back to MacDill AFB in Tampa, where I was an instructor in the F-4E, but left the service and started flying corporate jets in 1974. I settled with Sharon in Connecticut, and we raised three children there. They and their kids are still the center of our lives.

Tip stopped through several times in the late seventies. The first two times, of course, I had to put up with "Do you notice how nicely Tip dresses and how well his clothes go together?" As Wheels said, "Galer's a hot dog."

About the third time Tip showed up, he had a young good-looking redhead in tow. Actually, she had Tip in tow, but he may not have been aware of it at the time. They arrived in a tiny little auburn colored Pinto station wagon stuffed to the top with clothes and just enough room for a little dog. This from a guy who used to arrive at places in Corvettes and Porsches. After a day or two, when they drove away, I told Sharon, "Galer's gone. He'll be married within a year." I was right. No man in his right mind would have let Kim get away. They moved way out west and now reside near Park City, Utah.

Tip went on to spend a lot of time in OT&E (Operational Test and Evaluation) . A lot of that in F-15's. He retired and became and Airbus 320 captain for United Airlines. After leaving United, he started flying for Netjets, a large fractional owner jet operation. As Tip says, "can't get enough of this flying thing."

I flew several trips to Phoenix with the company and would usually drop by Luke just to see the old stomping grounds that had been where I went through the F-100 gun school with Wheels, where I went through the category-four checkout in the F-4, and where I learned to fly the F-4 as an instructor in the late spring of 1973.

Wheels went to Bitburg, Germany after he left Thailand, Not a volunteer for Germany, he swore he'd get out of that assignment at the end of his eighteen month commitment. He met a DoD school teacher during that time and, five years later, he left Bitburg.

During the Bitburg tour, he returned to Luke for the third time to learn to fly the F-15 and married Jeannie at the end of that checkout. A year and a half later he came back to Luke as an F-15 instructor and remained there for the next six years.

Wheels retired from the Air Force in 1987 and returned to Luke as a contract training development manager in the F-15C, F15E and eventually, the F-16.

Hugh and Kathy finished a career in the Air Force and then Hugh went on to Northwest Airlines, where he finished up as a DC-9 captain. As I said, I dropped in for dinner a couple of times while they were at Luke and I was going through one program or another. They also came through Connecticut with the whole gang at least once that I remember, and we went skiing at a local mountain. They were all good skiers and having been out West so much, they were not impressed much with our mountains, but we had a great time anyway. We saw them at the academy for the thirtieth reunion, and they split shortly after that. Hugh and family still ski and still fly. He is associated with the Cirrus light airplane. Kathy is now in the south. They and their new "spice" are both on the list of must-sees when I retire.

After Vietnam Jerry Becker flew a lot of T-38 missions for the next 12 years; first, as an IP at Moody AFB, GA where he met his wife, Chris; next as a Lead-In Fighter Training (LIFT) program IP when that program started at Holloman AFB, NM; then, thanks to classmate J.O. McFalls working in assignments, as an Aggressor pilot at Clark Airbase, Republic of the Philippines. Jerry extended a 2-year tour at Clark into 3 and a half. Jerry was the Ops Officer the year before he left. Jerry says this was the second best assignment of his career, right behind his combat tour in the "Hun".

Jerry returned to Holloman and the LIFT program where he was the 434th TFTS Red Devils squadron commander, then Director of Operations for the T-38 wing. He finished his 26-year career as the 5th AF Chief of Staff at Yokota Airbase, Japan, followed by a year at 12th AF headquarters in Austin, Texas.

Now living in Poquoson, Virginia, listening to the sound of freedom from the F-22 Raptors at nearby Langley AFB, Jerry has spent the last 14 years working as a warfare simulation instructor/controller at the Joint War Fighting Center in Suffolk, Virginia.

CHRIS KELLUM DID THREE YEARS at Columbus Air Force Base in Mississippi, as a T-37 instructor pilot. He escaped back into fighters at Nellis Air Force Base transitioning into the F-111 "supersonic scissors" He was medically grounded in Sep 1972 for diabetes.

Chris then talked the Air Force into sending him back to Purdue where he had flunked out after three semesters years earlier. The second time was a charm as he graduated with a 3.5 GPA in an Electrical Engineering Masters program. He finished 23 years in the Air Force in 1983 at Eglin Air Force Base as Chief of Operational Test of Anti-jam Communications

Chris became the "Chief of Maintenance" at the Sea Gull Motel in Hatteras, NC, his wife's, Mitzi, hometown. Mitzi died in May of 2009 and Chris moved back to his hometown of Kokomo, IN and later married the "girl I left behind" when he joined the Air Force. I see him at every Misty Re-union and try to keep up with him, on occasion, on the golf course.

Dave Jenny came out of Vietnam and flew the F-100 for a while in Europe before coming back to the states and upgrading into the A-7. While in the A-7 he flew two short tours of combat (A short tour is less than six months. Knowing Dave they were both probably 179 days). After that he checked out in the A-10 and remained in that airplane for years, becoming the high time Air Force pilot in it at one point. He flew the F-117 shortly after the Air Force took over responsibility for the plane from Lockheed and held various key command positions in that program. He eventually finished his Air Force Career in Alaska flying A-10's and F-15's I think. He spent his entire Air Force career flying fighters, never went to any professional military education and finished as a full colonel. That says a lot about what people above Dave thought of his ability to fly, fight, lead and inspire younger pilots.

Dave now resides on a small (500 acres) texas ranch in the Waco area. "C'mon down, Rosie. You can drink and drive on my ranch. Heck, you can drink and drive AND shoot all at the same time". I'm going to do that.

I also recently reconnected with a couple of guys from the F-4s. Jack Trimble went on to pilot training and finished a career in the air force, joined Federal Express out of Memphis, and is just retiring from that job. Tom Lampley and Bob Connelly have also recently been found. Yep, all three are on the list.

Preston Duke and I have written and talked to each other numerous times during the last thirty years, although we have never been able to get together. Pres finished his twenty in the Kansas Air Guard flying F-105s and F-4s out of McConnell Air Force Base. While in the guard, Pres flew for Federal Express and finished up as an Airbus check pilot. He and Emily live in Memphis, where they run a good-sized farm at the same time. He's now a rancher who has invited me to "come self-actualize in the 106 degree heat with me some time." He described himself in this year's Christmas card as "serving well in present position." I told him his picture, included in this book, looks like a satisfied man.

Clayboy and Ginger Lewis were with us at MacDill as F-4 instructors. They went to Hawaii, where Clay flew O-2 observation aircraft for a difficult three or four year stint. Actually, he did have the entire dash catch on fire on him on one of his final rides but managed to get it on the ground. Clay came back to the States, worked in general aviation, flew F-4s with the Texas Air Guard, got hired by Federal Express, and has since retired. They visited us two or three times during the years and we communicate several times a month. We did a ski trip together in the mid-nineties and tried to share with them the tension as their son, Mark, went to Afghanistan as a combat medic after surviving a similar year in Bosnia. They are close friends of Bud and Doris Day, so we get to see them at the Misty reunions in Fort Walton Beach every other year. One of Ginger's favorite expressions is, "they're in the other room, talking and shooting their wrist watches off. " That is in reference to the way a tale always gets told with two hands in the air, the left always being the bad guy.

Bill and Jackie Bowen live on the other side of town from us. Bill got out of the Sioux City Guard and flew C-141s for the reserves until he was picked up by Eastern Air Lines in the early seventies. His career with the airlines spanned Eastern, Trump, and US Air. I ran into Bill again in the New York Air Guard around 1975 where the 105th Tactical Support Wing was flying O-2s. That outfit, made up entirely of new second lieutenants and ex-fighter pilots or FACs, was extremely close, as only an old-time guard unit could be close. We transitioned to the Lockheed C-5 in 1985 and flew together in Panama, Desert Shield/Storm, and countless other earthquake-relief missions, special missions, presidential-support missions, and so on. We party often with them and travel together from time to time. It's wonderful having one of the old gang so close, especially one in which the wife is so close to Sharon.

Doc—Dean Echenberg—has led an extremely interesting life. He "disappeared" for a few years after returning from his second Southeast Asia tour. . Upon returning from his "walkabout," he ran his own family practice in San Francisco for years. One of his patients, a longshoreman, connected him to the Merchant Marine. He sailed as a commander/ship's doctor in freighters for several trips. Upon selling his family practice, he built houses for a living in addition to signing on with various volunteer United Nations medical teams going throughout the world as an epidemiologist. Now he dwells on top of a hill in Tiburon, California, in one of the most beautiful houses I've ever seen.

Wells Jackson left the air force in 1970 . At that time he was flying F4E's out of Torrejon Air Base in Spain. He sold real estate for a short time and almost immediately started a residential and commercial construction business in New Mexico which he ran for five years. After this he settled into the construction consulting business for the next 35 years where he analyzed failures and offered solutions related to the construction industry . He also served as an expert witness in forensic efforts. Typical of Wells, he owned several businesses and built some coffee farms in Boquete, Panama all the while raising a second family in Ft. Collins, Colorado. He retired in 2001, but after several years "down on the coffee plantation" he returned to productive work in Colombia, Germany and the U.S. He's now preparing for a "second retirement" in Boquete, Panama..

When Kelly Irving retired from the Air Force, he spent a year looking for "a real job." He tells me that he couldn't find one so he continued with his flying career. First came New York Air as a DC-9 pilot. Shortly thereafter Texas International bought Continental Airlines and kept that name (Continental). When Texas Air merged New York Air and Continental, Kelly moved to Denver to fly the MD-80. In his last four years at Continental he moved to the DC-10 and got paid "an embarrassing amount of money to sit on my ass and manage the flight director system." Since then he's worked for Foge (Ron Fogleman) as a judge on the Contest Committee at the Reno Air Races. The committee they serve on enforces adherence to the FAA Airshow Waiver that the Races must obtain. The picture of him "today" is from the deck of his house in Colorado.

Scotty Robertson, Ramsey Vincent, Pete Cleary, Lennie Lenor, Lee Gourley, Steve Cuthbert, Tom, Rog Rice, Clyde Seiler, and countless others didn't come home. They didn't get to raise kids and enjoy all that I've enjoyed for the last forty-two years. Their parents suffered their losses until the day they died, and their kids and wives still carry the burden of "what if" with them every day. And, in the background, always, there's Tom.

Tom was such a wonderful person that he drew a crowd wherever he went. Had he lived, I think we would have stayed a much closer group, because he really was the glue. He wouldn't allow someone to miss a get-together or go a year or two without a call. Tom loved you and required that you stay touch and do things with him. What a wonderful person he was.

I think it should be a law that to be a politician in this country, you must have been in the service, preferably a combat arm, whether in war or not. Once a man has endured the physical and mental stresses associated with such an undertaking, no matter what he does later in life, he will always know there's a group of guys that understand him completely. There will always be a group of guys that know what he's got inside, no matter what else he goes on to call his occupation. That would go a long way to stopping our habit of judging men by how much money they make.

Also, I think this country should levy a surtax and institute conscription any time it engages in armed conflict. Our wonderful volunteer military will be the first to go and hold the action until the new recruits can start feeding into the frontline. But after a few months, we'll have plenty of money and plenty of soldiers.

If these changes had all been in effect in the 1960s, some of the gentlemen who made decisions in Washington during the Vietnam War might have been a little more hesitant about starting and a little more determined about finishing that war. Also, with these changes, when a congressman waved a flag in the air, he would know that his children and his family member's children were at risk. There are too many "leaders" in Washington with no skin in the game. Brave men and women who enlist and volunteer deserve leadership that truly knows what our soldiers are being sent to endure.

My friends were called and went and went on. They have worked their whole lives as witnessed in this chapter, saved their money, made their plans, and now watch in awe the young folk flying such planes at the F-15, F-18, F-16, F-35, and the marvelous F-22.

I am honored to be a part of their group.

EPILOGUE

A N OLD FIGHTER PILOT DIES and arrives at the desk of St. Pete. Paging through the record of the man's life, the saint looks up and says, "You've made it. Under the guidelines, you're going straight to heaven."

Then St. Pete turns somber.

"I have to tell you that a lot of your friends are not going to be there, but that's the way it goes. The Boss leaves life's decisions up to individual's own choices. You've made good ones. Congratulations."

"The Boss" appears. The old pilot looks at Him and smiles. God smiles back. All is well.

"Welcome."

The word brings tears to the man's eyes, and he starts to walk through the Pearly Gates.

But there is a loud commotion over his shoulder, and he turns to see a crowd of men behind a large fence.

"Hey. Hey, is that you? Where you going? C'mon over here and say hi. We've been waiting for you."

As he walks over to the crowd, he sees that most of his old buddies are in this group. There's an early detachment commander who stood up for him when he was a foolish lieutenant. That commander lost his squadron because he wouldn't cashier his young friend. Three weeks later, he died when the wing of his F-100 failed as he pulled off a low-angle bomb pass.

Next is a classmate from the academy. The classmate married a beautiful woman who the man himself had tried to date. They had two adorable little children before he went off to Laos, where he died.

"Roscoe, PG Teuton de Beauregard." The Louisiana man recalls the confederate general's nickname he gave his old friend.

There's a quiet man who was wingman in a four-ship the day he'd been shot down over Laos. That man was later lost while on patrol as a Misty Forward Air Controller, seeking targets for strike fighters.

The "Great Muckrock" is there. He says nothing, just smiles and looks at the pilot. Memories of all the love that was between them flood back. The great times with Tom, Jerry, and Tom's adoring wife, Sandy, come back, and the pilot is overcome with happiness at the memories.

He turns to God and asks, "Why are these guys over here, all by themselves?"

"Because I don't know what to do with them. They aren't like the people we take normally. They don't qualify. I'm afraid we might not be able to let them in."

A tear rolls down the man's cheek. These are the guys that he ran with when he was young and crazy; guys who gave him strength; guys who he could turn to and see if they were as afraid as he; pilots who took the worst that an enemy had to give and laughed with him and jumped back into the fray the next day. They were men he loved.

"Hey, c'mon over. What's up? You flew for a long time down there. You done good, brother. Good on you."

They seemed to talk as one.

God asks, "Why are you crying?"

"Because I made it and they didn't."

"They knew the rules."

In a barely audible whisper, he says, "I can't leave these guys."

He falls to his knees, admitting the omnipotence of the creator, but loving his friends. What is he doing here? How did this happen? His voice is a whisper.

Before God speaks, all the power and strength of His perfection passes through the man. All the wisdom of all men of all times runs through the mere mortal and scares him to the core of his body. He trembles.

"I can't leave them."

God walks over to the group. He sternly faces them, and the old man is sure of the doom that will come from the Creator.

"You yeahoos win again. Each time one of these old fools comes up here, the result is the same. You were right about this one too. You all broke the code early. Go on in again. Try not to piss off the good folks. I'll be along later."

With that there is, instantly, a party, camaraderie, and food. The girls are back, all of them. Wives as beautiful as they were in 1966 and as old and adoring as they were the day they died. Girlfriends who pass by smiling and move into the crowd are there. Acquaintances and even transport pilots pass by and blend into the crowd. Overhead, all sorts of fighters fly by in formation and solo, wide open just off the ground. Open cockpits await anyone who wants to "go fly." It is all wonderful and surrounds the old man with love.

The cover artwork is "my" airplane-867 and was done by Mr. Anders Lejczak. (www.colacola.se) Anders uses computer generated images to create unbelievably authentic looking pictures of any F-100, with any paint scheme and design that may be desired. Although the paint scheme is 416th Tac Ftr Sqdn in the Summer of 1968, both Anders and I like the raw metal look better. We just considered it to be taken earlier in the war, before the camo paint jobs.

Made in the USA
Middletown, DE
10 September 2015